(From the original front cover flap)

Praise for Bob Vogel...

"Bob Vogel has served the people of Florida and Volusia County for more than a quarter of a century. He has done so with great integrity and honor. As sheriff, Bob has been a respected and brave soldier in our nation's war on drugs."

—Tillie K. Fowler
Member of Congress

"Bob Vogel is one of the most honored and innovative crime fighters Florida has ever seen. Throughout his career, he has been the scourge of drug dealers and other criminals. He never stops thinking of new and better ways to protect the citizens he serves."

—Bob Butterworth
Florida Attorney General

"Bob Vogel became famous with drug interdiction activities on I–95. Those same activities later brought him years of abuse in the press and countless legal battles. I have always thought that a few things get lost in the discussion of these activities. First, the public seemed to love what he was doing, demonstrated by Bob's staggering re-election percentages. Second, he never lost a court case. And finally, at the state level, those drug interdiction efforts have been expanded as part of the state's coordinated drug control strategy."

—Senator Locke Burt
16th District, Florida

"Bob Vogel's Marine Corps background is evident in his sense of duty. He has lived the Corps motto—Always Faithful—to the fullest in performing the duties of his offices. As a patrolman, his outstanding drug interdiction work received national recognition and his sheriff's office has consistently been rated among the best in the state. I am Bob Vogel's 100% admirer."

—John F. Bolt
LtCol, USMC (Ret)

Fighting to Win

Sheriff Bob Vogel
with Jeff Sadler

200 4th Avenue North, Suite 950
Nashville, TN 37219

445 Park Avenue, 9th Floor
New York, NY 10022

www.turnerpublishing.com

CONTENTS

DEDICATION

To the two most beautiful women in my life: Jeannie, my soulmate and Sheila, the twinkle of my eye. If I have made a small difference in this big, big world, it is truly due to your steadfast love and genuine support. Words cannot express my thanks for all your love and for walking through the fires with me.

My love forever.

FIGHTING TO WIN

Prologue:

ELECTION NIGHT, NOVEMBER 6, 1996

November 6, 1996 is a day my family and I will never forget.

It began with only the briefest of a night's sleep, as my wife Jeannie, daughter Sheila and I rose early for what promised to be a long day. We had been up late, closing down most of campaign headquarters, the twilight of another election campaign in sight. I had successfully run for Sheriff twice before and was looking to add a third consecutive term this night.

We brushed the sleep from our eyes, blundering around in the darkness, eager to get to the polls as we'd done the previous two election days. Adrenaline surged in each of us, for we knew this was the last day we could state our case to the public. We could only hope the results would be the same as in past elections.

The polls opened at 7:00 AM, and we arrived twenty minutes early per our custom. Jeannie and I had been first in line the last two elections, the first to cast our ballots at the Garden Club off Turnbull Bay Road in New Smyrna Beach.

Not today. Two other people were already there, ready to vote and get on with their daily routines.

This marked the first difference in what was to be a run of unusual occurrences for us on that warm, sunny November day.

And there was a second major difference today – Sheila would be able to vote. At 18, it was the first time she could vote for her dad. I was so proud of her! She was a tireless campaign worker just like her mother, and today she could actually register a voice that would be counted.

As we stood there, waiting for the sun to come up and the doors to open, I looked over at my wife and daughter. Jeannie, dark-haired and tiny, her already small, lean frame had shed more weight this campaign. Sheila, tall, blonde and beautiful, she would make any father proud. For two people that had less than four hours of sleep, they looked remarkably fresh. They both wore my campaign's now traditional T-shirts, yellow with black lettering spelling out "Vote Vogel!" Jeannie didn't want to wear them in plain view at the polling place, as she didn't want anyone to feel extra pressure to vote for me. We had always been sensitive about fair play. So she and Sheila wore sweaters over the shirts, while I wore my traditional shirt, tie and dress slacks for the day's campaigning.

Speaking of fair play, we had never put up our "Vote Vogel" signs at the voting precinct, either.

That was a third difference today. My opponent, Gus Beckstrom, had signs up here this morning, trying to make a splash in my home base. That had not happened in the previous elections.

I put my arm around Jeannie and hugged her. Both she and Sheila were a little tense, as was I, and I wanted to remind her how much I loved her, and that I knew it was going to be a marathon effort today. She smiled up at me, knowing I was also trying to relieve a little tension myself.

This would be the culmination of a year of fundraising and an intense four month campaign to be Sheriff of Volusia County. As the incumbent, I had the advantage and the polls seemed to be bearing this out so far. But if this was so, why was I a trifle uneasy?

The doors opened and we quickly cast our votes, Sheila finishing with a wide smile on her face. "Guess who I voted for Sheriff?" she teased, as we made our way to the parking lot. She was ready for the day ahead.

Jeannie said suddenly, "You know what's missing today?"

Sheila and I exchanged glances, but couldn't think of anything other than the differences we'd already noted.

"No cameras!" Jeannie exclaimed. "Remember how they followed us around first thing in the morning the last two election days?"

Jeannie was right. They usually camped outside the polling place ready to photograph us casting our votes. We had even been interviewed and asked to describe our election-day feelings.

Not today. Not a camera in sight. It was another difference in what was becoming a decided departure from what we knew as normal.

Election Day was typically a fun day for the candidate. You got to stand outdoors and reach out to the people as they went about their daily routines. You stood on street corners, parking lots, on bridges, waving at your constituents all day, looking to make eye contact, mentally tallying the votes as the day went along.

It was a last minute street sweep, a chance to bond one more time with the public, looking for signs of encouragement. As you stood and waved, you watched the folks drive by giving you a thumbs up (or down!), acknowledging your final run for the votes.

As always, we had designed a plan for the day. We left the Garden Club with three votes in my corner and drove north to the intersection of U.S. Route 1 and Dunlawton Avenue in Port Orange. We would start on the east side of the county and work our way north that morning. We passed several of our campaign workers, up early and clad in their T-shirts, ready to put in one more energetic effort on my behalf.

I felt so grateful to the people who put in time to support my re-election. It seemed that we had more volunteers than ever, putting in countless hours. I didn't even want to think about where I'd be without these wonderful folks. Many had voted by absentee ballot, so they didn't have to spend any extra time away from this day's campaigning. I was proud to represent them as Sheriff and personally appreciated their efforts.

When we arrived at the first designated spot, I was surprised to see one of my deputies waiting for us. Unbeknownst to me, Jeannie and those closest to me in the department were concerned for my safety, so Deputy Vinnie Vecchi had taken the day off to watch the backs of my family and I. I greeted him enthusiastically, but immediately said I didn't think the extra protection was necessary. He waved off my protest, and Jeannie and Sheila both thanked him for coming out.

It was another major difference about this Election Day.

It had been a tough campaign. I was extremely active, more so than in elections past, including my first campaign in 1988 when I literally wore the leather off my shoes. There were a substantial number of fundraisers that we held. There were an untold amount of phone calls and public appearances. We put up a record number of signs, a practice made necessary by the routine theft and destruction of these placards. There were negative, false stories run by the local newspaper, The Daytona News Journal. There was intimidation from the opposing side, and some former Sheriffs' deputies that had been dismissed during my tenure had joined the Beckstrom campaign. All of this created enough apprehension on my side to necessitate the presence of Vinnie on a normally fun day.

So while Vinnie watched, we waved. Motorists, on their way to work or taking their children to school made up the majority of cars seen early that morning. My mental calculator added up votes based on their reactions as I greeted them. At the first stop, I felt I was doing well.

Jeannie had us on schedule, moving from our first street corner to Beville Road to check on our campaign headquarters and hail more voters. We had closed the headquarters down the night before and the phones would be taken out today, another election in the books.

We worked our way up through Daytona Beach, the largest city in the county, then north through Holly Hill and then Ormond Beach, a growing area in the northernmost part of the county and typically a stronghold for me. As I stood in Ormond Beach on yet another street corner, it was a thrill to hear the horns of the cars sounding their support. People driving by would hold up one or two fingers, signaling how many votes in their household I could expect.

Even Vinnie, new to this type of thing, said he was amazed at the apparent show of support. I had to agree with him. For all the differences in this morning's routine, what I had seen so far was very encouraging.

After Ormond Beach, we went to Deltona, in the southernmost portion of our county. Sheila, Jeannie and I kept up our arm-weary waving, but this time we could see the difference in the support level. I had never shown well in this town, more a part of the Orlando-area than greater Daytona. The favorable looks were fewer and far between. From there we went to Deland, the county seat and site of my Sheriff's offices. The reception here was reasonably good, but there had definitely been a drop-off since this morning.

All in all, though, I had a good feeling about this day with the county's voters. The previous evening had provided me with a spark that had carried over into today's campaign marathon. In our first campaign in 1988, we started what had become a Vogel tradition the night before voters went to the polls. We split up the volunteers and some went to Deltona to line the bridge there, while others went to Daytona Beach. This year, I went to Deltona while Jeannie and Sheila led a group of our wonderful supporters to the Silver Beach Bridge that crosses the inter-coastal waterway.

Sporting their "Vote Vogel" T-shirts, cheering loudly and waving at everyone who passed them, the campaign volunteers made one final push for voters still going to the polls. Lined up across the span of the bridge, they looked like a yellow rainbow against the blue sky, now starting to show the orange tinge of the upcoming sunset. It was a sight that never failed to humble me, as large goosebumps dotted my arms.

Today, as darkness approached and the polls neared close, Jeannie, Sheila and I all thanked Vinnie for his reassuring presence. Once in the car and momentarily out of sight from onlookers, it was easier to see that the lack of sleep and tension of the day was starting to wear on us as we looked ahead to the evening's promise.

"Maybe we'll be lucky," I told them, "and we'll have an early night."

"Oh, it will be," they both said at once. I hoped they meant it.

At 6:30 PM, nearly twelve hours of campaigning finished, Jeannie, Sheila and I arrived at the Riverside Pavilion in Port Orange, overlooking the Halifax River. This growing town had been the scene of some of my most successful drug seizures as a state trooper, earning me a name and a reputation that had taken me all the way to the top law enforcement office in the county. It seemed only fitting that our campaign thank-you party for our workers should be held here.

The place was filling up fast; there were cars parked everywhere, each sporting Vogel bumper stickers. Black and yellow clothes dominated the landscape as crowds of people made their way inside. I felt my heart give another little flutter of pride and humility to see this kind of turnout.

Jeannie noticed something else. She pointed out the camera crews from Channels 2, 6 and 9, all camped out early, waiting for me to arrive. "Maybe this is where they'd been today," I thought. Jeannie said, "What are they doing here?"

She was right to wonder. Our previous two campaign nights had been remarkable for the lack of extensive coverage, except for a brief statement at the evening's conclusion. But they were here early tonight, and they gave me an uneasy feeling as their intrusive eyes followed us up the path to the main entrance.

There were smiles and cheers everywhere and we returned them with sincerity. I heard, "Congratulations, Sheriff!" over and over as people crowded in to see us, to clap us on the back, with "another campaign in the bank" type of feeling.

Sheila and Jeannie grasped as many hands as I did, thanking everyone as we went. I felt good, and you could see in these people's eyes that they had experienced the same warm feeling I did out there today.

But it wasn't over yet, and I cautioned those that seemed to think the night was ours already. "The votes still have to be counted," I reminded those around me. But there was no discouraging these individuals tonight. They were here to party—and celebrate another four years in office.

After we'd cleared the doorway, Jeannie made a beeline for Mel Stack, our friend and my former legal advisor to the Sheriff's Office. Mel gave Jeannie a friendly wave and smile, but Jeannie was pointing in the direction of the camera crews, standing like sentinels on the edge of the crowd.

"Mel, I don't want them here," I could hear her say. "They're making me nervous."

Mel put a reassuring arm around Jeannie and gave me a "thumbs-up". "They're here already, Jeannie. There's nothing we can do about it. Just ignore them and have a good time."

Jeannie finally smiled back and continued working the crowd, greeting as many people as she could, thanking them for their superb efforts. The room itself was decorated in yellow and black—Vogel campaign colors, of course—with balloons set to be freed and food and soft drinks available for all.

Sheila found her close friend, Michelle and her friend, Taylor, who had come down to share the campaign excitement with her. Sheila was also shaking hands on the evening of her first day to vote. She was both excited and nervous, wanting to hear some election returns to see how I was doing.

We had set up a big screen television in the main room with a large number of chairs available for everyone to watch the results. In the past, we only had a small television or two, but this year we wanted to make it easier on those who had given their time.

There was a back room set up for my closest friends and associates to monitor the results. As I continued shaking hands and thanking the people who had joined us, I could visualize Ron Johnston, the numbers guy, in the back room. It had been a tradition for us to have Ron on the phone with someone at the Elections office, recording the tallies even before they showed up on the television. I was sure he was there now, in touch with Gary Davidson who would be phoning in results to us as he had them. We considered Ron our good luck charm and were glad he'd agreed to come back for another election night.

Jeannie, Sheila and I finally made it to the stage in the main room, just as Jeannie's sister Marianne was writing down the first results that she'd heard. The polls were closed and some of the early numbers were already in.

Marianne smiled at us as she took the microphone and began reading the numbers out loud. Jeannie, Sheila and I held hands as we listened. As Marianne finished, something didn't sound right. Jeannie said, "We're losing?" as a question, not a statement.

"No, Marianne, those numbers can't be right," I said, and held out my hand for them. I looked at them and began reading the results out loud again and suddenly my hand shook as I realized that Jeannie's sister had read them right.

I was losing.

"It's early, folks," I reassured the audience, recovering from my initial shock at those numbers. It was time to get to the back room and find out what was going on.

Sheila looked pale and Jeannie put on yet another smile as we headed for the Pavilion's smaller room. The television reports were echoing those same early numbers as we worked our way out of the main room. My heart beat just a little faster as I entered the back room and spotted Ron Johnston.

Ron had his cell phone balanced on his shoulder, his ear to it as he wrote furiously on a pad of paper. As I waited for him to finish, I felt Jeannie's hand slip into mine. I looked down at her and tried to give her an encouraging smile. But she knew better, shook her head and squeezed my hand a little tighter.

Ron hung up and turned to face me, wordlessly handing me the numbers. This wasn't good, I thought, as I could see the sweat beading up on Ron's forehead. He was short, about 5'7", an outgoing, energetic, nervous type who'd always been glad to help us on this most important of nights.

The results were not encouraging. I sat down wearily and Jeannie and Sheila looked pensively over my shoulder. The smaller precincts generally turned in their votes first and these were from core areas of Daytona Beach itself. We didn't expect to do well there, and we weren't. I had never trailed on an election night, so on this day and night of firsts, I'd achieved another—less votes than my opponent in early returns.

Sheila looked to me for a sign that this night was going to be O.K. I smiled and hugged her and she said she was going outside with her friends for a while. I nodded and she hugged Jeannie and left, her brow wrinkling with worry lines. "The next phone call will be better," I assured Jeannie and others around me, but my voice sounded hollow to me. It seemed to appease the others though, except for my wife, who knew the inflections in my voice almost better than I did.

As I sat there in the chair, with the back room filling up with those closest to me, I refused to believe that these first results were an omen for the evening. I could not believe the good Lord would have brought me this far and not wish I would continue His work. As I sat there, trying to harness my wavering emotions, the voices around me began to fade and images of my childhood began to flash through my mind; of a boy with an independent streak, on the road to becoming the man I was today....

Chapter One:
From Emsworth To Hue City

The Woods

As a kid, I loved to hunt.

I would hunt anything that was in season. Rabbit, squirrel, deer, pheasant, bear, whatever. The challenge of searching out prey occupied a lot of my time growing up.

My dad gave me my first rifle, a .22; light, easy to handle and great for hunting. I would get up early, pull back the slide, load a dozen bullets into it and get dressed for the hunt. I would head out, looking for squirrel, knowing that if I caught enough, my mother would use the meat to make sauerbraten, one of my favorite dishes.

I would find a good spot, a place I knew would be frequented by squirrels, and I would hunker down and calmly wait for them. Once in my sights, I tracked them with my eye, patiently waiting for the head shot I wanted. I wouldn't shoot unless there was a clear head shot, because I didn't want to ruin the meat.

The squirrel would sit up, munching on an acorn, oblivious to the presence of the rifle. I centered my sights on its head and pulled the trigger. The squirrel flipped over, dead. Three more and it would be sauerbraten time.

I was eleven years old.

We lived on a hill (locals called it Nob Hill) outside the rural community of Emsworth, Pennsylvania, west of the city of Pittsburgh. I don't think the hill area even had an official town name. Emsworth was the closest thing to civilization, and even that was a stretch. You could drive up Nob Hill only on good weather days. Rain or snow would force you to park down at the bottom and walk up the incline.

But it was where young Robert and Louise Vogel raised their two children—Patty, my sister and two years my senior, and me. My parents were very young; my mother delivered Patty when she was seventeen and was only nineteen when I arrived.

We had very little. We lived in a house rented from Michael and Rose Rohanic. We had no indoor plumbing and instead used an outhouse on the property. My father was employed at an A&P grocery chain, working his way up to eventually be an assistant manager there. My mother stayed at home during these early years. She was not employable, having acquired no skills that she could put to use. Their families had made a big deal over me. I was the first boy on mom's side and only the third male in my father's family. My sister, who came first, was just another in a long line of females. As a result, my mother was very possessive and I used to look forward to the solace of the woods just to get away from the attention.

Looking back on it, I'm not sure my mother and father knew how to be parents. They were both barely out of high school when Patty was born, and my mother not yet twenty (Dad was 21) when she had me. They were teenagers, really, learning about life even as my sister and I were growing up. They had no inborn parental skills. My sister and I were just there, two other occupants of the same household. Maybe they didn't realize that kids needed encouragement and a good word occasionally. The confidence and strength I possess today was primarily self-taught.

The woods were my home. I treasured the solitude of hunting or fishing. I learned quickly how to adapt and survive in this forest of trees and brush. My father had sparked my interest in hunting. A hunter himself, he had no time for the activity, since the A&P demanded long hours and the commute alone was lengthy. He gave me that first rifle and regaled me with stories about his own hunting past. It was enticing enough for me and I looked after that .22 like it was a child.

Hunting occupied a large share of my free time in those days. There was no better feeling to me than taking on the challenge of the hunt. The experience of being close to nature and learning to survive in whatever element was something that I carried with me. At the time, I had no idea how much this activity would benefit me later in life. Only I could make a successful hunt happen, and this knowledge fortified my inner strength.

That's not to say the prey didn't occasionally exact its own revenge. There were a few cold days where I'd come home with little to show for my efforts. I remember walking home from school when I spotted a squirrel on a low hanging branch. I thought, who needs the .22? I can just grab this squirrel with my bare hand. And so I did, right by his bushy tail. I had caught him by surprise. I turned and began walking back to show my parents I could catch a live squirrel, when the animal curled up and bit me between two of my fingers. I learned the hard way that squirrels had teeth like razor blades. Blood oozed out of the wound as I dropped the squirrel and watched him scamper away. That ended a not-so promising career of live squirrel grabbing.

When I was twelve, I really wanted a Winchester hunting rifle, but I knew my parents couldn't afford it. They couldn't even buy me sufficient clothing. I took every kind of odd job I could to earn money. I delivered newspapers on my bicycle, through rain, sleet and snow. During blizzards I walked. No one on my route ever missed getting the newspaper. I helped clear land, chopping trees down with an axe and hacking weeds away with a sickle. After school and on weekends, I would work at a local bowling alley in a town called Bellevue, setting up pins after the bowlers took their shots. The alley did not have the automatic machines we enjoy today.

If I wanted something, I had to make the money to buy it myself. This included more clothes to wear. My parents never asked where I was going or what I was doing to earn the money for the things I bought. To get to the bowling alley, I had to walk two miles to get the streetcar. Coming back at some odd hours, I found myself walking home over a car path, a dirt road and a wooded area that could give you the creeps at night. I don't remember my parents ever waiting up to see if I made it home okay. But I was bound and determined to earn the money for that hunting gun.

The rifle I wanted, a Winchester Model 70 .30-06 cost $120, and I thought it was the greatest thing in the world. I had paid for it with my earnings and felt a tremendous sense of accomplishment. I knew early on that to get something you wanted, you had to make it happen yourself. It was possible, but not without effort. Many days I stood in the woods patiently waiting for game, and would give myself pep talks. I wanted something more out of life than just living in a town with no name. I wanted to make a difference somehow, and knew I could if I put my mind to it. I was dedicated to this proposition before I turned thirteen. I didn't know yet what I would do, but felt that whatever it was, hard work and determination could help me reach that goal.

To get anywhere from where we lived involved a serious trek. School, work, Boy Scouts, baseball, anywhere you wanted to go involved a combination of transportation. It began with that two-mile walk to the trolley station. As I mentioned, those two miles could be the scariest journey in Pennsylvania. A narrow path down the hill and a dark, winding street called Camp Horn Road used to add to the spooky atmosphere, especially in the winter days when darkness came early. There were times when I simply got off at the trolley stop and ran home, hearing noises all the way, quite certain that some ghost or other apparition was right behind me.

Even though my mother stayed at home with Patty and I, she had little to do with us. Once my sister and I were into our school routines, she eventually went back to school herself. She was training to be a nurse and had to be up early to catch the bus for the trolley to Pittsburgh. During those days, I would rise early, walk my mother down Camp Horn Road to the bus stop, walk/run back, change for school and make the trek with my sister all over again.

My father would take a little time off during deer hunting season in December to hunt with me. The year I bought the Winchester I couldn't wait until deer season. There were other small game seasons before it, but it wasn't the same. Deer was an entirely different proposition than squirrel or rabbit. It was a rare occasion for my father and I to spend time together, even if it was in the woods during season on the track of our quarry.

I was not close with my parents. But I did find a family in the hills of Pennsylvania. Our landlords, the Rohanics, lived next door and I ended up in their home quite often during these years. They had two daughters, Anna Mae and Rosemary, both of whom were slightly older than me. I quickly became the son and brother the Rohanics didn't have. The family atmosphere missing from my house overflowed at the Rohanics.

I had carved out a life of my own on the hill and in the woods. Between school, hunting and working at any job I could find, my days were primarily spent away from home. I know my parents must have had feelings for me, but I often felt as if they didn't know what to do with me. Being out of the house at least saved them from worrying about it.

I have said that my mother was very possessive of me, despite the lack of attention she gave. She was exceedingly jealous of my time with the Rohanics, fearful that Rose Rohanic was more of a mother to me than she was. She flew into a rage once over thinking that I had bought a greeting card for Mrs. Rohanic. I hadn't, but it was routine for her to flare up like that. But I was happy with our neighbors and continued to spend a lot of time there.

My parent's lack of attention ultimately cost me a few teeth. We rarely were taken to the dentist, and in the occasional visits I had, the cavities in my teeth were so bad the dentist had no alternative but to pull the teeth. I lost a number of my back molars during this time due to the lack of dental care. It wasn't something my parents ranked highly on their list of priorities.

I loved playing baseball as a kid. There were no parks on the Hill or in Emsworth, so it was a long journey to find a ball field to play in. In this rural area west of Pittsburgh, there were a lot of other boys in the same predicament. We didn't play in any organized league, but it became a Saturday ritual for all of us to ride our bikes several miles to a baseball field on Camp Horn Road. Whoever showed up played. We'd choose up sides and it was great fun, something we all looked forward to through spring and summer.

I was an average student. School was something I didn't appreciate much until later in life and I did whatever was necessary to get by. My life was consumed with other challenges. During the summers while I was in high school, I would work for my uncle in Pittsburgh. I was painting apartments and houses and it was a lengthy commute every day, but I was earning money.

My mother became a Licensed Practical Nurse, my father continued his promotions up to assistant manager at the A&P, and my sister and I went to high school. By senior year I knew I was in good shape to graduate, and there was a day when a buddy of mine thought it would be a good idea to cut afternoon classes. I had never skipped school before. Despite my loose upbringing, I was not a rule breaker. But my friend convinced me and after lunch, we went cruising in his car rather than returning for math class.

It was great, except for one thing—we got caught.

My father was furious. He didn't say much, but imposed the worse penalty he could think of for me. Deer hunting season was out for the rest of the year. It would come and go he said, and I was not going to participate.

I was devastated. He was right, it was the worst punishment I could have received. I kept thinking, how stupid could I be? I traded a half-day of horsing around and playing hooky for a season of deer hunting. It was a lesson I never forgot.

After graduating from high school, I went to work for the North Side Cheese Company. College wasn't a consideration. We couldn't afford it, my parents hadn't gone except for mom attending nursing school, so I did what a lot of high school graduates in rural western Pennsylvania did. We got jobs.

My sister Patty graduated the same year I did, having repeated a grade of high school. Like me, she had no parental support at home and no one encouraged her to do anything. Unlike me, she wasn't able to channel this neglect into hard work, hunting and the Rohanics. After graduation, she found work as a secretary at a car dealership and used her evenings to go to secretarial school to advance her skills. She would be married within a few years.

I was driving a truck and selling cheese to Italian restaurants and grocery stores. I was earning a lot more money than I had painting apartments or setting up bowling pins. I kept the same type of busy schedule. I went to electronics school at night and took up karate in what spare time I had left.

My karate instructor was an ex-Marine. While teaching me discipline and self-defense, he also encouraged me to consider the Marines. The Vietnam War was in full swing and soldiers were needed. I had already registered with my local draft board, but the karate teacher suggested I enlist.

It was January 1966. I would turn 19 at the end of the month and the idea of the Marines started to appeal to me. I always welcomed a challenge, and the Marines would certainly be that. I hadn't really decided what I was going to do with my life yet. I was studying to be an electronic technician and it was going OK, but it was something I could always pick back up on later.

I went down to listen to the local Marine recruiter. He was impressive, and after hearing him, I was jazzed up and ready to go. Before I could think about it any further, I had volunteered and signed up for the Marines.

THE CORPS

My dad was quiet. My mother cried. I wish I could say her tears were for me, but I knew better. She was upset at her loss, her inability to control what I did with my life, her fear of being alone.

I had never been away from home. Even though I'd spent most of my waking hours away from the house, I was a little apprehensive about leaving for the first time. I didn't know what lay ahead, but found myself somewhat wistful about this upcoming separation from my family.

My grandfather told me he'd watch me on television. I had a private conversation with him and he was the only family member who would publicly talk about the war in Vietnam. He said he watched the war on TV at night and perhaps he'd see me some evening.

The day before I left for basic training, my parents put on a party. It was a small gathering, my mother having alienated my father from his family and my dad not caring much about his in-laws, either. At least my girlfriend was there. The food was good, although there was a slight edge to the affair. I was, after all, headed into unknown territory and none of us knew what to expect.

The next day they drove me to the airport, from which I flew into Savannah, Georgia. From there, my fellow recruits and I boarded a Greyhound bus for Parris Island, South Carolina. It was March 30, 1966 and it seemed like the bus ride went on forever. There were a rag-tag-looking group of Marine wannabes on this tour and I wondered how many of us would last through boot camp.

It was nearly midnight when we arrived and, as we were all breathing a sigh of relief at having finally reached our destination and looking forward to a good night's sleep, the meanest guy in the entire world suddenly jumped on our bus. He let loose with a verbal barrage of insults about our appearance, our existence and our heritage. The last thing he said was that he'd better not find any cigarettes on the bus after we got off, and that sent a few scrounging around for any loose butts on the floor.

It was an introduction to our first drill instructor.

My whole life had seemed like a struggle up to that point, but I hadn't been through anything like Parris Island. Our first day, we were up all night. First, they shaved our heads. For some of us, it took longer than others. Second, they gave us our gear. Finally, they mustered us all in. But we weren't through.

They took us out to the farthest point on Parris Island. Our new best friend, the drill instructor, told us there were three ways we could get off the island. We could swim to Savannah, be carried off in a box or walk off as a Marine. He didn't highly recommend the first two options.

It was hell. It was the longest two months of my life to that point, but each day I was one day closer to walking out of there a Marine. A lot of guys didn't make it. But I had an advantage that I hadn't really thought about until then. I had literally grown up in the woods, and often felt during those early dreary days that I was back in those woods with only my own wits to help me survive. This reassurance helped me last through those two months until I finally earned the name Marine.

When I left, I walked out. There were tears in my eyes as I felt a real sense of accomplishment. I had made it! I was a Marine! I was doing something for my country and felt proud. Now it was on to Camp Lejeune in North Carolina for four weeks of infantry training. This time it was different. I had some confidence.

After Camp Lejeune, I was assigned to Communications School in San Diego. I felt like I was going back to electronics school. When I arrived, I was assigned as a Teletype operator for the three-month stint. There, I met Mickey Tidwell, from Birmingham, Alabama, a fellow Marine Teletype operator. It was good to have a friend.

The weeks went by and after we graduated from Communications School, we were both assigned to Camp Pendleton in California. The 5th Marine Division had just been re-activated for the first time since World War II. The Marines were the smallest branch of the armed forces, and more men were needed for Vietnam. We were excited about being part of the reincarnation of this unit.

The months went by and Mickey and I remained at Camp Pendleton. By now, we had both been with the Marines for more than 18 months and while men were being sent to Vietnam every week, we stayed back in California. The need for communications people was far less than for the ordinary grunt. As 1967 drew to a close, we decided to take matters into our own hands.

We didn't want to do our whole three years in the Marines and never leave the country. Vietnam was obviously where we were needed. We just weren't going to get there as Teletype operators.

Rumors were rampant around the base that the 5th Division would be shipping out as a group shortly to replace either the 1st or 3rd in Vietnam, who had received some heavy casualties. We had kept up a constant vigil on a large bulletin board where the postings wanted were listed. There was never a call for communications, but there were unlimited opportunities for O-3s, basic riflemen. We decided to apply as grunts.

They took us.

There were two weeks of advanced infantry needed, since we were Communications graduates and hadn't done much in the way of infantry training since Camp Lejeune. They let us go home for Christmas before the camp.

Before I arrived back in Emsworth, my grandfather passed away. I went to his funeral while I was home. My grandfather had been a nice, spirited man and I would miss him. I guess he wouldn't be watching me on television after all.

When I left, there was a stronger sense that this was some kind of parting, that I might not be coming home. I didn't feel that way, but I could tell my parents were doing their best to hold their emotions inside. We had never been a very demonstrative family and nothing changed that day. But I could tell they cared—and they were worried.

Advanced infantry training at Camp Pendleton meant a lot of weaponry lessons and maneuvers. When we finished the daily activities, we would return to a barbed wire enclosure for the evening. We were given minimal food, often just one cup of rice and some carrots as part of the preparation for what lay ahead in Vietnam. We all imagined this must be how POWs were treated. The training was tough, and this was after the other training we'd done in the last two years from landing on beaches to NCO school.

The weather that winter in California was unseasonably cold, and as the two-week training period went on I began feeling sick. I had chills, a fever, a cough, and I was weakening. I was an acting platoon commander for training only and there was a black Marine in my unit who I'd ordered to clean up our hooch. Others had done it and it was now his turn. He told me to go to hell. I reminded him that I outranked him and he had better get the hooch cleaned up pronto. We had a slight confrontation, and he ended up being reprimanded for disobeying a direct order. The last thing I heard from him was, "I'm going to get you Vogel when we get to Vietnam."

"Great," I thought. "We're about to go to Vietnam, I feel lousy and the first enemy I make is on our side."

The 5th Marine Division eventually received orders to go to Vietnam. The plans were to leave California aboard ship, which would take about a month. Because Mickey and I were doing some extra infantry training and there was just a few of us, we travelled by plane. It was the best thing that had happened to me in two weeks.

We flew to Okinawa, the final staging area before Vietnam. We left behind most of our stateside uniforms and assorted items and took minimal supplies with us. We also received our final inoculations there. There was one giant syringe they jabbed in your butt that contained a blood thinner for your system. That shot seemed to last forever, although I'm sure it only took a minute or two for all the fluid to be injected. It wasn't easy to sit down after that experience.

By then, the illness contracted in California had taken its toll and I was too sick to go on. Despite my protests, I wasn't going to Vietnam with Mickey Tidwell. I was going to the hospital.

Mickey was assigned to some outfit in Da Nang. I would take whatever I got once I arrived, but there was a good chance I wouldn't be with Mickey.

I hated the hospital, but I was truly immobile. I had developed pneumonia and it was three days until I could actually sit up and move some muscles with any regularity. By the end of the week, though, I was itching to go. I hadn't fully recovered, but I told the doctor I was feeling great and he released me.

It was February 1968 and I was finally headed for Vietnam.

NORTH OF DA NANG

I flew on a commercial plane into Da Nang. It was not exactly how I pictured going to war. All the Marines on board with me were going over to replace others who had either been killed or rotated out of country.

Once disembarked, I went to a receiving station and told the Marines my name. They gave me my assignment, 1st Battalion, 5th Marines, and then looked solemnly at each other. At that moment the 5th was square in the middle of some intense fighting. They pointed me to a C-130 cargo plane that had been stripped of its seats and used to haul supplies and cargo. Apparently the 5th was in need.

One other Marine boarded that flight with me, and we were off to a place called Phu Bai. It was located eight miles south of Hue City, an old provincial capital of Vietnam in the I-Corps area.

The two of us sat on the floor of the plane, looking like anything but Marines. We had utility outfits, no jungle fatigues and no rifles. Unbeknownst to us, the North Vietnamese had launched an all out surprise assault on U.S. positions in January. It was Tet, the lunar New Year and a national holiday, and everyone expected a lull in the fighting as there had been in the past. The 5th Marines had been dropped into the thick of the fighting at Hue City.

The trip was short and we jumped off the plane. All I could see was red dust around me. It didn't take long for a reddish tinge to settle on my clothes, the same outfit I had left Okinawa in hours ago.

I asked for the location of my unit and was pointed down a dusty, unpaved road. I smiled to myself, thinking the street reminded me of home. I started down the path, dragging my Sea bag (containing two stateside green utility uniforms, underwear, a camera and writing materials) with me towards 1st Battalion headquarters. I passed an officer on the way. I was a Corporal, but back in the states we were instructed not to salute a commanding officer (C.O.) in a combat area.

So I didn't. Man, he chewed my butt off big time for that oversight. Welcome to Vietnam, I thought.

Once I found headquarters, they sent me to Communications. I was here as a basic rifleman, but they'd noticed the communications tag on my papers. Red dust swirled everywhere, it was hot and the tents were rolled up all the way to try and circulate some air. It was late afternoon, I hadn't eaten since Okinawa, my sinuses were clogging up with red dust, the place was an absolute hole and I began to wonder what I had got myself into. I was as green as they come.

I tried to ignore the artillery sounds in the background and even the mortar rounds that seemed dangerously close. No one else appeared to be paying attention, and I didn't want to stand out on my first day. At the supply tent, I was given two sets of used jungle utilities (jacket and trousers) which were dirtier than what I had on. The rest of the equipment consisted of a rusty M-16 rifle, a new pair of boots, two canteens, a wet belt, a poncho, a backpack, a couple of magazine clips and a bandoleer of ammunition. Anything else I needed, I was told, I could scrounge up for myself.

I was pointed in the general direction of the COMM center. I guess I was back in Communications. The Sergeant in charge was a former infantryman who had been wounded and reassigned to head up the COMM center. He told me to go find some C-rations (which consisted of a can of food which represented your main course, a can of fruit, a chocolate bar and cigarettes) and pick out a cot. He pointed in the general direction of a tent and said that a lot of guys had been killed up in Hue, so I shouldn't have any problem finding a place to sleep. He'd take care of my assignment tomorrow.

He gave me the impression he was glad to see me. What the hell, I was a fresh, warm body.

Outside, I walked toward the tent, waving off the red dust that swirled with every vehicle passing or helicopter landing. It was still monsoon season, though, so there was a chance the dust could be watered down somewhat. For now, the cots were disgusting, covered in red like everything else seemed to be around here.

Darkness was approaching fast and I noticed that no one would talk to me. They must have realized it was my first day. I found out later that it was standard practice to ignore the new guy. You didn't want to get too close to anyone, since there was a better than even chance he'd be killed in the first month. After that, it was all right to converse with you. If you could get through eleven months, guys would still talk to you but were afraid of jinxing your nearly successful tour of duty. You could tell who the short-timers were as they used to put a piece of cardboard inside a band of rubber that wrapped around the helmet. The writing on the cardboard indicated how many days the person had left in their tour.

I noticed troops beginning to come back in, probably from Hue. I was stunned at how old they all looked, even though they must have been my age or, in some cases, even younger. I realized I had a lot to learn about this war.

That first day, I heard bits and pieces about what was happening. Twelve North Vietnamese Army (NVA) divisions had surrounded our whole 1st Battalion up in Hue City. Our battalion had about 700 people in it, but no one knew what the current count was since we had taken some heavy casualties.

Day turned into night so quickly I thought I'd fallen asleep standing up and missed an hour or two. Night in Vietnam was pitch black. There were no artificial lights to speak of in Phu Bai and you couldn't see the hand in front of your face. While I was deciding on whether to try and get some sleep, I heard someone yell, "Incoming!"

I had a pretty good idea what that meant, and suddenly we were being blasted. Phu Bai was the staging area for 1st Battalion and there were several trenches. As rockets exploded around us, one Marine grabbed me and pulled me into one. Somehow, it felt a little safer than ducking under the cot.

Shrapnel flew everywhere. Cots were blown up. Marines were still running for cover. It was chaotic. Some Marines jumped into the trenches on top of others. There were guys that were blown into the trenches, sometimes just a body part at a time. There was blood everywhere, along with yells and some agonizing screams that were as pitiful as any I'd ever heard.

Guys were yelling, "I'm hit, I'm hit!" and Marines lay dead and wounded all around me. The NVA mixed in some mortar shots with the rockets, inflicting still more damage. Later during my tour, I could tell you exactly what kind of rockets and shells were being used and give you their dimensions. Tonight, I just prayed I would get through the attack.

My leg was shaking with fear and I tried to breathe deeply to calm down. There was nothing you could do at this point except to stay down in the trench and hope that an air strike or artillery would come in and bail us out. I heard cries of pain from wounded Marines. There was screaming and the tremendous noise of rockets exploding everywhere. Showers of shrapnel strafed the trenches and the area all around me.

As I lay there, surrounded by body parts and a couple of other live Marines, thinking I'm going to die in a pile of red dirt, the thunderous roar around me suddenly receded and a spiritual calmness came over me that sheltered my entire being in a kind of peacefulness. As I lay there with the sounds of battle echoing faintly in the distance, out of this tranquil silence I heard my grandfather's voice saying, "Don't worry, Bob, you're going to make it."

The comforting sound of his voice echoed throughout my body and I could feel the fear rise up and drift away. My body relaxed, and while the noise of the attack continued to sound and I was still hugging the bottom of the trench, I felt the comfort that comes with knowing that somehow I was safe. It was as if a protective layer had been placed around me in which I alone resided, outside of the danger that resonated around me.

I had only been in Vietnam for ten hours.

The next morning after we'd cleaned up the remains of the night's attack, I met our Lieutenant in charge. He wore two silver-colored side-arm revolvers and looked like the Second Coming of General Patton. He had brought the new guys together that had survived the night shelling and was asking for volunteers to go out and train the local Vietnamese to help them defend their villages.

One of the things I had already heard about that duty was that volunteers had a relatively short life expectancy. I chose not to raise my hand.

Instead, they put some others and me on the back of a 2-1/2 ton truck heading up Highway 1 to Hue City. The NVA had concentrated the bulk of their forces in this part of South Vietnam with their offensive. Hue City itself was on fire.

In the truck, we passed some troops walking along the side of the road. You could tell who the newer arrivals were. They were the pale-looking guys with their pants slit open in the back, their bare butts shining in the morning sun just in case they had to go to the bathroom quickly. Dysentery was common in the first few weeks, and the sight of these "moons" on the road to Hue was one scene that wasn't mentioned in any tourist guides.

You could tell that Hue was a beautiful city. Despite the fierce fighting going on throughout its streets, the ancient buildings rose above the smoke and dust. We passed an old church and were shocked at the sight of two bodies hanging in the archway. They were two nuns who had been decapitated and strung up for all passersby to see. It was the first of many horrors I would witness in this country on the other side of the world.

Downtown Hue was just a large, urban city. We passed a bank and a grocery store where, on any other day you could visualize residents going about their normal routine. Today, we were trying to locate one unit that had been cut off from the others. We had lost complete contact with them and took up the search, street by street. After some time, we saw an American flag being raised in the north end of the city. Someone was there! We were jubilant!

After reuniting with these troops, we returned to the Perfume River south of the city and set up a firebase. I was placed in charge of security for this camp's COMM Center. We set up barbed wire and claymore mines all around the perimeter. The NVA were scariest at night and we wanted plenty of warning if they attacked.

We were at this firebase for several days. The NVA kept up their artillery shelling and mortar attacks. Ironically, the most beautiful sight in this country was the dropping of flares in the night sky that illuminated our perimeter to help offset any ground attack. Sharp, piercing light from tracer rounds and fiery explosions provided a sharp and deadly contrast with the ebony environment of evening. There were many nights when I counted the minutes until dawn, knowing that danger diminished during the daylight hours.

It became a daily survival battle. You had to take on the elements, the hardships, the limited nourishment, the carnage, and the tragedy. To make it, you had to transform yourself into an animal-like existence. Oddly, there were times when I thought about how grateful I was that I'd spent all that time in the woods back home. I realized I was a survivalist at heart, the instinct ingrained early in life and honed to a fine edge by training at Parris Island and other stops on the tour.

The day after we set up the firebase, some local villagers came out in the morning. (They also knew when it was safer to move around.) They were crying and gesturing at us, and someone finally interpreted that we had set up camp on a Vietnamese burial ground.

We advised them we couldn't move. This was the best location and we had already set up perimeter security. They requested the chance to dig up the bodies buried in this old cemetery and transport them elsewhere. So we agreed to help them.

The graves had no markers. Much of it was disturbed. In some places, there were circles drawn with stones that I hadn't really noticed before. It didn't matter. The locals appeared to know where all the bodies were buried. Some graves had been there for years while others were more recently dug. The smell was horrific; nothing is worse on the nose than a decaying body. The locals were all crying as we performed this ghoulish task, pouring perfume over themselves to fight back the nauseating odor.

During this stay in Hue City, word came through the ranks that Bob Hope was coming to Da Nang to perform in a USO show there. Certain guys were selected out of each unit and I was picked from ours to go. We were to take a plane to Da Nang from Phu Bai. But minutes before we reached the plane, it was shelled by a rocket. No Bob Hope Show, but we were all still alive.

It took a few weeks, but I started to get to know some people and adapted to my new surroundings, such as they were. My closest friend was Harold "Ace" Hendricks. We seemed to have a lot in common and spent many hours together talking about home. This closeness was rare. You were scared to get to know any-one real well since they could take a mortar round that night.

I learned a few Vietnamese words that enabled me to barely communicate with the locals. As a result, I befriended a couple of local kids. I kept them sup-plied with candy bars and they were my welcoming committee when I came back to base after a mission. They were typical kids. They wanted to hold the gun I carried. They asked endless questions about America. They had very little, so I always felt good about getting them whatever I could to eat. I found Asians, in general, to be very friendly.

I managed to learn quickly about the Viet Cong, known as VC, southerners that sided with the North Vietnamese. They were more of a guerrilla force, like partisans in enemy territory. We didn't see many of them near Hue City or Phu Bai, where we were. They operated further south. The NVA, on the other hand, was a well-trained, true military force. We didn't find much coordination between the two fighting forces, except they were dedicated to the same cause – Vietnamese independence.

Even though Hue was tough duty, we had heard worse about Khe Sanh, up near the border of North Vietnam. Our boys were getting hammered there. No matter where you were, you could always make a case for being better off than another hot spot.

We didn't see much drug use up in the fighting area of Vietnam. We had heard drugs were rampant in the cities, Saigon being the worst. Up here, we worried more about just staying alive and finding a decent meal. I was looking at life dif-ferently now. That happens when every day could be your last. You appreciate each moment so much more.

When I wrote home, my big request was always for my folks to send some instant Lipton Tea. The water here was awful, and tea seemed to at least make it easier to swallow. You always had to scrounge for stuff. I vowed to never take the simple things in life for granted ever again. One wish I had over and over was for ice cream. I used to close my eyes and try and remember how ice cream tasted. I'm sure it wasn't as good as I thought it was sitting out there in a rice paddy mined with God knows what, but it helped my frame of mind. I would even have settled for an ice cube.

Another wish was for a shower. After a few days, you reached a point where you were past being able to smell anything. The first weeks were ones of constant diarrhea. You didn't wear underwear and socks because of jungle rot. Jungle rot is like a fungus - a red, pimplish, moist, swollen rash that then dries as if you're skin is rotting away. I still carry some of the remnants of jungle rot with me today.

On patrol, there was simply no time for the unit to stop for you to go to the bathroom, so those that had to go simply went in their pants or through the holes cut in their trousers. As I said, you quickly moved past the time where smells or even dignity meant much to you.

Guys wanted out of there so badly they'd do anything. We were given a regular malaria pill to take every Sunday. It was a giant, scary-looking horse pill. Most guys didn't take it at all. They'd rather contract malaria then spend one more day in the jungle. That's how bad it was. I didn't take mine either, until enforcement of this procedure became tighter.

After a time, you could tell how long someone had been in country by the condition of the person's boots. The footwear always started new, but it didn't take long to beat them up. How used they looked meant the number of weeks the person had been on their tour.

You also could tell who was more affected by the experience. Not taking a malaria pill made perfectly logical sense to us. But there was a huge difference between veterans who still maintained their sense of humor and ones who were simply serious all the time. The latter were guys I thought would have trouble adapting if and when they returned home. They had crossed some boundary inside themselves and would never be the same.

While we were stationed near Hue, we received word about a secret NVA hospital on top of a mountain. Our battalion commander, a Colonel, got a group of us together and went to take a look. It was a typical search and destroy mission.

It took us three days to maneuver to the top of the mountain. It was equivalent to climbing a mountain in the Rocky Mountains of the United States, except you went up through jungle. The trees and vegetation formed a kind of canopy over our heads, enveloping us in near total darkness on the ground even during daylight hours. This cover provided a cool contrast to the normally hot, humid air, but it was slow moving and scary as you felt danger could lurk around every dark corner. Parts of this journey provided us with incredible scenery, running streams amidst lush undergrowth. It was hard to imagine this was a war zone.

It was through these streambeds that we made our way up the mountain. We knew we wouldn't leave a trail to follow and the sound of the water covered our own noise.

During that trek, we would travel until dark, but take patrol turns at night to protect ourselves. We were paired up in twos and at night we often combined with another duo for watch purposes. One individual would take the first two hours while the others slept and then another would take his place and so forth through the night. Despite this routine, we rarely caught more than a couple of hours sleep. One morning, there were a few guys we couldn't get up due to exhaustion. They said they'd sleep for a couple of more hours and catch up. It was daylight. They weren't worried. When they didn't show, a couple of us went back to look for them. They had been killed as they slept.

It seemed to take forever to go up that mountain. It was steep and somewhat treacherous in parts. It poured rain most of the way and when it subsided, the mosquitoes came out in droves. When you tried to sleep at night, you wrapped every inch of bare skin inside some clothing to prevent being badly bitten.

We finally reached the top early on the fourth day. Sure enough, it was a full-fledged operating hospital. We found a series of tunnels; passageways where the wounded and supplies would be brought in or were utilized as an escape route. It had been used that morning, but the place was now deserted. There was fresh blood and bandages on the operating room floor, so the enemy must have dragged the wounded out through the tunnels.

We blew these tunnels up and then checked through the supplies to see if there was anything we could use. There were a bunch of chickens running around, which we rounded up for food. We also found some rice donated, according to the packing, by the University of California at Berkeley.

There were loads of heroin here. It was frequently used as medicine, but also for another deadly purpose. There were wounded NVA who would wrap themselves up tightly in thin communication wire, shoot themselves up with the stuff and come right through the barbed wire perimeter around the base to attack you. When you would shoot at them, the wire would hold the bullets inside their bodies and the heroin would mask the pain, allowing them to keep driving forward. These were purely suicide missions, and I was amazed at the number of NVA who would participate in these attacks, trading their life for a life.

The NVA had left behind a large cooking kettle, so we cleaned the chickens and put them in the cauldron along with the rice and our C-rations to make a kind of Marine Mulligan Stew. It was good eating. We then finished destroying the hospital so it couldn't be used again, and we headed straight down that mountain in a hurry.

It took us days to go up the mountain, but only eight hours to run down it. That's about how much daylight we had left. We had requested the helicopter after the last detonation and we did not relish the thought of another night out in the jungle here. We weren't even sure we would be picked up as the area was labeled a hot landing zone, and it was up to the pilot to decide whether the aircraft's descent was feasible.

We made it before nightfall, but the helicopter wouldn't land since it was not a secure area. So we spent another night. The NVA figured we were still up on the mountain somewhere, underestimating our determination to get down that incline. They spent the night shelling it, trying to kill us. We were glad we'd made the run even though we had to stay one more night. They picked us up the next day before the NVA found us.

When we returned to base, we were surprised to see a big dinner and a USO show awaiting us. While we looked forward to the promise of round-eyed girls in the production, we knew there was something else coming. A big meal and show like this meant they were shipping us someplace. Our guess was Khe Sanh, a hot border area about to ignite. Nobody was very enthusiastic about our potential assignment.

We were wrong. Several helicopters flew in before sunrise to pick us up. They shipped us instead to An Hoa, close to the border, where the Ho Chi Minh Trail comes into South Vietnam. It was about 35 miles west of Da Nang and was all VC territory. The ARVN (Army of the Republic of Vietnam, the South's military force and our allies) would be accompanying us. They dropped us into a hot landing zone and we were under fire as we disembarked from the helicopters. It wasn't exactly the welcome wagon for our new home.

An Hoa was another mess. There were constant raids on our base. Our re-con missions often turned into shoot-outs. Ace and I somehow managed to get through the weeks unscathed.

I also met two German doctors who were stationed at a neutral hospital on assignment. They appreciated my name, Vogel, and accepted me as one of their own. As neutrals, they were friendly with everyone: the NVA, the VC, the ARVN and other civilians. They treated anyone who came to the facility. They invited me over to dinner one night and I took Ace. After we ate, they took us through a hospital where they worked and even pointed out some of the NVA wounded they were treating.

We didn't do anything. This hospital was neutral ground. I kept thinking, here are these people out on what passes for a road northwest of Da Nang. They were unprotected. They had no weapons. They maintained this hospital for anyone that was hurt or needed medical attention. To me, they were a courageous bunch and were always nice to me when I came by.

In An Hoa, we had a Master Sergeant named "Top" Smith, who was proud of a jeep he had out there. None of us could figure out what Top was doing with this jeep. I mean, where was he going to go with it? It wasn't like you could take it for a ride anywhere. The roads were impassable and often mined. There weren't exactly any sights to see.

But, man, was he proud of that vehicle. He had scavenged it from the Army and had stuck Marine decals all over it. He was clearly attached. Finally, during one shelling we took, a mortar round found Top's jeep and blew it all to pieces. He was crushed. We all tried to keep a somber mood in his presence, but suddenly someone started to laugh and we all broke down. I know Top didn't find it quite as humorous as we did.

During occasional respites, I met up a few times with Mickey Tidwell in Da Nang. I had bumped into him once or twice when our units crossed paths, but the R&R gambits with him were a pleasing distraction to the disturbing atmosphere of daily life in Vietnam.

When a major operation was being planned, all units often came together in one large assembly area. One such time, we found ourselves among the Green Berets. During the evening hours, we decided to embark on our own mission against them. These elitists were all snug and cozy when we stole all of their guns. The next day they were all over us, hopping mad! But our Colonel told them that if they couldn't protect their guns, what use were they anyway? What if we were VC? They'd have all been killed, probably. They got in their helicopters, left on their assignment and we ended up with some decent firepower.

One particular night we were getting shelled badly. Rockets and mortars were coming fast and furious, sending shrapnel everywhere. You just huddled down in a bunker and hoped you didn't take a direct hit. Suddenly I heard someone cry out, "Ace is hit!" I cried out, "Who?" The return shout confirmed it was Ace.

Immediately, I forgot everything I had learned in training, jumped out of that bunker and ran towards the source of those shouts. I was running across open ground, explosions going off all around me, yelling "Ace! Ace! Where are you?" It was pitch black, so the explosions actually illuminated the ground for me. After a few tense moments, I hear Ace hollering, "I'm over here!"

I ran to his voice, fell headfirst into his bunker and scrambled up to see how bad he was. I grabbed him by the shoulder and said, frantically, "Where are you hit? Are you OK?" Ace just nodded and said, "Yeah, I'm OK." I relaxed and said, "Thank God! Where are you hit?

"In the lip," Ace replied and another mortar went off nearby, providing some light. There was a small trace of blood coming from his mouth caused by a tiny piece of shrapnel.

"This is it!" I shouted. "This is where you've been hit!"

Ace wiped the blood from his chin and acknowledged that this was his war wound.

"Great, Ace," I said, a little put out. "I ran across an open field for a cut lip?"

"Hey, I didn't tell you to do that!" Ace protested.

But I was glad he was all right. We spent the rest of the attack, huddled together in this bunker, hoping we could stay as lucky.

We made it through another night.

My last month there was insane. I was a short-timer so, except for Ace, nobody talked much to me. We were overrun a couple of times by the enemy.

During one of these firefights, one incident stands out in my mind. One of our Sergeants had just extended his stay six months. As was common, he had been given a free month's paid leave anywhere he wanted to go. He used this time to return to the States to marry his childhood sweetheart. He then came back to begin his new six-month tour. He had just returned hours prior to this latest firefight. During the battle, he caught a mortar right in the chest. There was nothing we could do to save him.

I remember sitting next to his body, with only a couple of days to go myself thinking, why him? Why now? Why that mortar round in that location? None of it made any sense. His girl was widowed before she had much chance to be his wife.

Down to my last two days, I was in base hoping for no more mission assignments, when I felt the urge to use the bathroom. I left my gun in camp and took off down this little trail for a few moments of solitude. As I was walking down the path, I spotted another Marine coming the other way. I didn't think much of it until the man drew closer. Suddenly, I recognized him. He was the black Marine I'd disciplined back at Camp Pendleton for failing to obey my order to clean up our hooch. His last words to me as I recall were about getting me when we got to Vietnam.

This was his chance. He was almost on me now and was fully armed. I was mad at myself for leaving my gun.

He recognized me, too, and I nodded at him, watching his face as he carried his M-16. He said, "Is that you Vogel?"

"Yes", I answered.

A small, faint smile slowly appeared. "How many days?" he asked.

"Two," I replied.

He nodded thoughtfully and responded, "Good luck back in the world!"

I thanked him, wished him well and we parted. He set off down the trail to wherever he was going and I watched him go. I was relieved! I'd never witnessed anyone shoot another Marine over here, but we had heard about it often enough. After that verbal exchange, it was obvious that my disciplining him back in the States seemed so trivial after all we had both been through. I was sure that he, like me, had more troublesome images on his mind from his tour of duty.

In early January 1969, the NVA launched another offensive that continued right through February. I had arrived during one a year earlier and hoped to quickly leave this one behind. The monsoon season was in full swing. It was a brutal one, raining heavily on a continual basis. It was always cold and wet, and the rain and the wind were relentless. We were constantly damp. I was down to about 120 pounds, I had jungle rot, I was malnourished, but I hadn't been shot. Twelve months and 18 days and I had remained wound-free. How, I have no idea.

But this latest NVA offensive and the weather didn't let me get away easily. We were under constant threat of attack and each night the VC overran us. They broke through our perimeter and we were engaged in a firefight within minutes. These battles had raged on with frightening regularity, and I fought as hard as I ever had.

The rain made it impossible for helicopters to fly in. I was down to the wire on my tour and I prayed for the rain to stop, as I knew the next helicopter that came in would be my ride home. My anticipation hung heavy in the air, like the humid weather we breathed in every day.

We managed to turn back assault after assault and then artillery or an air strike would send the rest of the VC scurrying back to the jungle for cover. Once again, I had emerged without a scratch. I had to get out of there before my luck changed for the worse.

Our mission had been to engage the enemy on as many fronts as we could and we had done that. Now all I wanted to do was go home. When the rain stopped, and the buzz of the helicopters coming in became a reality, I knew I was going to do just that. The helicopters brought necessary food and supplies and it was all unloaded in a matter of minutes. The wounded were loaded, and there was more than enough transportation for me to go out with this first wave. Those few brief moments were all the time I had to say goodbye to people who had been like my family, who had shared experiences with me like nothing any of us had ever seen. I hugged Ace and repeated the familiar parting words, "See you back in the World."

As the helicopter lifted off the ground, I was glad this tour had come to an end. Our unit had received many medals during my stay from the Presidents of both the U.S. and South Vietnamese governments.

That was the end of my days as a Marine. These would be times I would never forget and I would have nightmares for some time to come. Backfire from a car or truck would send me to the ground until I readjusted to the familiar surroundings of the States.

Mickey Tidwell and I exchanged Christmas cards for a while. I even visited "Top" Smith up in Quantico, Virginia after I had come back, but eventually lost touch with him. My buddy, "Ace" Hendricks, was the best man at my wedding and we still see each other on occasion today.

I visited Parris Island not long ago with my family. I found my old barracks. There were a few recruits there being trained. I watched them for a few minutes and noticed some other old Marines standing around. One of them turned out to have been here in 1966 with me. The drill instructor came over and we talked about the past and then drove about a mile or so to the rifle range.

There were monuments there, for the legendary Marine sites of Iwo Jima and Guadalcanal, fought during World War II, and for the Chosin Reservoir in Korea. But there were also two monuments commemorating the 5th Marines at Hue City and the 9th at Khe Sanh. To be sharing the same commemoration as those other historic events brought tears to my eyes as I remembered the hard work and sacrifice, and my comrades who had paid the ultimate price. We didn't exactly get a hero's welcome when we returned. In 1969, the country was bitterly divided over the war and whether we should stay or go. The sight of that memorial humbled me. It meant a lot that someone cared enough to remember the brave soldiers who had given their lives there.

Before we left, I signed the guest book. As I wrote down the date, March 29, 1996, it struck me that I had first entered these grounds almost thirty years to the day, March 30, 1966.

I had time to reflect on my experience in the Corps after I came home to Pennsylvania. I knew that my boyhood spent in the woods had prepared me for Vietnam. I could only wonder then what my tour of duty in Vietnam had prepared me for next.

I knew one thing. I had lost my desire to ever hunt again.

Interlude:
ELECTION NIGHT, 1996

In the back room of the Riverside Pavilion, the scene of my election night gathering, close friends and associates had come together to share the evening with Jeannie, Sheila and I. We were anxiously awaiting the next results being phoned in by our contact, Gary Davidson, to a cell phone held by Ron Johnston, who was presently standing next to me, a dark look of concern clouding his face.

The chairs around the small conference table in this room had filled up. A pair of French doors looked out on the Halifax River, a beautiful view that no one seemed to be noticing. By now, everyone had heard the first numbers that had me trailing my opponent Gus Beckstrom, among the early reporting precincts. Ron had a complete list of precincts and was looking down at the numbers he'd already written in, as if his stare could somehow change the results.

Sheila was out in the main room, while Jeannie "hosted" this back room group. One of the people joining us was Major Leonard Davis, the man in charge of the largest division within the Volusia County Sheriff's Office, the Law Enforcement Services Division. An African-American, Leonard was a long-time employee of the Sheriff's Office, having started in 1971. He cut an imposing figure at 6'4" and over 300 pounds, and was known for his jolly, caring and kind personality to those closest to him. Though sporting a tough exterior, inside Leonard was more of a teddy bear and was proud to be a graduate of the prestigious FBI National Academy.

Also taking a seat was Captain Dale Anderson, the head of one of our four District offices around the county. Dale was an impressive-looking man, muscular, athletic, slightly balding, a great street cop and also a graduate of the FBI National Training Academy. I had a tremendous amount of confidence in Dale; he was the type of officer who would have taken a bullet for me and I knew I could always trust him with my life and that of my family. He reminded me a little of

Sean Connery in the movie, The Untouchables. He and his wife, Debbie, had four children, the oldest of which went to school with Sheila. They had lost a child early in their marriage, but now cared for four boys ranging in age from 19 to 2, a wide span that constantly kept them busy. When Dale first appeared tonight, he'd grinned at Jeannie and held up a cigar. "It's our lucky cigar!" he told her, reminding us that he had brought one on election night in 1992 and lit it up after the results were clearly in my favor.

My second in command, Major Bob Rickmyre, had just come in to the back room. He was in charge of our Administrative Services Division. Bob was thin and worked out actively to maintain his slender appearance. He had proven to be a good decision-maker for me and had passed along plenty of welcome advice in my first eight years as Volusia County's Sheriff. Bob's son had contracted leukemia nine years earlier at age 10, an experience that had changed Bob's life. After treatment at Shands Hospital in Gainesville, Florida and much caring and praying, his son continued to be a survivor, now 19 years old. It had transformed Bob into a religious believer, and now, I thought, we could use his prayers tonight.

Major Connie Locke headed up our Community Services Division. She was already a retired Commander from the Metro Dade (Miami) Sheriff's Office, and was now serving with us. Her husband Art was the police chief in Orange City, a town in the southwestern part of Volusia County near Deltona. She was an outgoing, robust woman, a natural leader who served on a number of national boards including the FBI's National Crime Information Center (NCIC). I relied on her to network with the public, and she thrived on working with local community groups. She was the type that could take on any task—and get it done.

Also joining the back room contingent was Sergeant Jody Palermo, who had acted as an unofficial bodyguard for Jeannie and Sheila during the campaign. There had been some threats from the other side, and Jody took them seriously. I was grateful to him for his concern and effort. He was also the kind of person I could always count on, and I cherished my relationship with him. Of Italian descent, he was in his late forties like me and had worked in the Broward Sheriff's Office in Fort Lauderdale before coming to work here in Volusia County.

Finally, Captain Terry Sanders rounded out the current group seated at the conference table, waiting for the phone to ring with good news. Terry was in charge of our Special Services Unit, consisting of aviation, marine, traffic and reserve deputies. Now in his early 40's, Terry had practically grown up in the Volusia County Sheriff's Office. Terry was another loyal member of this team, an intelligent, hard-working man. He was married with two children, and also owned a couple of feed stores on the side. He was another person I knew I could count on.

This core group was my support team in the Sheriff's Office. Together, we had turned the Volusia County Sheriff's Office into a professional law enforcement agency, a far cry from the disorganized institution I had inherited in 1989.

We still had some room for improvement, and we were all dedicated towards continuing the high standards we had set for ourselves.

Of course, I had to win this election first. The conversation in the room was muted, many of them silently considering their own futures in the Sheriff's Office if I was not re-elected. I only wanted to hear the next results.

The phone's ring nearly paralyzed the people waiting for the call. The room looked like it was in freeze-frame, everyone afraid to move a muscle until Ron Johnston recorded and read the results.

Jeannie had stopped talking and was looking at Ron intently, trying to read the results from his face. She was not smiling, so I knew Ron wasn't either. Not a man to hide his feelings well, Ron must have been listening to election figures similar to what we'd already heard tonight.

Finally, he stopped writing and clicked off his cell phone. The noise of the revelers in the main room seemed to lower as Ron read us back the results.

I was still trailing Gus Beckstrom, and several key precincts had reported in. I was doing well in Pierson, a small community on the western fringes of the county; Ormond Beach, a usual strong supporter to the north; and my home base of New Smyrna Beach, a town the local newspaper predicted I would have difficulty carrying this year.

I was losing in Daytona Beach, Deltona, Deland and Oak Hill. I had never done well in Deltona and Oak Hill was always iffy, but it was too small to make a significant difference. I had always carried (if not by wide margins) Deland and Daytona Beach, but this year those votes were not going my way.

I looked quickly around the room. Leonard was staring at the floor, Ron was wiping his forehead with a handkerchief, Connie and Terry were looking to me for reassurance and Dale had put away his lucky cigar.

"It's still early," I said, as confidently as I could. I had never been in this position before in an election and wasn't quite sure what to say. But I had been in this spot before in my life and was sure I would be again. I could feel my inner resolve kicking in, steeling myself for a long night, knowing I was going to be in there until the last vote was counted. "We're not behind by much," I said, trying to console the suddenly grave bunch that sat around the table. "There are plenty of votes to come, and we'll have four more years to show for it when it's over. Hang in there!"

As I finished, my eyes found Jeannie's and I could see the pride in her and the confidence that we would get through this no matter what. Just as I tried to motivate the troops, Jeannie was—and always has been—my inspiration. We didn't need words between us now to know what was going on. We had long been able to read each other's, a strength that I couldn't imagine having with another soul.

As we looked at each other now, I thought back to the first time we had gazed into each other's eyes when I had knew immediately that this was the woman with whom I wanted to share my life....

Chapter Two:
TROOPER VOGEL

JEANNIE

I sat next to her in Psychology class at Seminole Community College (SCC) in Sanford, Florida, a small town located in Central Florida north of Orlando. She was tiny, a little over five feet tall and thin, with long brown hair almost to her waistline. In 1972, Jean Marone was eighteen years old while I was 24, a Vietnam veteran still figuring out my future.

The first time I looked into her eyes I sensed a strong connection. No other woman had made that kind of impression on me and I knew immediately that Jeannie was special. How special would become even more apparent over the years, but at that moment in that classroom, time seemed to stand still for me and I realized I had found my life partner. Somehow fate had conspired to put us in this same room on this modest community college campus.

I had come to Florida in a roundabout way. When I returned from Vietnam in March 1969, I knew only one thing – I wanted to readjust to life back in the states. The war was still with me; a haunted kind of feeling that was difficult to simply shrug off. Upon discharge, there was an active effort to recruit me into a law enforcement career. Many Marines coming home had opted for this profession, while others had gone back to school. I had a job offer from the California Highway Patrol, and police departments in Los Angeles and Washington, D.C. were also on the lookout for ex-Marines. Their strategy was no test, just come to work.

I wasn't ready to make that decision yet. There had been only twelve hours difference between huddling in a wet foxhole and sleeping between comfortable clean sheets when I came home. There simply was no transition for a Marine. Any readjustments were left up to you. At the time, I was merely thankful for being alive. While law enforcement had a certain appeal, I wanted to think it over carefully, maybe take a few months to decide and enjoy some of the time I'd missed while I was in the Corps. I was mustered out of the Marines, a few days that consisted of a multitude of paperwork and empty hours.

I wanted to integrate back slowly, get used to old routines and habits all over again. The best place for me to do this, I decided, was back home in Pennsylvania.

My mother, ever the possessive one, seemed glad to have her son back again. Emsworth was all I'd known until joining the Marines, so I felt I had an advantage in acclimating by returning to the familiar surroundings of my youth.

I even went back to work for the North Side Cheese Company. I first tried an electronics job with Muzak, since I had gone to school to study this kind of work and had utilized these skills during my stay in the Corps. But driving a truck and servicing some regular accounts for North Side Cheese held more appeal to this veteran, and I enjoyed the daily contact with people.

Eventually, my friend Tony and I decided to open up a pizza place in Emsworth. We set it up in part of a building owned by Tony's dad and opened for business in 1970. It was the first chance at owning something significant of my own, and I enjoyed the control and freedom of this opportunity. My Marine buddy, Ace Hendricks, came down from Michigan to help decorate the place. We were located not far from the town's drive-in theater, and kids on their way to the movies would stop in and order a pizza or a hoagie before the show. At times there were long lines, and we worked hard to fill the orders. I really felt part of something and the memories of Vietnam slowly began to recede.

A short time later, I had to make another decision. My parents were still struggling financially, and I helped them out with errands and money as I could. My dad was also suffering physically. Along with his promotions to manager at the A&P came a prolonged bout with ulcers. By late 1970, they were ready for a change.

There was a chance for my father to transfer to an A&P store in Deland, a town in the Central Florida area between Orlando and Daytona Beach. My sister was married and gone, and the appeal of re-location to a better climate was strong for my parents. They could sell their place (they had finally accumulated enough to own a small home in North Hills, five miles from our rented house in Emsworth) and buy something in Florida, where they hoped to eventually retire. It would be their last stop, they thought, and here was the key chance to go.

They went, and I wondered how long it would be before I heard from them. I didn't think they'd miss me personally as much as they'd missed the things I'd always done for them. It didn't take long to receive that phone call. My father said I needed to come care for my mother. My mother went on and on about how she couldn't live without me nearby, and at one point informed me that she was on the verge of a nervous breakdown unless I moved to Florida.

I was still trying to find myself, as were other members of my generation at that time. The stints with Muzak and North Side Cheese had bought me time to adjust back, and even co-owning the pizza place was a temporary situation, much as I was enjoying it. When my mother appealed to me to move to Florida, I really had no ties keeping me in Pennsylvania other than the business. I decided to head south.

Dad had gone to work for the A&P, and I was determined to come closer to a career decision. I enrolled in the local community college to obtain a degree in Criminal Justice, and went to work in comfortable surroundings—an Italian deli. The rest of the time was spent attending classes, studying and helping out my parents.

And it was there, in Psychology class, that I first met Jeannie. Unbeknownst to me, her sister Marianne had been a regular at the deli and had already told Jeannie about me. She kept telling Jeannie that she needed to come down and meet this guy that worked there. But Jeannie was engaged to a man who still lived in New Jersey and saw no reason why she should meet anyone else. Jeannie's family was from there and had also recently relocated to Florida.

After class, I asked Jeannie if she wanted to get a cup of coffee in the break room. We talked for a while and she asked me what I did. I told her I worked in an Italian deli, and she immediately wondered if I was the guy that her sister had been raving about. Jeannie was studying languages here at SCC. I could listen to her for hours. We parted, but I couldn't get Jeannie out of my mind.

Jeannie told Marianne she had met a guy that worked at a deli and together they came down to the store to see if they had picked out the same guy. They had. Jeannie couldn't believe it, and I knew that somehow we were meant to be together.

I asked her out after our next class together. She declined, saying she was engaged. But I didn't hear the rejection. I kept right on talking. I had to talk her out of this engagement thing. How could a guy that wasn't even in the same state compete with me?

But Jeannie continued to firmly decline. Desperate measures were called for. I had strep throat that week and was on antibiotics, so I took out the prescription bottle of pills to show her, saying I only had three months to live, how could she turn me down?

I was joking, but it made an impression on this gullible 18-year-old whose image stayed with me every hour of the day. Jeannie told Marianne about my "illness" and her sister said, "Of course you have to go out with him! He's terminal!"

Our first date was to the Central Florida Fair in Orlando. Jeannie was a little apprehensive at first. I was older, a Marine veteran, and she felt a bit intimidated, but it didn't take long for us to relax and enjoy the date. When I took her home that evening, I kissed her hand. I had fallen for Jeannie Marone.

Over the next couple of dates, it became clear that Jeannie was feeling the same way. She sensed the same strong connection that had drawn us together, that brought us from Pennsylvania and New Jersey and put us next to each other in an obscure community college classroom. By now, Jeannie knew I didn't have a terminal illness, but seemed to forgive that blatant exaggeration easily once she realized our unique bond.

It wasn't long before I was formally introduced to her parents. Her mother Frances had a long history in politics, which was unusual for a female in the 1950s and 60s. She was the town council commissioner back in New Jersey, and Jeannie and Marianne were seasoned election campaign veterans at an early age. Their New Jersey dining room table was piled high with precinct lists, campaign workers coming and going at all hours, and countless fundraisers. While other girls played with Barbie dolls, Jeannie and Marianne were helping plan election campaigns with their parents. Jeannie was a Goldwater girl (for Barry Goldwater's unsuccessful run against incumbent President Lyndon Johnson in 1964) and her mother knew Richard Nixon. It was a distinctive childhood.

When the family moved to Florida, Jeannie thought they would get away from all that. But her mother founded the Seminole County Women's Republican Club and was Bill McCollum's first campaign manager during his initial run for Congress. By the time Jeannie was 18, she was fed up with politics.

Her mother didn't care what my religious affiliation was; the first personal question she asked me was to which political party did I belong? I answered, "Republican," which was the correct response. Jeannie knew better than to bring home someone of any other party affiliation. After that first visit with Ralph and Frances Marone, Jeannie's mother told her that I was going to be a member of the family. She was certain of it.

Jeannie's engagement was to a New Jersey councilman's son. He was determined to follow in his father's footsteps. This gave me another decided advantage in addition to being in the same state with her. I had no interest in politics. One of the first things Jeannie asked me was whether I had any intentions to run for an office. I truthfully answered in the negative. By this time, I knew that law enforcement would be my future. Politics seemed well removed from that career aspiration.

Jeannie's fiancé made a long-awaited trip to Florida to see his future bride. He was too late. Jeannie and I were so closely linked by then that we could see no future without each other. The only problem was she didn't know how to tell him. He was a friend of the family and would actually be staying at the Marones. He had been Jeannie's first date. Her fiancé was comfortable, like a pair of old shoes Jeannie had said, but now it was time for her to move on.

So I told him. He was a nice enough fellow, but I informed him that I was dating Jeannie now and there was no other future for her. He didn't put up much of an argument. He could tell from my voice that I was thoroughly convinced that Jeannie was the woman for me. It was a little awkward for a couple of days, but everyone parted friends. Jeannie was grateful that I had broken the news to him and saved her from the task. But it wasn't that difficult for me.

Jeannie was the one with whom I wanted to spend the rest of my life.

STATE TROOPER

Meeting Jeannie had closed another chapter in my life—that of readjustment. I had been back from Vietnam for three years now and while there were still some bad nights, I had come home successfully. I had postponed the career I felt would suit me best—law enforcement—but now it was time to leave the Italian delis and pizza places behind. If Jeannie and I were to have a decent future, it was time to start thinking long-term.

I talked with a police officer I knew, a Lieutenant Fagen who worked in the Sanford Police Department, and asked him to recommend me for the Florida Highway Patrol (FHP). I had less than a year to go in school, but thought I could work on my degree while I was holding down a regular job.

I passed the FHP test and celebrated by asking Jeannie to marry me. She agreed. I then promptly left for Tallahassee for three months of training. It was July 1972.

After boot camp, the Marines Corps and Vietnam, this training was easy by comparison. I had forty-four companions for these sessions and all but one were veterans. I missed Jeannie's company, but we called and wrote to each other as often as we could. After only a few short months, I knew Jeannie was my soul mate and the person with whom I wanted to spend the rest of my life. I wanted our future to start off right and dedicated myself to being the best State Trooper I could be.

After graduating from the training academy, I was sent to Homestead in Dade County for my first assignment. In FHP, you were stationed in Dade County because you were either new, single or had messed up somewhere else in the state. Homestead consisted mostly of migrant labor camps and was a marked contrast from Central Florida. Over time, it became more suburban and houses sprung up as a natural extension out from the city of Miami. This is the area Hurricane Andrew devastated in 1992.

I had a few days to get my act together and report for duty. Jeannie and I drove down and back in one day (about eight hours total in the car alone) and found a one bedroom furnished apartment for $185/month. I had received a raise after graduation from FHP academy and was earning $665/month. Our life together was beginning.

FHP had a procedure where a veteran state trooper broke in a new arrival. You worked with that individual for the first few weeks, spending every shift together. My "tutor" was Buck Buchanan, an old Florida cracker from Madison County in North Florida. It didn't take long to see that he was well liked and had the respect of his fellow officers and the local community. Buck possessed a knack for being in the right place at the right time to apprehend a criminal.

There was a story about how Buck, earlier in his career, had walked into a construction office during the lunch hour just in time to see the receptionist being robbed by a gunman wielding a .38 revolver. Buck charged in and the man turned, shot him in the face and went to run out the door. Buck used his left hand to retrieve his own weapon while the right one attempted to staunch the bleeding from his head. He fired at the robber, hitting him in the spine. The wound would leave the criminal paralyzed from the waist down. The man was given life imprisonment; Buck had earned a commendation and a few scars for his trouble.

Buck taught me a lot about the job. He was tough, street-wise and full of advice. He even had some for Jeannie. The first time he met her he asked her why she wanted to marry a state trooper. They didn't make any money, the divorce rate was high, and they ran the risk of getting shot in the face. He even showed her his scars, but Jeannie was not put off by his speech.

We were married shortly after I had started work in Homestead. Jeannie and I honeymooned at the just-opened Walt Disney World in Orlando before settling down in South Florida. This was Jeannie's first time away from her parents, but she quickly adapted to her new environment. She worked first at an office job in a construction company office in nearby Perrine before finding work at a local Homestead bank that was starting up and looking for bi-lingual employees. Jeannie could speak Spanish and was hired on the spot. The bank was located directly across the street from our apartment so she only had a brief walk for her morning commute.

Buck and I were a good team. We responded to all sorts of calls: robberies, murders and highway accidents. There was more crime than we had law enforcement to cover. Most weekends there were numerous serious crimes being committed. The highway mishaps were often due to drunk driving. In addition to tending to the accident, you often had to convince the vehicle occupants to drop any weapons they were toting. Daytime shoot-outs were played out in the hot Florida sunshine, just like the old westerns you'd watch on television.

Buck and I were once called to the scene of an accident that involved a minister named Reverend Logan. When Buck asked him for his registration, the man replied it was in the glove compartment and that he'd get it, but Buck quickly told him that he would retrieve the papers. The man argued and Buck finally handcuffed him, opened the glove compartment and found a gun. I learned an important lesson that day—everyone down here was packing. Even Jeannie. After some of my early experiences, Jeannie carried a gun to cross the street, to work or to the Laundromat.

Life was different here. A man in his 40s driving drunk lost control of his car, slammed into a cement power pole and was killed. When Buck and I went to tell his wife all she wanted to know was the location of his wallet.

The migrant labor camps would take busloads of workers out into the tomato fields. At one stop in Homestead, a man boarded and began looking for someone. He was obviously angry, and when he spotted his quarry, he drew out a gun and fired at him. He missed his target, hitting another man instead. The original target then pulled his gun and returned fire. He, too, missed and shot the bus driver. The bus careened off the road and stopped on a sidewalk. When it was over, three people were dead and workers were bailing out of the back of the bus in a hurry. They left twenty-three guns behind in their wake.

After my initial training with Buck, I was released to work on my own. I was given a personal vehicle, and waxed and shined it until you could see your reflection while looking down on the hood. I put on a new, neatly pressed uniform and headed out for my first day alone. I wasn't out but an hour or so, when a car pulled up beside mine. The passengers were people from the migrant camp and one of them was very pregnant and in labor. I called an ambulance and tried to comfort the woman. She was much calmer than the other occupants and within a few minutes she delivered a baby right into my arms.

After all the death I had seen in Vietnam, it seemed fitting that my first day as a state trooper on my own would be one where I helped bring life into the world. The ambulance arrived and mother and son were bundled up and taken off to the hospital. She already had several children and seemed to think it was no big deal. I, on the other hand, called Jeannie immediately to tell her about my first day.

I worked a territory from South Miami down U.S. 1 to Monroe County, the start of the Florida Keys. It was a considerable distance and there was something happening all the time. You had to be constantly aware of the availability and use of weapons. At one accident scene, I remember asking the female driver for her purse. She was reluctant to part with it, but I insisted. She refused. Eventually, I handcuffed her and secured the purse. Inside were two guns, three knives and a straight razor. This woman was ready for action.

Cockfights served as evening entertainment for the locals. One large operation was exposed by an undercover investigation by the Florida Department of Law Enforcement (FDLE). They had located a major arena down in Florida City, complete with ticket sales and seat numbers like a regular sporting event. It was big business. An FDLE operative was in the arena, wearing a wire and being monitored outside by some fellow FDLE officers. He was caught and the wire discovered. He barely had time to radio his partner for assistance.

Concerned for his safety, they called FHP for assistance and prepared to go in. I responded to the call. All hell started to break loose as I arrived on scene. The arena was emptying out fast once its occupants realized an FDLE officer had been found inside. People ran everywhere, mostly into the woods nearby. One of those in flight was the Mayor of Hialeah, who'd left his car in the arena parking lot. We located the undercover cop, who was grateful for our timely entrance. He told me he thought he was a goner when they found the wire.

The man that owned one of the labor camps in Naranja Lakes was a splashy type; single, wealthy and incessantly bragging about dating airline stewardesses. He had a scheme in which he sold guns to his workers, docking their paychecks for the cost. Once the debt had been paid, he would tip off the local cops. They would conduct a raid, and guns would be left behind in the confusion. Then, the man would sell the same guns all over again to a new set of workers. He made a mistake by selling a machine gun, though, and ATF (Alcohol, Tobacco and Firearms) operatives nailed him for it. This scam partially explained the never-ending flow of guns.

Vehicular accidents were common and one of the bleakest aspects of the job. One Sunday afternoon, I remember responding to a call in which a family was heading for the Florida Keys on US 1 and met with tragedy in a horrific accident. Five people were dead, with another barely alive, and I had to tell the surviving seven year-old boy, who had been staying with a neighbor, that his family would not be coming home—ever. This was something to which you never became accustomed, and it remains one of the most difficult parts of the job.

Our life in South Florida had settled into some kind of routine. We were proud of that first apartment, but soon began looking for a bigger place as we started to accumulate furniture. We both loved antiques and spent a lot of our free time casing the furniture stores, looking for deals. We bought a lot of used, older pieces when we could afford it. I spent my off-days or the occasional weekend re-finishing our acquisitions. We soon had to move to a two-bedroom apartment after a year.

We were making ends meet, but I was always looking for ways to stretch our income. I guess this was a product of my childhood. The manager of our new apartment offered me a deal to provide security in exchange for an $80 monthly reduction in the rent. "Having a trooper's car in the parking lot was worth it," he said.

I made a friend with another state trooper named Jimmy Benton. He was a little on the wild side and had come to Dade County for the third of the three possible reasons—he had goofed up elsewhere. He had managed to get into a fight with another trooper behind his patrol station, and thus ended up with the dead-end transfer south. Jimmy loved rodeos and for a while actually wrestled bulls. FHP put a stop to that when they discovered Jimmy's avocation.

During one of our shopping trips, Jeannie had spotted an antique brass bed in Coral Gables for $200. We didn't have the money for it, but it became one of our early monetary goals. We were out on a double date with Jimmy and a friend of Jeannie's from the bank. Talk turned to the brass bed Jeannie and I wanted and its price. We were at the dog track, and Jimmy was set to bet on the next race. He asked Jeannie to pick a winner and he would bet on him. She did and Jimmy made the wager. It was a long shot, but Jeannie's dog won. The winnings amazingly, came to $200.

Jimmy wanted Jeannie to take the money, but she wouldn't. It was his money, after all, that he bet. They argued good-naturedly about it and Jimmy seemed to forget it as the night wore on. But the next morning, an envelope was taped to our front door with the $200 in it and a note from Jimmy saying, please go get that bed!

We did. It was a great bed, our first major purchase. We still have that bed today as it sits in our guest bedroom. Jimmy's luck, though, wasn't as good as ours. Only a few months after the night at the dog track, he was struck and killed by lightning while at an accident scene. He was one of those people who come into your life for a brief period whom you never forget. When we look at that brass bed today, we think of Jimmy and Jeannie's long-shot pick.

Tragedy struck closer to home for us that year. Jeannie's mother Frances developed cancer in 1974. We were devastated by the news. At that time, they were testing some sort of new chemotherapy and used it on Frances. To all of us, the cure seemed worse than the disease. As she was violently ill, her bones became brittle, and she lost her hair in large chunks. She finally resisted the procedure all together and tried to regain a sense of normality.

Both Jeannie and I felt we should be closer to her. She had quickly adopted me as her son and I felt as close to Jeannie's parents in the short time I had known them than I ever had with my parents. Like the Rohanics before them, there was a warm, comfortable family atmosphere in the Marone household that I loved. I had never received that parental stability at home and knew in my heart that we should be as near by to Frances and Ralph Marone as we could.

I asked for a transfer to Central Florida. I had put in my time in Dade County and now no longer satisfied any of the reasons someone was sent there in the first place. FHP had a policy that you couldn't work in your home county for the first ten years of your career. Since Seminole County was now considered home for me, I looked elsewhere in Central Florida. The closest county in which I could find work was Volusia County, a widespread area that was home to Daytona Beach. The vacancy was in a town called Edgewater.

We had no idea where it was, but we packed up and headed for it at the first opportunity. All we knew was that Jeannie's parents lived an hour away. That was good enough.

CENTRAL FLORIDA

For not knowing anything about Volusia County, we picked a great place to live. New Smyrna Beach was a cozy ocean-side community located about 20 miles south of Daytona Beach. The mainland was divided by the inter-coastal waterway and the barrier island on the ocean contained a lot of homes that were lived–in part of the year by outside residents. Floridians who owned these places would come in the summer while northern homeowners, usually retired people, would winter here. On the mainland was a growing community of young families, and we felt comfortable there from the beginning. It was only an hour's drive to Jeannie's parents' house, and I could continue my career with the Florida Highway Patrol.

My patrol in Dade County had me working on U.S. Highways 1 and 27. Here, the main route of travel was down Interstate 95 north and south and Interstate 4 east and west. These were major road arteries and would ultimately play a significant role in my career. Gone were the migrant workers packing guns and the frequent murders and robberies that kept you occupied right through your shift. Volusia County was much quieter on the surface.

Jeannie's mother made a strong recovery once she stopped the chemotherapy. She was soon back into a relatively active lifestyle and Jeannie and I were glad of our close proximity. I could also keep tabs on my own parents.

I took the midnight shift so I could go back to school and finish my degree. I enrolled at the University of Central Florida and continued the Criminal Justice program I had started at Seminole Community College. It took a couple of years, but I worked hard toward that degree. Disappointingly, FHP did not encourage its troopers to pursue education. In their point of view, the only reason a trooper would obtain a college degree was to leave FHP for some other position. At this point, I was pleased with my work as a state trooper and intended to stay. To me, an education gave me an advantage in situations I would confront and in investigating cases. But FHP's top brass didn't see it that way.

In 1977, Jeannie became pregnant and we now had another new experience to share. We were both so excited about the prospect of becoming parents. I continued to split time between work and school and the day when Jeannie went into labor, I was in a quandary. I was her labor coach, but I had to take a final exam that day. The doctor said Jeannie could spend a long time in labor. While I didn't want that, it allowed me to go take the final and come back. I couldn't remember much about the test as my thoughts were elsewhere, but I knew enough to pass. I returned to the labor room in plenty of time and coached Jeannie through the birth of our daughter, Sheila.

Jeannie had also enrolled at UCF to complete her degree, but the combination of caring for an infant and attending classes didn't mix. The evening Jeannie dropped Sheila off with her mother, only to get to class and realize she had brought the bag with the diapers and bottle instead of the school books, cut short her degree effort at that time. I did graduate from UCF with my bachelor's degree. I wanted to press on with graduate school, and I'd even taken the GMAT exam to qualify. I entered Rollins College in Winter Park and completed three graduate courses before preoccupation with work and family life finally made it too difficult to continue.

I balanced it all precariously. Work, family and school kept me on the move for the better part of most days. Sleep was almost an intrusion and I got by on very little of it. Going through Marine Corp boot camp, I learned there was no such word as "can't". Just when you thought you couldn't do another push-up, you found the strength to do ten more. When you believed you couldn't run another mile, you'd do one more. You came to understand that your mind and body have a tremendous capacity if you pushed yourself. The Corp drove you further than you ever thought possible. I was in great physical shape. I simply had to convince my mind of that.

The midnight shift patrolling Interstate 95 in the southern half of the county--Edgewater, Oak Hill, New Smyrna Beach and Port Orange—brought some interesting occurrences my way. One night, I was working with a young man named Gary Watkins, the son of one of our sergeants. Gary was considering becoming a law enforcement officer, and his dad had asked me to take his son around on a shift one night as a favor to show him the life of a trooper. I had been dispatched to an accident scene in Daytona Beach Shores, had concluded the investigation and headed with Gary back over the bridge to the mainland. At the same time, a pickup truck going over the bridge on the other side was moving at an excessive rate of speed. I turned around to give chase, flashing my lights as I made the maneuver.

This was during Daytona's famous Bike Week and the driver pulled his truck into the parking lot at the Boot Hill Saloon, a well-known Daytona Beach biker bar. I could see the place was lined with motorcycles as I pulled in after the man. As I began to write up his speeding citation, the party in the bar had turned its attention on us as people began streaming out into the parking area to see what was going on. I had a decidedly unfriendly audience as I wrote up the traffic ticket for the driver.

As I was doing this, a man named Mazuka walked out towards my car. I didn't see him, but my inexperienced passenger did. He watched helplessly as the man proceeded to puncture my tire with a pocketknife. Gary yelled over to me what had just happened. I couldn't believe it! He pointed out the culprit to me and I waded into that hostile crowd, grabbed the man by the shoulder and hauled him out, telling him to come with me.

As he turned, I noticed the cast on his arm. It diverted my attention momentarily, and I suddenly received a close-up view of this piece of plaster as the man struck me in the side of the head with it. I went down for the count. The next thing I knew the crowd had gathered up some courage and moved in, while Mazuka was kicking me in the groin and stomach as I lay face down on the ground.

Fortunately, Gary came through. He called in the fracas to the dispatcher, asking for help and then pulled the shotgun out of our vehicle. He went into the crowd, backed them off with the gun, and pulled the man with the cast off me by grabbing a fistful of hair. The man screamed in anger and pain and sat down next to me on the ground. I struggled to sit up, still feeling a bit dizzy as Gary kept the crowd at bay with the shotgun. Thank God I had someone with me that night. The Daytona Beach police arrived moments later and made the arrests, while I went to the hospital for x-rays. I had a concussion, a sprained ankle and some assorted bruises. Gary probably saved my life that night.

In contrast, one late night situation on a fairly cold and rainy Florida winter night involved an automobile that skidded off the interstate and onto the median. The young woman who had been driving immediately got out of the car as I responded to the accident. Standing there in the pouring rain, she was soaked through to her skin. I called a wrecker for her, as the car had sunk into a ditch and needed to be pulled out. She said she had a suitcase in the trunk of her car and asked if she could change her outfit. I agreed, as she was clearly going to catch cold in the damp clothes she was wearing.

She followed me back to my patrol car, and I told her she could change in the backseat. I walked back to her car to wait for the wrecker. When it arrived, the driver and I exchanged a few pleasantries and he began to attach the tow- line to her car to pull it back onto the road. At this time of night, there wasn't much else going on.

It had been about twenty minutes, and I went back to check on the woman. I was stunned to see her sitting in the back of my car stark naked. She had no problem taking off her wet clothes, but seemed to be in no hurry to put on the dry ones. I didn't know why; it was a miserable night and she was likely to freeze sitting there like that. I was thankful no one else was out that night. How could I have explained this?

I pleaded with her to put some clothes on, but had little luck. She must have been on something, but I didn't recognize it when I'd brought her back to change. I thought I was doing her a favor and maybe she thought she was doing me one in return, but all I wanted was for her to get dressed and be on her way. I walked back to where the wrecker was pulling the car out of the ditch. A passing truck's headlights illuminated the back of my patrol car, and this must have finally encouraged her to don some clothes. Either that or she finally did start to freeze, even in the car.

This was a long way from the cockfights and bus shoot-outs in south Florida. Even though I also doubled as a homicide investigator for FHP in this part of the county, the work was less eventful early on compared to my Dade County stint.

The times, however, were changing. With a substantial step-up in drug trafficking in Florida, my Central Florida beat was about to alter dramatically. So was my career.

~ ~

ILLEGAL DRUGS

Illegal drugs are killing this country in a number of ways.

Illegal drugs have caused more problems in the United States than any other criminal enterprise.

Most people don't realize how much of the tax bill they pay goes towards this problem. We pay for it in prison space because substance abuse, directly or indirectly, accounts for most of the prisoners incarcerated in our jail cells. We pay for it through community hospital bills in the form of drug overdoses, cocaine babies and maintaining support systems for severe drug addicts. We pay for it in our homeowner's bill because of damaged or stolen property taken to support a drug habit.

Illegal drug sales are a $300 billion dollar business worldwide, and we are picking up the tab.

I learned a lot of this at a Drug Enforcement Agency (DEA) school in Tallahassee that focused on the magnitude of the problem. FHP had sent me to hear more about the drug trafficking problems in our state. The interstate highway I was patrolling was the central artery for dispersing drugs in this country. While I stopped people for traffic violations, investigated a hit-and-run, or aided a motorist in trouble, drug dealers were bringing in millions of illegal substances right through our county for sale elsewhere.

South Florida was the principal port of entry. After that, it was up to the various drug lords to figure out how to sell it elsewhere. That generally meant a trip through my county. It was astounding to find out the extent of these illegal operations.

Florida's primary struggle is with cocaine and marijuana. There are some countries that keep the United States stocked with a growing supply. Poor farmers in these countries grow the crop just to feed their own families. Drug traffickers capitalize on that need.

These countries take the position that if there weren't a demand for drugs, they wouldn't export it. But they'll also protect it at any cost. These countries don't have the same laws we do. They'll shoot down helicopters and kill our undercover DEA agents. They'll threaten, extort or kill police officers, judges, attorneys, anyone that might block their way. It is guerrilla warfare.

What's behind it of course is money. $300 billion is a lot to spread around. Corruption is rampant. Our politicians generally ignore the problem. When they do talk about it, it's mostly political rhetoric they think the masses want to hear. When it comes down to crunch time, their support for stepped-up law enforcement wanes significantly. All too frequently, they turn it into a race or ethnic issue.

It's not. This is about life and death. This is about violent crime in our own neighborhoods.

Marijuana and cocaine. Those were the two drugs talked about at length during this DEA school.

It was news to me that marijuana is actually cultivated and grown right here in Florida, even in Volusia County; often, ironically enough, on government land. We were taught what to look for to alert us to a marijuana field. The growers look for a fertilized area to plant their seedlings. They irrigate the land properly, supervise the growth regularly, but don't live on the land being used. They often booby-trapped these fertilized areas, so you had to be careful when you were searching suspected fields. We were given descriptions of the equipment used to help us locate the contraband.

Cocaine, on the other hand, is not grown in our state. It comes in most often by air or sea. Up until then Vice President George Bush pushed an interdiction agenda in the mid-1980s, drug dealers had nearly a free ride into Florida. They would bring in cocaine and marijuana unconcealed, in large quantities, like it was no big deal.

Once formal interdiction was established, the drug dealers adapted. They hid their illegal freight and brought it in lesser amounts. They used commercial transport and smaller boats, concealing 40 kilos at a time instead of 1,000. Twenty and thirty boats were needed instead of one. They would do air drops at night with powerboats standing by to pick up the parcels.

They had created a foothold in Florida and weren't about to let it go. They stepped up efforts to continue to bring drugs ashore. Large drug dealers brought in enough to send 20-30 drivers (called "mules") to transport drugs to the north, bringing the contraband to safe houses for later distribution through their networks. They would solicit legal and illegal Central and South American immigrants to do this conveyance. They used whatever pressure they could to force these people to work with them, relying on the language barrier. Often, these drivers would have families back in the countries they'd left and the drug gangs would threaten to execute family members if the driver was ever in a position to cooperate with law enforcement.

They had big-time operations worth billions. A little risk was no problem for these criminals. Most of the time they just weighed the money being exchanged for the drugs rather than counting it. What was a few thousand dollars difference to these guys? They found banks where they could effectively "wash" their money. If they couldn't find a bank, they used restaurants or real estate deals to get the cash back into the monetary system.

If they had to, they would resort to other measures, like buying winning lottery tickets from the winners for 10 percent above value. They would find out where a winning ticket was sold, usually a convenience store of some kind, and they would make it known that they would pay for the ticket plus 10 percent in a lump sum. The lottery winner, especially if it was someone on vacation would be attracted to this offer. The money would be paid up front in cash and there were no taxes to be paid. For the dealers, they cashed in the ticket and effectively laundered the money into a nice annuity. The taxes and 10 percent fee were a minor business expense to them.

Small-time dealers were more hands-on. They often made the deals themselves and transported the drugs personally. If they were concerned about driving it, they hired cheap labor to do it for them; people who were desperate to make a few extra dollars but who were amateurs when it came to the drug business.

Once the drugs were in our state, typically brought into South Florida, the drivers had to bring it north. It was the only way to go and one of the prime pipelines was Interstate 95. A sea of drugs began traveling north.

This is where we could make a difference in the cocaine crackdown—stop the flow of drugs and hurt the dealer in the wallet. I saw drug interdiction as something I could do to help our communities. If I was successful, not only would I help my own Volusia County by keeping the drugs out of it, I would be assisting other towns where the illegal goods were destined.

There are few chances any of us get to make a difference. After the DEA school in Tallahassee was over, I returned home with a new mission in life.

➢ ➢

CUMULATIVE SIMILARITIES

Being sent to drug detection school was one thing. Working it into your routine trooper activity was something else. FHP wasn't training me to be a drug agent. This was one of many tasks I had as a state trooper. I would be reminded of this on several occasions.

Still, I vowed to dedicate myself to putting a roadblock in the path of drug couriers. Even if it meant working extra hours, I could make it part of my routine without much difficulty. Inside me, I felt I was cut out for this type of work.

I shared some of my thoughts with Jeannie and she agreed that this was an area that needed focus. Sheila was growing up and had started school. Jeannie had returned to UCF to finally finish her degree, and came away with a B.A. in education. With Sheila in school, she went to the classroom herself, this time in front of it as an elementary school teacher.

Drug interdiction was an evolutionary process for me. I never went into it with a specific plan to integrate drug interdiction into my work. I made some traffic stops, some of which ultimately resulted in drug and cash seizures. I started keeping track of the successful busts to see what patterns existed amongst the couriers. This seemed to be the best approach to me. If there were similarities between those individuals I stopped who turned out to be transporting illegal drugs, I could build on a series of indicators that, when present, would alert me to the possible presence of contraband.

This did not happen overnight. It took time and research for me, all on an informal basis. I had also examined the possibility of a roadblock to stop cars coming through the county late at night. We had statutory guidelines that spelled out the proper procedure to set up a legal roadblock. A well-lit area, plenty of uniformed police and advising the local residents so they were aware of it—all of these were principles of proper roadblocks. We could stop on a random basis – every third car, every fifth car, etc., to be determined by the amount of officers that we had on hand to handle it effectively and avoid any long traffic lines. We could detain passenger cars and let commercial vehicles go. Tractor-trailers were especially problematic for K-9 dogs, as they were too high off the road for the animals to pick up a scent.

But roadblocks were intrusive, and it meant stopping a great number of innocent people and delaying them unnecessarily. Instead, I decided to keep track of my successful arrests and attempt to establish a pattern (if there was one). Rather than stop a sequence of vehicles, as you would do at a roadblock, you could only stop cars that had committed a traffic violation. The stop was made on the basis of that offense, nothing else. Since this was part of my expected activity, this seemed like the most practical method to me.

There were indicators you could note before you stopped a vehicle. In addition to the traffic violation, you could observe the direction of the car (northbound on I-95), its occupants (young male, 20-45 years of age), and the license plate (out-of-state, rental tag).

Once the person was pulled over, I could begin to look for additional traits that indicated the possible presence of illegal drugs. High mileage on a new car, new tires on an old car, luggage in the back seat that would normally have been in the trunk, a map in the front seat of the car with cities circled, and a radar detector in a rental car, were among the tip-offs that there could be more going on here than was obvious on the surface. The existence of one or two of these peculiarities was not necessarily meaningful, but if an individual exhibited a number of these indicators, circumstances dictated that I take it further.

I could ask them for permission to search their automobile.

I would never go this far unless I had a strong sense of the presence of illegal drugs. But when I added up a variety of factors, I was nearly certain that there was contraband in the car before I solicited consent to search.

If I were alerted to the likelihood of drugs in the car, I would write up the traffic citation or a written warning. During this process, I would initiate a conversation and ask more questions. I would walk over to the car and visually observe its interior during this verbal exchange. Often, if more than one person were in the car, I would casually talk with each individual separately. When two passengers were involved, they often didn't know each other's names, let alone have the same story about where they were heading and the purpose of their trip.

I asked them to read the "voluntary consent to search" form and then sign, acknowledging they had freely agreed to the search. This was all done after the traffic citation was written and all documents returned, so they could feel they were free to go and didn't have to sign the form. No signature, no search. It was that simple.

I spent countless hours attending courses and lectures about search and seizure laws. I had numerous conversations with the state attorney's office and the FHP attorneys to be certain of the lawful procedure to follow. As I proceeded ahead with drug interdiction, I wanted to be as informed and legal as I could be that any arrests I made could hold up in court.

There was only so much preparation you could do and then it was time to set the wheels in motion and learn from practical experience. I had reached that point.

When I made a traffic stop for a violation, I would look the occupants of the vehicle over carefully. Everyone is a little nervous after being stopped by a police officer. However, there were those who were more nervous than the average person would be, who would avoid eye contact, who could not stand still and would constantly shift from one foot to the other. Those who were driving cars not registered in their name, and who had the spare tire in the back seat instead of the trunk, were obvious people with whom to pursue questioning.

It was interesting to me how willing many of these people were to agree to a car search. Perhaps they thought I wouldn't search if they were cooperative since it appeared they had nothing to hide. Or, they may have felt the drugs were secreted so well in the vehicle that they figured I wouldn't be able to find them anyway. Saying "yes" to the question about searching the vehicle could also give them a defense later if needed, like "why would I give the officer permission to search my car if I knew drugs were there?"

I found cocaine, marijuana, cash used for drug deals, guns and other assorted paraphernalia. The more I searched, the better I became at uncovering the illegal substances. The couriers hid it in door panels and gas tanks. There were secret compartments in the trunk and trap doors underneath seats and seats that were opened and sewn up again to hide the contraband.

My successes were starting to accumulate data for me. It took a number of arrests and a study of these results to perfect my list of cumulative similarities that indicated the person I stopped for a traffic violation could also be a drug trafficker. This list included the following attributes:

What you see before you stop a car:
1. Direction of travel -- northbound
2. Traveling at or less than the posted speed limit
3. One or two occupants in the car
4. Male
5. 20 --45 years of age (median is 32)
6. Cars displaying out-of-state tags or Florida rental plates (At the time I started this in the mid 1980s, rental cars had a specific tag letter - Z; now it is no longer so obvious. Also, some out-of-state license plates were more prevalent than others like New York, Pennsylvania, North & South Carolina.)
7. Daytime occupants would avoid making eye contact as they passed by a trooper's parked patrol car.
8. Driving with both hands on the steering wheel.
9. Weaving, especially at night, indicating a lack of sleep or possible personal drug use.

10. Late model, four-door vehicles. (not the typical car for a younger driver)

What you see after you stop a car:

11. Occupants don't know each other well, or don't know each other's name, or tell different stories about their destination and plans.
12. Car is not registered in driver's name.
13. Occupants appear more nervous than an ordinary person would under the circumstances.
14. When occupant reaches into glove compartment for registration, a tube of toothpaste is present, indicating a long distance trip without stops.
15. Spare tire, jack or luggage in the back seat.
16. Presence of radar detector, CB radio, hand held police scanner.
17. Occupants throw something out the window as car stops, or appear to be hiding something.
18. Occupants wearing casual sportswear, including designer jeans.
19. Driver may have driver's license from another state than where car is registered.
20. Fast food restaurant bags inside the car.
21. The odor of fabric softener.
22. High mileage on a new car.
23. No trunk key on the key ring.

Taken alone, or even someone who has two or three of these traits, did not indicate a person transporting illegal drugs. However, if multiple factors were present, there was a strong chance you'd pulled over a prime drug suspect.

As noted above, some of these characteristics I noticed before stopping a vehicle. But even if you could see the car had out-of-state plates, the driver was young, in a four-door sedan, avoiding eye contact with you, there was nothing you could do until they committed a traffic violation. If that happened, whether it's exceeding the speed limit, changing lanes without signaling or following too closely, the opportunity existed to take it further.

After you made the stop, you would observe the other possible indicators that would demonstrate the strong potential presence of illegal drugs. Many drivers that I pulled behind with my lights flashing used their turn signal to move over to the highway shoulder. Those who ultimately turned out to be carrying drugs were generally the most polite and would never even argue about the traffic ticket. They simply didn't want to be there any longer than they had to be. They just wanted to get the ticket and leave.

I would ask questions in a quiet manner, review their documentation, write up the traffic citation and return their documents before proceeding further, so they would have everything in their possession and wouldn't feel the need to consent to search.

At that point, I would then ask permission to search the vehicle and give them a consent form to sign. It was written in both English and Spanish. If the person signed it, you searched. If not, and you felt sure there were drugs in the car, you called in a K-9 dog to check for the contraband. It was very rare that an individual did not sign the form. Every time someone denied to sign the consent form and a K-9 dog was either there or could be brought to the scene within a few minutes, the animal would find drugs.

≈≈

THE FINGER

I started working the midnight shift again. Drug trafficking was generally a nighttime activity and the early morning hours were the times of fewest vehicles and, so the couriers thought, fewer police.

In a sense, they were right. I was a lone ranger out on the highways for several years. I worked alone, late at night, without backup. I was obviously taking a chance, but I felt the end result of putting away major drug dealers was worth the risk. But the danger existed. There was a case of a state trooper who made a traffic stop, was captured by the occupants of the vehicle, taken out-of-state and executed. It happened. I knew it.

Going to confront a drug dealer without backup is a survival test. It was like Vietnam in that sense, except the elements were easier. There was no jungle, no monsoons and no diarrhea. But Vietnam had prepared me for this new assignment. I was always aware of my surroundings, just as I had been in Southeast Asia. I never tried to put myself in a bad position. These were instincts I had learned over there.

When I stopped a car, I always put the driver between me and a potential threat from inside the car. I made sure that if there were shots fired at me, they would likely hit the driver first. I learned to vary my patterns, my approaches, keeping this same thought in mind.

I tried to take proper precaution for my own safety. I wore a bullet-proof vest, carried a survival knife around my neck, had an extra pistol strapped to my ankle and even carried an extra handcuff key in my back pocket in case I was captured and cuffed with my hands behind me. These were not items I would normally have. But I had to be prepared for the unexpected. Who knew if the car I stopped contained people high on drugs who wouldn't hesitate to shoot anyone let alone a perceived law enforcement threat? So I was in a constant state of alert for this type of action.

That being said, I rarely pulled out a gun, let alone the survival tools. I didn't want to coerce anyone into granting me permission to search the vehicle. I took a low-key, friendly approach to the stops, tried to put people at their ease and then quietly ask them for permission after a few minutes. Most people agreed and signed the consent to search form even though they were often transporting illegal narcotics.

By this time, I had made a number of significant arrests. From February 1984 to March 1985, I made thirty felony drug cases. With each arrest, I added in the characteristics of the case to my statistics, looking for the patterns that would help me modify my list of cumulative similarities. My ability to sense which traffic violators I should press forward on to uncover illegal drugs earned me the nickname "The Finger". I had a counterpart in FHP named Barney Stallworth, who worked up on Interstate 10, an east-west route that ran through our state from Jacksonville to Pensacola. He was called "The Nose" for his talent in being able to sniff marijuana.

I don't think I would have had this early success without the help of Mel Stack in the state attorney's office. He was instrumental in helping to shape the process I used with each stop. Mel even told me to call him in the middle of the night during a stop if I had any questions. I took him up on that offer on several occasions.

I remember an early stop where I had secured consent by its occupants to search their vehicle. The search of the car yielded nothing, but there were three suitcases in the trunk. The occupants would not admit to who owned the luggage.

I had permission to search the car, but not the suitcases. My suspicions told me that at least one of the suitcases probably contained contraband. I called Mel for guidance while the people waited for me to finish. Mel told me to remove the suitcases from the trunk and separate them from the vehicle without opening, putting them by the side of the road, clearly away from the vehicle. He then told me to use the K-9 dog to sniff the luggage for drugs. The minute the narcotics dog got near one of the suitcases, he reacted.

That suitcase was then opened to reveal the drugs. It conveniently contained identification. The dope was contained in plastic bags, which are ideal for lifting fingerprints. We could then fingerprint the occupants of the car to see if there was a match. It would be hard for them to deny knowing the drugs were there if their prints are on the plastic bags containing the illegal substance. Or, it could match the owner of the suitcase in which case we had another arrest possibility. In this case, two of the occupants' fingerprints were found on the plastic bags.

This was how the stops routinely progressed. I stopped people for traffic violations on the highway. I also spent time checking the rest area off I-95 in Port Orange. If the car had a problem like a faulty taillight or tag light or some other equipment defect, this was also a violation that allowed you to proceed further if you harbored suspicions about the driver's activities.

Drug dealers and their mules were often encountered at rest stops. Their operations were structured whereby individuals would drive down to South Florida, make a buy and immediately turn around and drive back to their destination.

They didn't stay at a motel. The mules would always stay with the drugs and, if necessary, sleep in the car.

Depending on where the trip originated, these people could be several hours and even days on the road. The mules were bound to be sleepy and would often pull into the rest area to refresh themselves, maybe even take a short nap. Sometimes they used the drugs themselves to try and stay awake.

People who fit this profile were ones with toothpaste in their car (usually in the glove compartment), limited luggage, wearing casual sportswear, were unshaven, and had red, sometimes swollen eyes. In general, they looked like they had gone a long time without sleep.

Typical of the type of activity I had at the rest stop was one early evening around 5:00 PM, when I pulled in behind a car with Pennsylvania tags. A man exited the driver's side of the vehicle carrying a towel. He appeared to have about two days' growth of beard and walked very slowly, almost as if he was in a stupor.

When he went into the rest room, I checked the outside of his vehicle. The front windshield was cracked. When he came back out, I asked him about the windshield. He said it wasn't his car. He was clearly tired, bloodshot eyes reflecting a definitive lack of sleep. I asked for permission to search the car. He agreed.

I found several kilos of cocaine concealed inside a door panel.

On occasion I worked with a partner, usually one with a K-9 dog. One night a car came by while I was sitting by the side of the road with Trooper Earl Collins and his canine. This car went by, committed a traffic violation by weaving in the roadway, and I stopped it.

The driver came out of the car at my request, and I could see he was extremely nervous. His hands were shaking, he couldn't stand still, and had bloodshot eyes that stared at the ground, avoiding contact with me. The car had Duval County (Jacksonville) plates and it was not registered in the driver's name. A female passenger was sitting in the front seat.

The man certainly possessed a number of my cumulative similarities. However, he was not about to give me permission to search the car.

I asked him politely to turn the car engine off while I wrote up a written warning. Typically, an engine's fumes will irritate the K-9 dog's nostrils. Only after the car has sat silent for a few minutes is the dog effective.

After a short time, Earl walked the dog around the car. The canine went straight for the trunk.

When the dog senses drugs, this is considered probable cause and permission is no longer necessary to search the car. I asked the man for his trunk key. He said he didn't have it and started walking back to the car.

I ordered him to stop, but he reached inside the car and grabbed his keys. I asked him again for the trunk key as he tried to hide the keys from me. He started to run, but Earl and I grabbed him and wrestled him to the ground. The girl inside the car was yelling, "You're killing him! Don't hurt him!" There was no one else out on the Interstate at that time in the morning, so we were the only audience for her protests.

As we tried to subdue the struggling, panicked driver, he somehow managed to work the trunk key off the ring. Suddenly Earl shouted, "He swallowed the key!"

At that point, he stopped resisting and Earl and I both looked at him. We fought to keep a straight face now, and just shook our heads at this guy. We safely secured him and called a locksmith who came out and opened the trunk for us. Three hundred pounds of marijuana was there waiting for us. No wonder the guy was nervous. We weren't with him when he passed the key out of his system, but we both bet it was an uncomfortable few moments for him.

The man had scared us for a second, though, when he rushed back to the car and reached in to grab the keys. Some dealers are extremely dangerous, and he could have just as easily pulled out a weapon. Small-time drug dealers are the worst; they have more at stake and more to lose than the big-time criminal does. The big drug dealers would write off the loss, tell the drivers to let it go and keep quiet. They could afford to lose some shipment; small-timers could not.

It was a violent, dangerous world, but one officer *could* make a difference. Years later when I was campaigning for Volusia County Sheriff, I was at the local Daytona Beach Flea Market shaking hands with the various vendors. One vendor refused to grasp my hand and noticed my look of surprise. He said, "You don't recognize me, do you? You put me in jail! I had two kilos of cocaine in the gas tank of my car and you found it." I told him I hoped he wasn't doing that anymore.

Another time, Jeannie, Sheila and I were at Scotty's Hardware to pick up a few items and a man began following us around. After a few minutes, I was concerned for my family's safety so we left for the car. The man followed us out into the parking lot and I finally turned on him and said, "Look, what do you want?" He replied that he just wanted to thank me. "You arrested me for drug trafficking and put me in jail. But it changed my life for the better. Drugs cost me my wife, my furniture and finally my house. But I'm working in a decent job now and living a normal life."

Not all the endings were that positive. But I knew if I could change a few lives through drug interdiction, I was doing the right thing. It became my cause. I felt I was put on this earth to serve my community by battling drugs. I worked long hours every week during this time patrolling I-95. There were nights I would come home and go to bed, sleep for a couple of hours, wake up and go to court to testify in the cases I was making, and then go back out on the road. Knowing that river of drugs was moving up my portion of the interstate made me more determined than ever to do my job. I was tenacious and focused on the task. Once I made up my mind to do something, I tried to be the best at it.

I worked late at night and generally alone. I didn't consciously think about it. I prepared in advance with my survival gear, and stayed constantly alert during each stop. Cumulative similarities became second nature with experience. I was able to size up a driver quickly after a stop and knew whether I had pulled over someone transporting drugs or an individual merely driving poorly.

I took my time with each stop, trying to relax the people as much as I could. You couldn't rush through this type of situation. While I was setting the people's mind at ease with my deliberate manner, I was studying each individual, reading non-verbal cues and body language. This often tipped me off as to whether I should pursue the investigation further. At the same time I was being careful, watching my back and building my case if it came down to that. It was just as important to do a proper traffic stop as it was to pursue the drug investigation further. Doing my job properly meant the difference between a successful arrest or not.

You couldn't show fear. That didn't put anyone at ease.

Asking questions was also critical. You could learn a lot from the answers. Many of these cars contained people who were strangers to each other. Very often, they didn't have their stories straight as to who was who, where they were going or how long they had been traveling. This was a definite indication to pursue my questions.

Still, no one was required to give permission. They could go on their way and some did. Still other stops revealed occupants who were simply travelers, not drug couriers. One night, a red car with New York plates went whipping by me a few miles over the speed limit. I followed quickly and pulled the car over. There were two occupants, male and female, and the woman had clearly been sleeping when I approached the car. They were older and said they were on their way back home. A check of their license and registration found them to be orderly and a couple of further questions confirmed that these people were who they seemed to be. I gave the driver a warning and told them to drive on.

I didn't go by hunches or a sixth sense or anything like that. I just observed and asked questions, looking beneath the surface for what I had. Patience and knowing what characteristics were more indicative of drug trafficking made my eventual searches quite fruitful. I didn't ask permission on a whim. It was the rare circumstance where one of my searches came up empty.

Jeannie was very supportive of me during this time. I was onto something, that was obvious. My success rate was amazing, even to me. We both knew it was dangerous and this actually strengthened our marriage. We had always communicated well, but going out each night to face danger also forced us to settle arguments quickly. We had disagreements as others couples do over various matters, often trivial in nature. But I never left the house until we had talked it out. Neither of us wanted to part badly—just in case.

While drug stops dominated my work activity, it was by no means my solitary duty. One day, a BOLO (Be On The Lookout) had come in on a car suspected to be involved in a kidnapping incident. A man jilted by his girlfriend had managed to grab her and force her into his truck. They were headed north on interstate 95. They had stopped at a gas station in Brevard County (just to the south of Volusia County) and she begged the man to let her use the bathroom. She somehow managed to slip a note to an attendant, who called 911 to report it. As luck would have it, I spotted the car when it entered Volusia County. I radioed it in, but the nearest backup was 50 miles away. I reluctantly pulled the car over without any backup due to my concern for the woman's safety. When the vehicle stopped, the woman immediately bolted from the truck and the man surrendered without incident. The woman was certain he was going to kill her. I was in the right place at the right time.

I received a citation as Florida's outstanding law enforcement officer of the year for this arrest. But it wasn't anything spectacular. I merely acted on the information I received and was in a fortunate position to intervene and capture the criminal before he could do additional harm.

As a state trooper, there were always vehicular accidents that I was required to investigate. One such circumstance occurred on U.S. Route 1 south of Port Orange. Two young women, girls really, ages 17 and 16, had spent a good portion of their day at an establishment called Uncle Waldo's. It was a billiards place in Daytona Beach and the girls had consumed several pitchers of beer, even though they were below the minimum drinking age of 18. The bartender knew the girls were drunk and even walked them out to their car. He let them get in and drive off. At the time, there was no legal basis for liability on the part of the bartender for this action, other then serving drinks to minors.

The girls soon came up along another driver whom they knew, a male classmate, age 18, who had been drinking, too. They waved to each other and soon started drag racing down U.S. 1 at 70-80 miles per hour. There's a dangerous curve on this street just south of Port Orange and, as they hit this turn, the girls' car never made it, slamming into the guardrail which actually went right through the car, separating it in half.

The other car left the scene, but was noticed by stunned onlookers who reported it quickly. When the driver finally was stopped, some people who had followed him made sure he didn't go anywhere until we arrived at the accident scene.

Both girls were badly injured. The passenger, Charla McGill, was barely clinging to life. The young female driver was arrested for her part in the accident.

While Charla was rushed to the hospital, we also arrested the 18-year-old male for leaving the scene of an accident and vehicular homicide. He was not legally drunk.

Charla had an identical twin and she and her family kept a vigil at the hospital. Charla's injuries were horrific though, and her chances slim. I went to the hospital to see how she was and talked with her mother Joyce for some time. We discussed the senselessness of it and how it might have been avoided. One issue we both felt strongly about was the bartender; not that he served underage patrons as much as that he let them drive away from the place knowing full well they needed assistance just to get to their car.

Charla died two days after the accident.

But the end of her life signaled the beginning of her mother's crusade against drunk driving. Joyce was determined that Charla not die in vain, but that her misfortune could in some way benefit others. The bar owner was fined as a result of this incident. An investigator from the state beverage department was unsuccessful at bringing any charges against the bartender. The state attorney general, Bob Butterworth, led the charge to initiate some legislation to hold owners of these establishments responsible for their patrons and being able to prosecute them should drunken driving result. I wanted to help put this kind of law on the books about extended liability to bartenders and bar owners who let people drink and drive away.

Joyce McGill started a local chapter of Mothers Against Drunk Driving (MADD) and this organization was extremely effective at lobbying the legislature to pass laws against drunk drivers and drinking establishments. Charla McGill's presence is still being felt today as crackdowns on DUIs have helped slow the vehicular death rate due to drunk driving.

≈ ≈

THE DRUG CASES

With my successful number of drug arrests, it felt as if I was really making a difference out on the streets. Somewhere there were drug dealers mad as hell at me for stopping their shipments. I had cost them lots of money and taken many of their operatives and couriers off the street.

The increase in the number of arrests had now attracted some attention, especially from defense attorneys. They went after my methods any way they could to get their client off. The more arrests I made, the longer the cases dragged out as attorneys slowed down the process in an effort to discredit me and have the case thrown out.

One defense attorney in particular, Dan Warren, led a crusade against me. Although drugs had adversely affected three of his children, he deplored my practice at making successful arrests on drug charges and set out to attack from all sides to find something successful to use on his clients' behalf. He was quoted often in the media about the way I operated.

Warren tried every angle. He brought up the question of race, telling Presiding Judge McFerrin Smith that I was biased against minorities and that virtually all my stops were evidence of that since these were the people I primarily arrested. He made this point when he was in court for the arraignment of several people I'd arrested on drug charges, four of which were represented by Warren. He was arguing my bias to the judge on behalf of an African-American client whom I'd caught transporting illegal drugs. Judge Smith looked first at Warren, then at his defendant, and finally the other three people he represented that day. The judge said if my bias against minorities was an issue in this case, what defense was Warren going to use for his other three clients, all of whom were Caucasian?

The race question was one Warren and other defense attorneys latched onto, desperate to put a stop to my successful Interstate drug interdiction. But race was never a motivation for me, nor was it on my list of cumulative similarities that would lead me to question a person further after a traffic stop. I arrested all kinds of people; white, black, Hispanic, and so on. I didn't select who would be transporting drugs. I made a traffic stop and continued on from there. There were minorities I pulled over for a violation who drove on after I gave them a warning or a ticket. If they didn't match the essential characteristics that indicate the possible transportation of drugs, I didn't detain them further nor ask permission to search.

Dan Warren refused to believe this. He continued to try every method he could to win a case. A judge had tossed out one of my arrests because he didn't feel the traffic violation—weaving within a lane—was an adequate reason to stop a car. The stop had led to the discovery of 50 pounds of marijuana. Warren pounced on this and said I was using the law—weaving within a lane—as an excuse to stop a car and search for drugs. But weaving is a danger to other vehicles on the road. Weaving could also indicate a tired driver, one who had potentially been up a long time and was a possible danger farther up the road. To me, I was doing a service by stopping those cars, many of which I let go on their way with a warning and a suggestion to stop at a hotel and get some sleep. The stops didn't always result in searches. Some people were genuinely tired, and not from being up all night transporting illegal substances.

But Warren wrote the FHP and anyone else he thought would listen to him about stopping cars that weave within a lane. Warren became so enraged with me that during one trial he stated my home address in court, in full hearing of his defendant, an accused drug dealer. Law enforcement officers' home addresses are protected from release by statute. There were a lot of people who wanted to know where I lived and this blatantly casual mention of my street address was inexcusable. It was only a matter of time before there would be a problem for my family.

Jeannie and her mother Frances had organized a garage sale. They set up a number of items to sell in our driveway and waited on arriving customers. Sheila, now seven years old, was playing in the front yard. It had been busy in the morning, but traffic had slowed now that it was midday.

A car pulled up and parked in front of the house. Two men in shiny suits got out of the car and came up the driveway. The one who sported a red handkerchief in the pocket of his sports jacket asked Jeannie, "Is this Trooper Vogel's house?"

As Sheila continued to play only a few yards away, Jeannie thought quickly and said, "No. It used to be, but they moved." She hoped the men would not see her leg shaking. The men studied her and then nodded, turning to go. One of them pointed to Sheila and said, "That wouldn't be Trooper Vogel's child, would it?" As calmly as she could, Jeannie told them, "I don't know what you're talking about." The men paused for what seemed like an eternity to Jeannie. Finally, they said thank you and returned to their car and drove off. Jeannie held her breath until they drove off and finally exhaled, sitting down to stop the nervous twitching in her limbs. She was so flustered, she didn't get the tag number of the car. Frances just stared at her daughter and asked, "Why didn't you tell them who you were?" Jeannie looked over at her mother, seeing Sheila in the background, who was oblivious to what had just transpired. "Believe me Mom, we didn't want these men to know who we were."

I was concerned over this incident, but it didn't repeat, so perhaps word had gone out that the Trooper making all the successful drug arrests had moved. Jeannie had an incredible presence of mind and the internal composure to call the men's bluff. As a result of this situation, we increased the internal security of our home.

I refused to cut down on my vigilance. Jeannie was more determined than ever that I work to slow down the drug business and try to move it out of Florida. There was no extra pay in it for me for the hazards. I didn't care. I wanted to plug up the drug pipeline up Interstate 95 and would continue to work toward that goal.

I was asked to train other law enforcement agencies in light of my success. Word had spread rapidly through police channels about my ability to locate drugs once a car was stopped for a traffic violation. I even created a video that became a prominent training tool. I taught a number of officers about successful drug interdiction.

There were a number of memorable drug stops during those Trooper years. I stopped one car that had an Ohio tag. There were two passengers in the vehicle. The driver got out of the car and as he did, the other man locked all four doors and rolled the windows up tight. I asked the driver who was in the car. He told me it was his brother. The driver was young and nervous, and I looked over his shoulder to see the other occupant moving about in the car. I walked carefully over to the auto and tapped on the window, motioning for the passenger to roll it down. He was surrounded by several brown paper bags and was doing his best to try and conceal them.

He began inching the window down. My idea was to wedge my flashlight in the window and reach down and open the door. I wanted the passenger out of the car. I was concerned about a gun and my own safety.

As the window slowly moved downward, I went to push my flashlight into the opening. The man in the front seat could see this movement, though, and he quickly rolled up the window before I could work the flashlight into the opening.

I asked the driver if there was a gun in the car. He vehemently denied it, and I then asked him to tell his brother to get out of the car. But the brother was preoccupied. There was a flurry of activity and the paper bags were being lifted up and down. The car windows were steaming up and it looked like it was snowing inside the vehicle.

It was obvious he was trying to dump out whatever cocaine they had been transporting. I waited patiently until he finished. The man finally emerged and gave new meaning to the word "snowman." He was covered from head to toe in a milky white substance and I could barely suppress my laughter.

He had been trying to dump the cocaine into an ice chest that housed some cans of soda the men had been drinking. The ice had melted and I suppose he thought the cocaine would dissolve in the water. It didn't. Not much. And, instead of being charged with possession of one pound of cocaine, he was charged with the total weight of the water and melted ice too, which increased the possession charge to 12 pounds.

Two days later, another Ohio driver committed a traffic violation and I attempted to pull them over. I had my light on and the siren, but he wouldn't stop. He wasn't speeding or trying to flee. He merely refused to stop. It was broad daylight, so I decided to wait the man out. There was an older gentleman driving and a younger man sitting next to him. The passenger was squirming around, doing something I couldn't see.

When he finally did stop, I asked the passenger to get out of the car immediately. His clothes were damp. I noted that he had urinated on the front of his trousers. Apparently what he'd been doing was pouring cocaine into an empty soda can and then urinating in it to destroy the evidence.

As it turned out, this was the father and brother of the Snowman. Dad had come down to bail out his two sons and brought son number three with him. While they were in town, I guess they thought they might as well pick up some more drugs. I had to admit that they had some unique ways of disposing of evidence. Thereafter, I referred to this case as "All in the Family."

One early morning in August 1985, I drove into the Port Orange rest area off Interstate 95 and noticed a small U-haul truck with an Oldsmobile parked next to it, both with North Carolina tags. This was not the usual place to park a U-haul, so my curiosity was aroused. As I pulled into a space next to the car, a black male sleeping in the front seat of the Oldsmobile woke up and looked startled at the sight of the FHP vehicle. He quickly bounced up and out of the car and opened his left rear door. It looked like he was trying to hide something.

I approached the car and asked the man what he was concealing. He didn't reply. I saw a couple of marijuana cigarettes in an ashtray and a flashlight on the floor. I asked him for some I.D. and he produced a Canadian citizenship card with his picture and the name St. Horace Livingston Robinson. He said he was on his way to North Carolina to pick up his car that had broken down there. He had a Florida driver's license, but the Oldsmobile belonged to another man, a North Carolina resident.

I handcuffed him and placed him in the right front seat of my car, buckling the seat belt around him. At that time, we didn't have cages in the patrol cars that you see today. I then read him his rights and told him he was under arrest for possession of marijuana. A further search of the car might turn up more evidence. Robinson refused to acknowledge that he had been read his rights and then complained that the handcuffs were too tight. I loosened them for him and went back to search the car. The obvious presence of marijuana had given me probable cause.

There were bales of marijuana in the trunk. I began photographing the car and its contents and requested a wrecker with my radio. While I was preoccupied with the Oldsmobile, I heard my car start up. Robinson had somehow managed to work the handcuffs around to his front and he drove off with my car.

It was a little embarrassing, standing there watching my car head off into the morning sun, but I quickly recovered and called for assistance. There was about 135 pounds of marijuana in the trunk.

Robinson didn't go far. He got off at the next exit, apparently aware that he was driving a conspicuous FHP vehicle, and a new one at that. He parked it off to the side of the road and was walking east on this highway when two Port Orange policemen apprehended him. They had his description by now, which I had radioed in, of a man without shoes, wearing black socks on his feet.

I stayed with the drugs, while other FHP troopers drove to the spot where Robinson had been taken into custody. The car was found off the road, in a pile of mud.

The car keys in the ignition had also contained the handcuff key that Robinson had used to remove them from his wrists.

With his flight, Robinson had now added a couple of charges to his arrest sheet, which I explained to him as we rode to the station. He didn't speak English very well, but he did manage to tell me that he was the father of four children, his wife living with two of them in Miami, the other two residing in Canada and Jamaica.

At the station, his English was good enough to ask us if he could call his lawyer. He didn't ask for privacy, so I remained there while he made the call. When his attorney came on the line, Robinson told him, "The policeman put me in his car and I drove away with his car." Wow, a confession on top of everything else. It had been a wacky morning.

The Port Orange rest area was home to a number of drug traffickers who had stopped for a breather. On another occasion, I drove in about the same early hour as I had when I spotted Robinson. I was out of my car and stretching myself after a long night when I observed a red Dodge Aries car with South Carolina plates. Two white males had emerged from the rest room and were approaching the car. When they saw me, their faces betrayed their nervousness, their eyes widening as if I had caught them doing something they shouldn't.

On the floor of the backseat was a Clorox bottle. I later found out that many dealers used Clorox to test cocaine to make sure it was the real stuff. I asked for their identification. The car was a rental; Troy Chapman the driver and Paul Smith the passenger. They said they'd just finished visiting relatives of Chapman in Fort

Lauderdale. Smith's hand was shaking when he handed me his I.D. He was obviously nervous, more than he should have been for some routine questions. These guys were guilty of something.

I asked them about the Clorox and they said they'd just washed their clothes. I then asked where their other clothes were and they replied that they were in the trunk. I asked to see their luggage and they agreed. There were several suitcases there with a change of clothes and two Colt .45 pistols.

The drug search turned up two clear plastic zip lock bags of cocaine.

These two country boys were rank amateur drug dealers. They had records, but dealing drugs was a new venture for them. They collected about $30,000 from their friends and went to South Florida to make a drug buy. The Beverly Hillbillies Go To Miami. They brought a couple of guns just in case. It was their biggest drug deal to date. They met the seller—a Colombian—in a hotel room. They wanted to test the cocaine. They had brought a bottle of Clorox with them because they'd heard if you poured Clorox in a glass and then sprinkled in some cocaine, if the residue went to the bottom of the glass, you had good stuff.

But they didn't have a glass, only a paper cup. They were so nervous, they spilled Clorox all over themselves. Cocaine was going for about $18,000 a kilo. They paid $30,000 for their one kilo buy. The cocaine had also been cut, so it wasn't as pure, further diminishing its value. They thought they could make about $5-6,000 on the kilo; they should have made $25,000 on it.

Once this was all explained, I asked, "You mean you risked up to fifteen years in jail for a $5-6,000 profit?" Maybe it was a lot of money to these good ol' boys. But drug dealing was definitely not their game.

They decided to cooperate with us in an attempt to go after the dealer who had sold them the cocaine. It was a good move on their part, since their drug-dealing career had come to a screeching halt. When they contacted the dealer about making another buy, the guy probably broke a few speeding records getting up here to make it. After all, when you could sell $18,000 worth of cocaine for $30,000, why not do it again?

We had recorded the calls setting up the buy. The dealer came and sold them some more cocaine. We then arrested him—chalk one up for the country boys.

This was an example of what drug dealing in the 1980s was all about. Amateurs mixed with professionals and everyone thought it was an easy way to make a buck. I stopped a dentist who was transporting drugs to pay back his medical school bills. I arrested him when my search turned up about 100 pounds of marijuana. Everyone wanted to pick up a little drug money on the side.

It was an era of radar detectors in rental cars and of double trunks and double gasoline tanks in which to hide the contraband. One night I stopped a car with Ohio plates. The car was not registered to the driver. He fit the typical characteristics I would use to justify asking to search. I made the search request, but he denied it. I asked for the phone number of the owner. He did give that to me and I called the man in the middle of the night. He also declined my request to search. I went to Plan C. I contacted a K-9 unit to come out.

I told the driver that he was being detained on suspicion of transporting drugs. I told him to stay close to the car. This is where my work got a little tricky. You could only detain like this for a short time. If the K-9 took too long to arrive, I would have to let the man go. Sometimes the dog would be over on the other side of the county and we couldn't get the animal here in a reasonable time frame.

This was the most dangerous time of any stop. The car occupants knew what was in the car and we all waited together for the dog to come to turn up the inevitable drugs. I was always alert for trouble at this point, knowing these people could consider themselves in a desperate situation from which they could only escape through violence.

Tonight, the K-9 unit was nearby and responded quickly. The dog alerted us to the presence of drugs and we found a large amount of cocaine, concealed in a door panel.

Sometimes you crossed unknowingly into another investigation. One night I stopped a car containing a male driver with both a male and female passenger. I asked for their consent to search. There appeared to be a modified gas tank, where part of the tank contained gas and the other was a secret compartment. It wasn't something you could check without putting the car up on a lift. The people even consented to driving to a service station. When I had the car put up on the lift, an extra compartment containing three kilos of cocaine was clearly revealed. I arrested these cooperative suspects.

The next day, the DEA called. They wanted the car from our previous evening's arrest. They also asked me to drop the charges on the three we arrested. I declined unless they told me more. They refused, demanding that I put the car on the Auto-train and ship it to Maryland. The only thing they would say was that the car had been used in a murder, but they wouldn't tell me anything about the passengers in the vehicle. I didn't drop any charges. These people were traffickers and unless there were extenuating circumstances, the charges stayed. I asked again for further explanation. They refused. The suspects remained in jail.

I generally worked well with the Drug Enforcement Agency (DEA). I didn't know what happened here. For a time, I had a DEA agent working with me named Frank Chisari, out of the Orlando DEA office. The DEA had taken an active interest in my successful stops. They wanted to participate but couldn't make traffic stops. I had that authority, so Frank and I worked together as a team and made a number of successful arrests. It was obvious that drugs were being transported up the interstate and out of Florida in substantial amounts.

At one point, Frank and I put together a program to set up roadblocks on I-75, 95 and the Florida Turnpike, all the major routes out of our state. We wanted a one-shot deal—to pick a time period where there was little going on so we wouldn't disrupt the average innocent motorist or hold up peak traffic. We wanted to do it in the early morning hours, prime time for drug transportation. It would give us an idea of the percentage of cars that were actually transporting drugs. We met with Frank's DEA supervisor, Felix Hernandez, who was all for the plan. But FHP's attorneys rejected our plan.

Despite my successes, I never wanted to leave Volusia County. I turned down promotions that would have required me to move. Jeannie and I were happy here, Sheila was in school and I was doing what I wanted to do—stopping the flow of drugs. During a three and a half year period in the middle 1980s, I confiscated 3-1/2 tons of illegal drugs worth over a billion dollars on the street. That hurt someone in the pocketbook and prevented countless other crimes that were a direct offshoot of drug use.

<hr>

RECOGNITION AND A NEW DIRECTION

My success brought local and national recognition for a job well done. I didn't do the work for the awards, but I did receive a number of honors. In August 1987, the local Oceanside Rotary Club of Daytona Beach did a salute to me entitled, "We Like Your Profile" and made me an honorary member. That brought a telegram from President & Nancy Reagan, congratulating me on the honor.

The night was a pleasant one. Colonel Burkett of FHP attended to say a few words. At this time, I was speaking to a number of agencies to provide tips on drug interdiction, including the FHP Training Academy. Nothing like this type of recognition had ever happened to anyone at FHP before.

That evening, Burkett praised me for making FHP a household name in America, thanks to my drug interdiction efforts. He told the audience that I received no additional pay for the extra hazard of meeting armed drug dealers night after night; dealers who wouldn't hesitate to shoot if they thought they could get away with it. Florida, in 1987, ranked 47th in the country in pay for state troopers.

The master of ceremonies, in his remarks, said that he had never heard of one Mayor in any of the Volusia County municipalities saying they'd received a letter about Trooper Vogel stopping a citizen and doing something wrong. Not one letter saying someone's constitutional rights had been violated by Trooper Vogel.

I was pleased to hear him say that. If I were going to be recognized for anything, that lack of citizen complaint would be my preference. I worked diligently to avoid violating anyone's rights and making cases well within the legal bounds of my authority. My job was to ultimately protect people's freedom, not take it away. I liked that reputation.

Another reputation I enjoyed was evident when I awoke a passenger after a traffic stop in which I had already made a search and arrested the driver. The man angrily said to the driver, "I told you not to drive through Volusia County! Didn't I tell you to stay out of here?"

Bob Butterworth, who at that time was the Director of Highway Safety and Motor Vehicles which oversaw the Florida Highway Patrol, had a habit of sending out congratulatory letters to law enforcement officers who had made a significant arrest. He sent so many letters to me that he finally purchased a rubber stamp that read, "Congratulations Trooper Robert L. Vogel, Jr. You did it again!"

The *Atlanta Journal & Constitution* had done a sizable feature story on me in their Sunday newspaper. One of their reporters had come down and rode in the patrol car with me to observe a routine night of drug interdiction. Someone from the CBS television show *60 Minutes* read that story and called to say they wanted an interview. This show had a reputation, too. Usually when they called, you didn't answer. But I had nothing to hide and told them I would be glad to talk with their reporter.

The reporter turned out to be Harry Reasoner and we had a good visit. He was a pleasant man and a true professional. He had severe arthritis at the time, to the point where his hands were somewhat deformed as a result. I put a bulletproof vest on him and he came with me on a typical night's tour and was impressed with the results I was getting. He came with his producer, Jim Jackson, to our home and met Jeannie and Sheila. He graciously allowed us to have our picture taken with him. He did a generally positive piece for the show. If drug dealers watched *60 Minutes*, they'd probably avoid Volusia County now. I had become more effective than I'd ever dreamed after I left the DEA School in Tallahassee a few short years earlier.

Jeannie was at my side during this period of recognition. I always felt as if we walked as one, and there was no reason she shouldn't share in this success. She'd wondered often enough if I was going to make it home. I'd told her once that if something happened to me, it would be another car that would pull into our driveway, bringing the news. They never called on the phone. When Jeannie would hear the car turning in, she'd sometimes check to be sure it was mine and upon seeing it, know I had made it through another night.

I tried to minimize the danger. I always let the dispatcher know where I was regularly and what I was doing. Jeannie could always find me just by checking with the station. Sheila didn't understand the dangers as much and we didn't elaborate on them to her. She just knew her Dad was a policeman and that was it.

I was invited to speak at a DEA conference in Atlanta, the official kickoff of a program called Operation Pipeline, a nationwide effort of drug interdiction. Colonel Burkett came with me in a show of FHP support. I wanted to help any law enforcement agency I could. If my experience could be used to successfully stop the drug flow elsewhere, I was glad to lend a hand. It didn't do us much good to divert the drug trade from Florida if it just flourished somewhere else instead.

One month I received a letter citing my lack of DUI arrests in the previous month. Interestingly, I had made 23 felony arrests that month, more than most of the troopers make in a year. I had also testified before the Governor's Highway Safety committee on dram shop legislation as a result of the Charla McGill case. In addition, I had solved two hit-and-run homicides that month. But he was right. I had no DUI arrests. My supervisor must have had his butt chewed out for a lack of DUI activity and simply passed that responsibility along to us.

I promised myself that if I were ever in a position to supervise, I would do a better job than that. I was obviously doing my work. You don't alienate good people like that. I believed a supervisor got into trouble if you only looked at numbers. This encouraged officers to go out and make bad cases just to get their numbers up. That was not effective law enforcement. Officers should be recognized for their positive actions, not simply numbers. I had numbers in drug arrests, but was more proud of the rate of convictions on those arrests. An arrest is only successful if it holds up in court. I vowed to look for more in an officer if ever placed in a supervisory position.

As 1987 wound down, I started to think seriously about my future. I felt my time at FHP was drawing to a close. I had applied for a vacant position as police chief of Port Orange, an appointed position. Although I was one of the finalists, I wasn't accepted for this job. Even so, I knew my days at FHP were over. There was talk of Volusia County's Sheriff Ed Duff retiring. He was in his late 70s and had been Sheriff in the county for twenty years. I was receiving plenty of encouragement to seek that office, and I thought it was something I could do. But first I wanted a little more experience outside of FHP.

I made contact with the State Attorney's office and went to work there with my mentor and friend Mel Stack, who had guided me through my formative years in drug arrests. It would give me a little more on my resume to run for office, if I decided, and united me with someone with whom I liked working.

I took a job as an investigator, and a new chapter in my family's life was about to be opened.

ELECTION NIGHT, 1996

Precinct numbers continued to come in as the evening wore on. The results were not particularly encouraging. While I hadn't fallen much further behind, I was still a few hundred votes behind my opponent Gus Beckstrom.

As I looked at Ron Johnston's precinct list, I knew there were still several key areas to report in. In addition, the absentee ballots had to be counted. I figured to do well there, with many seniors and my own campaign workers representing the majority of these votes, giving me a sure edge.

There were bits of conversation going on in the room, but nothing like the celebratory nights of the two past elections. My key leaders were still here, refusing to believe that we'd lose, just waiting for the next phone call that showed me surging ahead.

My daughter Sheila was in the parking lot of the Riverside Pavilion, sitting in the back of a pick-up truck with her girlfriend Michelle and her friend Taylor. They were listening to the radio for results, and Sheila was trying desperately to calm her nerves over the early evening results so far. The back room was too intense for her, and she preferred the relative quiet company of her friends, conversation vastly different than her dad's latest numbers.

Jeannie and I had been circulating in the back room, saying the reassuring words people wanted to hear. Internally, I knew we both felt less confident, but like past times we both understood how to rally in the face of difficult odds. We were a team and still believed in our hearts that this night wasn't yet over.

Ron's cell phone had died out after the last call from Gary Davidson at the Elections Office and I hoped it wasn't an omen. Our "good luck charm" seemed down on his own luck tonight.

Jeannie talked to the Pavilion's manager, and they set up another phone for us in the back room. Ron called Gary to give him the new number for updates and hung up. Moments later, the phone rang again.

The phone had a speaker function and Ron hit it so we could all hear the numbers at the same time. But it wasn't Gary Davidson. It was Mary Jo Phillips from the Florida Sheriff's Association in Tallahassee, making a routine call to an incumbent Sheriff running for re-election.

Everyone sat numbed as Mary Jo greeted us in her typical melodic manner. Cheerful, bubbly and obviously unaware of what my numbers were to this point, she chatted about the day, the weather, the news and other assorted topics. The silence in the room was deafening as my inner circle of friends sat dumbfounded, listening to Mary Jo talk as if the election was over and I'd won by a landslide.

Finally, she asked us for our numbers, likely not dreaming of what we were about to tell her. She was routinely tracking the results for the Association, and I know she thought I was already safely home.

It was Jeannie who actually spoke, who put a voice to what we were all feeling. She gave Mary Jo the latest count and told her it wasn't going all that well at the moment. Now it was Mary Jo's turn for silence. After a few seconds, she apologized for not knowing what was going on and put in her own plug for us, saying she would call back later for what she was sure was better news. She hung up.

At that same moment, there were loud cheers coming from the main room. Jeannie and I walked out to see what all the noise was about. The scene we saw was incredible. Dilys Harris, a close friend of ours and the editor of the newspaper Seniors Today, was standing in front of the large screen television, leading our campaign workers in a series of cheers.

We found out later that Dilys had been doing this all night. Every time the results were posted on the television, Dilys stood in front of it and shouted that she would not accept any bad news tonight – and neither would anyone else. When the local news cameras came on to film the reaction of the Vogel campaign to the losing numbers, all they recorded were a cheering, raucous bunch rather than a group of dejected volunteers.

It was this kind of spirit that I loved about our campaign. Virtually all the people that had helped us over the years put their heart and soul into it. They truly believed in me and I was always humbled at the thought. I couldn't let these people down. These numbers had to improve!

Jeannie and I then saw Kemp Newman coming over to us. He was a lifelong friend, a good ol' boy from Georgia who had worked with us on our first campaign. He asked how we were doing and Jeannie said, "Please don't tell anyone, but we're scared." He nodded thoughtfully and said, "Don't worry, it'll be O.K." We thanked him.

Seeing him reminded me of his daughter, Stacy, who Kemp and his wife had lost at the age of 19 to diabetic complications. On our first campaign in 1988, Stacy was one of my youngest volunteers. She had broken her arm and had to have a cast for several weeks during my run for the Sheriff's Office. Rather than feel down about it, she went to the Volusia Mall and had the words "Vote Vogel" airbrushed professionally in bright letters on her cast for everyone to read. She probably secured more votes for me that year than any other thing I did.

As we walked back to join our friends, I thought back to the thrill and excitement of that very first run for office....

Chapter Three:
SHERIFF VOGEL

VOTE VOGEL

Volusia County Sheriff Edwin H. Duff II was elected to the key law enforcement position back in 1968 while I was still in Vietnam. A native of New York, Duff retired with the FBI after nearly 30 years of service when he decided to run for Sheriff.

Much had transpired in the twenty-years between 1968 to 1988, but Ed Duff was a constant in Volusia County. After running successfully in 1968, he won re-election four times. Duff had a reputation for excessive swearing. In the last few years, he spent countless hours hunting recreationally. Now, according to various rumors, the 77 year-old Duff was not planning to run again.

I was working in the State Attorney's office as an investigator as the year 1988 dawned. After fifteen years with the Florida Highway Patrol, I wanted to take a different avenue in law enforcement. This investigator's job was my first step.

My work consisted primarily of investigating sunshine law violations (statutory requirements that were not being met), drug cases and other serious crimes. I spent a substantial amount of time running down businesses that had failed to account for and pay the proper state sales tax.

I was also still concluding my FHP career. A number of late cases I made during my last few months were now coming up for trial and I had to give depositions and testimony to complete my work.

I had applied for the Port Orange Police Chief's position the year before and, although a finalist for the job, I was not selected. I was disappointed, but Jeannie's mom had said at the time "when one door closes, another opens." Perhaps that door opened into the Volusia County Sheriff's Office.

I had promised Jeannie years ago that I wouldn't run for public office. Her fiancé from New Jersey had been a town councilman's son and he was supposed to be the one to enter politics. Now, more than fifteen years later, he was a successful restaurant entrepreneur who had never sought political office, and I was entertaining just that thought. Things change, I guess.

Whatever decision made would be one Jeannie and I made together. We loved Volusia County and wanted to stay there. What better opportunity than to run for the top law enforcement office? If I could be so successful at drug interdiction by myself as a state trooper, what could I do for the citizens of Volusia County to stop the flow of drugs with several other well-trained deputies patrolling our major highways? That thought was inspiring to me.

I didn't consider myself a politician. I was a law enforcement officer. Invariably, there would be the hand-shaking, speeches, barbecue chicken dinners and fundraising that all campaigns require. I like people, so it seemed reasonable that I could handle that part of it. More importantly, I truly felt I could make a difference in the lives of our county residents by reducing crime and making Volusia County a safer place to live and they would hear that conviction in my voice. If the work that the Sheriff's Office could perform under my leadership would help Volusia citizens sleep a little better at night, it would be worth all the hoopla of a political race.

My life growing up in the woods of Pennsylvania had prepared me for Vietnam. Vietnam had then readied me for the danger of late night traffic stops as a state trooper. Now, that FHP experience could be used to move on to another influential level where I could have a positive impact on others' lives.

Jeannie, despite her long-ago plea that I never seek political office, almost immediately agreed that running for Sheriff of Volusia County was the right thing to do. She warned me that political candidates are targets; they're right out front for both criticism and praise and I would likely face both. I thought the *60 Minutes* episode would help me with name recognition, and Jeannie pointed out that residents of this area had already been reading about my drug interdiction efforts for years. We had received for some time both written and oral encouragement to run for office. To us, it finally felt like the right time to act.

The official qualifying period for Sheriff's candidates to file their intent to run for office wasn't until July 1988, but several people were already unofficially in the race. Like me, they probably figured that Ed Duff was about to retire and the race would be wide open. It was time for a new direction in law enforcement. Duff was kind of a "laissez-faire" Sheriff, definitely more "hands off" than "hands on."

At this point, there were four individuals that had already declared their plans to run for Sheriff. They were Noel Ouellette, a captain with the Daytona Beach Police Department; Bruce Wragg, the chairman of Daytona Beach Community College's criminal justice department; Joe Benedict III, chairman of the Volusia

County Growth Management Commission and a former county councilman; and Richard Falardeau, a former administrator in the Volusia County Sheriff's Office. Falardeau had resigned in February to run for office.

I wouldn't be forced to resign my position in the State Attorney's office, though I would have to take a leave of absence to run for office. I wanted to talk to Mel Stack and State Attorney Stephen Boyles about the possibility and solicit their feedback.

One thing this election wouldn't have was political parties. It was a non-partisan race and if all the candidates qualified, there would be a primary in September. If no one person received over 50 percent of the vote, the top two would face a runoff in November.

Ouellette had been a candidate since the previous September and had been planning his campaign since that time. He was still employed with the Daytona Beach Police department, in charge of the patrol division, but had planned to take a leave of absence in July to campaign. At age 47, he was nearing enough service years to retire and wanted to move on to the county's top law enforcement office. He was a large, overweight, balding man who lacked enthusiasm for the challenge. He was a backslapping, overbearing good ol' boy who practically shouted during his speaking engagements and intimidated some voters.

Wragg, like me, was a graduate of the University of Central Florida. He had also continued his education in graduate school at Rollins College, acquiring his Masters in Criminal Justice. He had been chairman of the Criminal Justice Department at Daytona Beach Community College since 1985 and had formerly served in the Ormond Beach Police Department as a patrolman, detective and patrol sergeant. Wragg was of average build and he had the habit of wearing sunglasses during his speeches. He had a tendency to use big words during his talks, which did more to confuse the audience than impress them as they seemed to have no idea what he was saying. At one talk, the other candidates and I noticed a price tag hanging on a string from his suit jacket. He was speaking from behind a podium and it was obvious he had forgotten to take it off. Each of us battled to keep a straight face as we looked out at the audience.

Benedict had eight years on the Volusia County Council, and had been its chairman for two of those years. Governor Bob Graham had appointed him in 1980 to the East Central Florida Regional Planning Council. Benedict was a farmer in Samsula, running his own place with his two brothers called Benedict Farms. He had developed some allergies to chemicals that made it difficult for him to carry on his farming work, and was looking for other avenues of employment. Apparently, he felt the Sheriff's Office was that avenue.

The 49 year-old Falardeau had nearly 30 years of combined military and law enforcement in his background and had been director of operations for Ed Duff until his recent resignation. He was small in stature, with dyed, slick, jet-black hair that he combed straight back like NBA basketball coach Pat Riley. He wore dark-colored, expensive tailor-made suits, with a pocket kerchief. He looked like he could have walked onto the set of the film *The Godfather* and fit right in.

Then there was me. By the end of March 1988, I had made up my mind to run and had the support of my family and friends. Mel Stack thought I was the perfect candidate and I thought highly of his opinion. It wasn't going to be an easy race, I felt, and there were likely to be other candidates before the qualifying period ended in July.

I was fortunate to find an excellent campaign manager. I met Alice Jones of Deltona, ironically enough, during one of my sunshine law investigations for the State Attorney's office. The alleged violation was by a member of the hospital board that she served on as a director. The charge ended up having no validity and the board was exonerated. But it gave me the opportunity to spend time with this political insider.

Alice was in her 60s and her husband Parker was over 70, and both were active members of the local Democratic executive committee. I was a registered Republican, but the race was non-partisan so political affiliation didn't matter. Alice would take some heat from Democrats for agreeing to become my campaign manager, but she liked me and felt I would do an outstanding job as Sheriff and that mattered more than party ties.

Alice and Parker had met during World War II. They both served in the U.S. Army and she outranked him, Captain to Sergeant. Both had successful careers as physical therapists, self-employed in the Boston, Massachusetts area. They had come to Florida and maintained an active role in Democratic politics, with Parker serving as President of the Democratic Club in Deltona.

They had the kind of know-how that Jeannie's mother possessed about political campaigning. Unfortunately, we were not able to use Frances' expertise as she had recently succumbed to a second bout of cancer. She had survived a number of years after voluntarily stopping her chemotherapy years earlier, and we were glad we had moved back to Central Florida to be near her. We would miss her for this campaign, but knew that she had approved of Alice.

Alice, Jeannie and I put together an informal advisory board of people like Mel Stack and CPA Brent Millikan (who would be my campaign treasurer) to offer opinions, advice and guidance during this run for the Sheriff's Office. Also on this board was Clyde Mann, a neighbor and retired Marine Corps General. He had been the Chairman of the County Council and was experienced in local politics. T.C. Wilder, co-owner of the Settle-Wilder Funeral Home in New Smyrna Beach, was the area representative for Congressman Bill Chappell. Sandi Cone was a physical education teacher in Holly Hill who had run unsuccessfully for a place on the city commission. John Long, who was in advertising, had designed ads for the campaign of former Florida Governor Claude Kirk. The board represented a substantial amount of local campaign experience and would be quite helpful to me during this campaign.

This advisory board suggested I make the formal announcement of my candidacy at the Port Orange rest stop on Interstate 95 where I had made so many felony drug arrests. At the time of my April announcement, I was the seventh candidate for the Sheriff's seat. The fifth individual to throw his hat into the ring was an individual named Don Riley who, like Duff, was the former senior resident agent for the Daytona Beach FBI office. Riley was 55, tall, graying and friendly, although he appeared to lack the spirit for the position. He might have just been looking for something to keep him occupied during his retirement years.

The other person declaring his intent to run was Ralph Henshaw, a former deputy in the Volusia County Sheriff's Office who had been fired by Ed Duff back in 1979 for drinking and smoking marijuana on the job. At the time, Henshaw said the charges were false and he took his case to a Personnel Board. The Board ruled that the firing was unjustified, but Volusia County Manager Tom Kelly, who has the final say on all personnel decisions made in the county, overruled them. His overrule later stood up through an Appeals Court hearing. Henshaw was not a political rookie, having run against Duff unsuccessfully in the 1980 Sheriff's race. He was currently a used truck salesman, short, balding, gray, and street-wise with an edge to him. His grammar was extremely poor, reflecting a lack of formal education.

I was the lucky seventh to officially announce my candidacy. Jeannie called us the Seven Dwarfs. All were nicknamed according to their characteristics. Riley was Sleepy, for his tendency to nod off during candidate debates. Henshaw was Dopey, Benedict was Sneezy, Wragg the professor was Doc, Falardeau was Happy, Ouellette was Grumpy and I was Bashful for my reticence in the public eye.

Over 100 people showed up on April 7 for my campaign kick-off. Alice had made up some campaign buttons that showed a Sheriff's star with the phrase "Vote Vogel." There were people from all over the county and many held placards that stated where they lived—Deltona, Deland, New Smyrna and other towns within the county. The media had turned out in full force. I wasn't unknown, having received recognition for my success as a state trooper, so the media had a natural curiosity as I turned my attention from drug stops to campaigning for votes.

We decided early on to emphasize my drug enforcement experience in the campaign. I did that at the kick-off, telling onlookers that Volusia County had a crime problem that could only be addressed by a courageous and hard working Sheriff. I had the courage to face a drug smuggler with a gun in the early morning hours along the interstate and, if elected, I wouldn't be afraid to leave my office to fight crime. It was a strong message that played well with the crowd that day. I began telling my story!

Jeannie's memories of her childhood campaigns on behalf of her mother kicked in. And it didn't take long for Sheila, now nine years old, to get in the swing of it. Jeannie loved the organization behind a campaign: the planning, the fundraisers, the strategy. Seeing the people was something we both thoroughly enjoyed and made the long race a bit easier to take.

Our campaign was grass roots all the way. I remember one woman coming to our campaign headquarters on Beville road in South Daytona on a bus. The bus pulled up outside our office doorway and this woman in her 80s slowly descended the stairs and emerged from the vehicle into the sunlight. She came into the office and removed a tattered purse from a handbag that was equally withered. She took a dollar bill from it and handed it to us, saying it was all she could spare but wanted us to know she was behind me for Sheriff. Alice didn't want to take it, but the woman (her name was Mary) insisted. She then took a campaign sign for her yard and, refusing the offer of a ride, got back on the bus for the return trip. More than seventy years separated her and another volunteer, Stacy Newman, who had the words "Vote Vogel" stenciled onto the cast she had to wear on her arm. These were the kind of supporters I had and wanted and for whom I would do my best if elected.

Mel Stack was of tremendous help during this campaign. His advice, suggestions and simple friendship meant a lot to me through the years, especially during this run for office. He was enthusiastic, being in the State Attorney's office, about having a "hands on" Sheriff, unlike the effort Duff had been putting in for several years now. He played a key role on my advisory board and we grew as close as brothers.

From the beginning, I was astonished and humbled at the amount of support I received. Campaign contributions poured in from all over the county, generally small amounts given by concerned residents that seemed ready for a law enforcement change. In no time at all, I had collected more dollars for my campaign than my opponents combined.

There were a number of speaking opportunities, including candidate forums, leading up to formal candidacy in July. Ralph Henshaw, Don Riley and I spoke at a Chamber of Commerce meeting in May and the emphasis was on drugs. I was comfortable with that and spoke easily of my experience as a state trooper. I wanted a unit permanently patrolling our highways to stop both drugs and the cash that would come into our state to buy drugs. I promised a full-fledged enforcement of narcotics laws to make our county safe. I told the people present that the active support of the community was also critical. It was important for residents to be the eyes and ears of law enforcement and to tip us off about illegal activities. I spoke of volunteerism and reducing crime in general.

As predicted, Sheriff Duff announced his decision just prior to the July qualifying period that he would not seek re-election. Not surprisingly, he threw his support to Don Riley, a fellow former FBI agent whom Duff felt was the most qualified to be Volusia County's next top law enforcement official.

The campaign had its share of negativity. It sure seemed as if the other candidates had teamed up to be "on message" about me. They all said repeatedly that I had virtually no administrative experience and thus was not qualified to seek the position of Sheriff. There seemed to be a particular venom that accompanied these put-downs, but Alice reassured me that the only reason they didn't like me was they were afraid I was going to win.

None of the candidates actually had much administrative experience. To me, being heavily qualified administratively was not necessarily an asset. Law enforcement is made or broken on the street. If you don't do it right out there, all the administration in the world isn't going to help. I continued to emphasize my experience in the field as the best reason to elect me to office.

Joe Benedict, the farmer, was the first casualty of the race. He dropped out before July qualifying, apparently realizing he was out of his element. Everyone else was in for the September battle, which was fast approaching. Between the six of us, there was nearly 125 years of law enforcement experience. The Volusia County Sheriff's Office had grown dramatically in the years since Duff took over in 1968. At that time, there were 14 deputies. In 1988, between deputies and administrative staff, there were nearly 500 employees. The sheriff's position had risen in importance as the county's population size increased rapidly. In September, these residents would be facing a ballot without Ed Duff on it for the first time in twenty years.

I felt I would do well in the primary. There seemed little chance anyone could command a 50 percent plus majority, so the top two would go on to the November ballot. I was optimistic based on the campaign to date that I would be one of those two candidates. The support was there. We had numbers and that's what it was all about to me—the people. That was to whom the office belonged, not to me or any one individual. It was Volusia County's Sheriff and the people would choose.

We tried to use our campaign funds wisely. One technical piece of equipment we lacked was a fax machine. Bill Chappell, a Congressman running for re-election, had his campaign headquarters a half-mile away. Many of his staff were among my supporters and graciously offered us the use of his fax machine if we needed it.

While Alice Jones took some criticism from her party for working for me, another Democrat, Florida Attorney General Bob Butterworth, endorsed me for Sheriff. His party similarly reprimanded him, but ours was a non-partisan race and Bob truly felt that I was the best candidate. Bob was a friend when I was a state trooper. He had headed up the Department of Highway Safety and Motor Vehicles and had initiated FHP's drug interdiction effort.

Bob forwarded a written endorsement to be used in a campaign ad to appear in the newspaper. He faxed a copy of the endorsement to the *Daytona Beach News Journal* to run, and faxed a back-up copy to Bill Chappell's office. When we called the *News Journal* to verify receipt, they said their fax machine had torn it up. This was Friday afternoon and we wanted to run a big ad featuring this endorsement in Sunday's paper before the Tuesday primary. I took the copy that was in Chappell's office and brought it directly to the newspaper. Incredibly, Josephine Davidson, the managing editor and spouse of the newspaper owner, edited the advertisement without contacting either Bob Butterworth or I. They changed his title from Chief Law Enforcement Officer to Chief Legal Officer of the state of Florida. When the ad ran, I called Bob to apologize. He said that Josephine Davidson had actually called him to verify the endorsement. He just laughed it off and said you never knew what to expect from the media. I didn't realize at the time how prophetic Butterworth's media comments would be.

When the results came in, I was amazed. A lot of people had said they were going to "Vote Vogel" and they did. When the dust cleared, I had 23,915 votes, 45.2 percent of those cast. A distant second was Noel Ouellette with 11,657 tallies, good for 22.1 percent of the vote. Rick Falardeau received 9,081 votes (17.2 percent), but he was eliminated as only the top two move on. Rounding out the voting were Ed Duff's choice Don Riley at 4,431 votes, Ralph Henshaw with 2,645 and Bruce Wragg pulling in 1,130 votes. Absentee ballots put me at 48.5 percent of the vote.

I had almost ended the race in September. In a six-candidate race, to pick up 48.5 percent of the vote was a real confidence-booster to me. Jeannie, Sheila and I knew the support was there, but not until we saw it translated into numbers did we realize how widespread that support actually was.

Ouellette took the opportunity to hammer me on experience again, saying if he doesn't do his job properly over the next 2 months of the campaign then Vogel, without experience, will be the next Sheriff. Falardeau also stated that he was supporting Ouellette and encouraged his supporters to back the Daytona Beach police captain.

No matter. I was going back to my grass roots campaign. I was ready to continue campaigning and build on the votes in the primary that were not cast for me.

Ouellette worked hard to discredit my credentials to be Volusia County's next Sheriff. He spent the two month campaign time trying to hack away at me, thinking he could make up ground and perhaps cause some of those who voted for me in September to think again.

I chose to take the high road and give people a basis to vote for me, not reasons to vote against Ouellette. Some police officers in the Daytona Beach police department that hated Ouellette told us of a police report on an incident involving my November opponent. According to the case file, he was directing traffic near the Ocean Center, an auditorium that housed a number of concerts and other events and that was located near some neighborhoods. One woman who did not want people parking in front of her house came out to talk to Ouellette about it. They exchanged words and it escalated into a verbal altercation. The senior citizen shook a finger at Ouellette and he grabbed it, breaking it in the process.

I wouldn't bring this report to public attention. I wanted people to vote for me because they thought I was the right man for the job, not due to Noel Ouellette breaking a woman's finger.

Ouellette was a throwback to the old days of law enforcement. But the South had progressed beyond the Rod Steiger (*In the Heat of the Night*) and Jackie Gleason (*Smokey and the Bandit*) type of Sheriff. I was certain Volusia County residents would prove it again in November.

Ouellette had picked up some support from other candidates. Ralph Henshaw donated $500 personally to Ouellette's campaign and the truck dealership Henshaw worked for gave him another $1,000. Retiring Sheriff Ed Duff, with his hand-picked successor Don Riley out of the election, also donated money to Ouellette's campaign.

Rick Falardeau did a turnabout. Publicly throwing his support to Ouellette on the night of the primary, he changed his mind two weeks later and announced he was endorsing me for Sheriff. Ouellette naturally charged that I had made a deal with Falardeau to retain his top position in the Sheriff's Office if he supported me. Those that know me would tell you that I would never make that kind of promise. I had met with Falardeau to discuss my ideas shortly after the primary, and he decided that I was probably the best candidate after all. I was apprehensive about his support and I wasn't sure how much good it would do me, since he had just publicly criticized me days earlier. This is the stuff of political campaigns, I guess.

As the campaign escalated even more, I could feel the fatigue starting to set in. One night in late October, I had just come home from a lengthy day of campaigning. I was sitting down and taking off my shoes. Jeannie gasped and pointed to the bottoms of my shoes. I had almost worn them through. No wonder my legs were tired at night. I had only a paper-thin support underneath me.

In November, Volusia County residents gave me 20,000 votes more than Noel Ouellette and a total of 68 percent of the vote. I won every precinct in the county, including Ouellette's home turf in Daytona Beach. That widespread support was especially gratifying. I owed a tremendous debt of gratitude to so many people, especially Alice and Parker Jones, who drove over every day from Deltona to Daytona Beach to put in a fifteen hour day of campaigning and strategy.

Florida Attorney General Bob Butterworth administered the oath of office to me on December 29, 1988 on a stage in front of the county courthouse, with Sheila holding the Bible and Jeannie standing next to me. Jeannie would later say it was the bluest sky she'd ever seen and the future looked just as bright that day. Jeannie wore a white suit and Sheila held flowers, some homegrown orchids given to us by a supporter. Another supporter, Bob Granstrom, designed and handed out bumper stickers which read "Sheriff Vogel—Do Your Thing". Father Jerome from Sacred Heart Catholic Church gave the opening prayer. I stressed in my remarks that I would be a visible, working Sheriff. I emphasized my goal of proactive law enforcement.

There was some bitterness on the part of the other candidates that carried over into 1989 in public remarks. Interestingly, a letter to the editor of the *News Journal* was published in February from one of these candidates—Ralph Henshaw. His comments: "I am writing because I have heard many statements from my supporters and the supporters of other candidates that are not in the best interests of this county. I realize that sour grapes are the by–products of elections, however the race is over. Now we must all give Bob Vogel our support. He needs every bit of help that is available from the public. Crime is a problem that affects all of us. Bob Vogel is our Sheriff. He put forth a great effort to get elected and did it without any degrading remarks or advertisements. I take my hat off to Sheriff Vogel and extend my hand and support. I ask all of my friends and supporters to do the same. Please give Bob Vogel a chance to use his plans to reduce crime and make our county a safer place."

These comments were right on. It was time for a new beginning. The past was just that—past. That Henshaw could write these words was all the more remarkable for what came later.

We had not heard the last from Ralph Henshaw.

A New Beginning

What I wanted to accomplish in the Sheriff's Office would not happen overnight. The department I took over in 1989 lacked organization, discipline, vision and modern technology. It was an inefficient operation that needed overhaul, and it was sure to be uncomfortable for some of the holdovers from the Duff regime. Change is always difficult, but it had to be done so that we could become an effective and efficient law enforcement agency.

I wanted to make the time between the election and my swearing–in meaningful, and attempted to meet with Ed Duff. He never gave me the opportunity. I was not welcome in Duff's office. I heard later that on the day I was to formally occupy the Sheriff's Office, Duff tossed the keys onto the floor. The Sheriff's name is on so many documents in our county. I wanted to be able to come to the office in January with that documentation handled and ready to go so I could work on other aspects of change.

Legal papers, ID cards, stationary, business notices and signs on the waterway all had the current Sheriff's name and had to be changed. Fortunately, some forward—looking employees handled it anyway without being told. I did attend an "Incoming Sheriffs School" in Tallahassee, which had over two-dozen new Sheriffs; a number of those were former FHP state troopers.

Duff had essentially let others run their specific operations within the department, and they had proceeded to build their own empires. I needed to dismantle those, so that everyone in the department operated from the same book. Sid Massey was the captain of the Patrol division; Joe Nasser was in charge of the Communications Center; Ed Carroll was the captain in charge of the Investigations division; and Howard McBride oversaw the Judicial Services division. The operation needed restructuring to squeeze out inefficiency and bring law enforcement closer to the citizens of the county.

McBride retired shortly after I came aboard. I moved Ed Carroll out of investigations and into a "special projects" assignment working in an administrative capacity. I put Sid Massey in charge of McBride's Judicial Services division and I promoted Lieutenant Leonard Davis, an African-American, to head–up Patrol and renamed it Law Enforcement Services. Leonard was the highest–ranking black officer in the department and an individual well–deserving of that honor. With his dedication and discipline, I could see nothing but bright days ahead for him. I hoped that he could also help me recruit more minority deputies. We had a total of ten in the Sheriff's Office in early 1989, yet we had a county that was 17 percent African-American. Clearly, we had work to do in this area.

The Civil Division was in good hands when I arrived. Run by Lieutenant Judy Wiley, she was the best in the state at what she did and I was not going to change it.

District offices were established, and I decided to move some investigators out into decentralized field offices. The majority of crimes investigated were either persons or property crimes, and I felt the investigators should be closer to the victims and patrol deputies. Those investigators could then report to their district commanders, who in turn would report to Captain Leonard Davis, the division commander.

There was a lot of energy expended making these changes. Not everyone was happy about it. People who had little supervision before now had to take responsibility for their actions and be accountable for their decisions. Responsibility, accountability and progressive discipline were all implemented.

One of the biggest difficulties I faced early on was securing an administrative assistant for me. I asked Alice Jones if she would take the job. I had relied greatly on her wisdom and decision-making during the campaign and felt she would be a real asset within the Sheriff's Office. She agreed. That was the easy part.

Former Sheriff Duff had two young ladies performing the same tasks for him. Based on their skill levels, they were undoubtedly there more for appearance than anything else. I transferred them to other administrative positions, created an unclassified position with the approval of the County Manager and hired Alice.

I also brought in Mel Stack to work in the position of legal advisor to the Sheriff's Office. He agreed if I understood that he wouldn't serve the full four years. He would help me get started and stay for a time, and then look around to find a suitable replacement. Mel wanted eventually to go into private practice. Mel is a good, honest person, a far cry from the people described in the usual attorney jokes. He was a local boy, having grown up in Daytona Beach and attended Seabreeze High School here. He was highly respected within the community, by the Bar Association, judges and other law enforcement personnel. He knew how to prosecute drug cases and how to make the cases stand up in court. He had helped me stay within acceptable legal guidelines, and was personally responsible for the high rate of convictions my arrests turned out simply because he supervised the methods I used. Since I wanted to create an assigned group of deputies to work Interstate 95, I believed that Mel, once again, would be a critical factor in its success.

I began to implement community–based policing early in my first term. Based on results elsewhere around the country, this seemed to be an effective method of law enforcement. We had a district substation in Deltona and I wanted offices in Ormond Beach, New Smyrna Beach and Deland. I wanted Lieutenants in charge of these districts and wanted to build on the supervisors we already had in place. Rollins College professors developed a specialized evaluation and training program designed to enhance key administrators' strengths and weaknesses. I divided the county into four quadrants and began to build the district offices accordingly. The Citizen Observer Program was placed under Len Jansen, a tall, muscular man who had retired to Florida from New Jersey where he had owned a restaurant, some real estate and several businesses including a construction company. He was an avid New York Jets fan as was his wife, Fran, who became the volunteer secretary for the Citizen Observer Program. Even though he had a large presence that commanded your attention when he came into a room, underneath he was a gentle man.

Automation was a major problem that had to be fixed. Some people that were brought in had no computer to use. Virtually nothing was computerized. Records management was a manual task. The Communications Center had some of the most deplorable working conditions I had ever seen. It was like walking into a bunker. There were no windows. Morale was understandably low. There weren't enough headsets to wear. There weren't enough chairs to sit on. The building environment was further impacted by the permission for some employees to smoke inside the building. Employee sick time was the highest in the department.

Citizen complaints came in daily, with protests about slow response time, insensitive deputies and uncaring dispatchers. My first month in office saw nearly thirty patrol cars damaged in traffic accidents.

One accident involved a large pick-up truck with a six-inch steel pipe front bumper and a drunk driver. It was after midnight, and one of our deputies spotted this truck weaving and speeding. He activated his siren and lights, but the truck wouldn't stop. The deputy's supervisor, who was nearby, responded to assist with the call. The supervisor passed the deputy and drew up alongside the truck. The truck, still weaving, struck the right side of the supervisor's car, who occupied the inside lane of a four–lane highway. The supervisor, angered now, called in several other deputy cars, and they all played bumper car with the pick-up. Five or six deputies pursuing one drunk driver in a pick-up truck had resulted in thousands of dollars in damage instead of a simple stop and arrest.

The division commander drew up large diagrams for staff presentation of all the vehicle positions. The supervisor remarked about how everyone did a great job and did things strictly by the book. By what book? The original deputy was the only one with a head on his shoulders. He was going to pursue the truck as safely as possible and wait for him to stop or run out of gas. He could then apprehend him—case over. But the involvement of the supervisor created a hazard on the roads far greater than one drunk driver.

Policies were changed. Emergency vehicle driving and refresher courses were required along with the implementation of a progressive discipline program. A very limited pursuit policy was established. Deputies could only chase if a violent felon was being pursued.

I also began to re-evaluate our communications process so that we could improve response time. In some areas, our deputies were clearly overwhelmed with calls and that hurt their ability to respond quickly. All citizens wanted deputies responding within a reasonable period of time. They had a right to expect that and we had an obligation to deliver that service.

The key was to figure out where the calls were coming from and how best to improve our response time. Our analysis showed that a great majority of calls came from the western part of the county —Deltona and Deland. We isolated the location of the largest number of calls and reallocated our allotment of deputies to put more in areas that had the highest call rate.

We set up a program where volunteers could come and work at the Sheriff's Office. It cost us very little, and these folks could perform some tasks to help the people who were there on salary. The paid workers were concerned that they would be replaced by volunteers, but all I wanted was to get more done in a given hour with more hands at no increase in price. I had people perfectly willing to volunteer and I wanted to take advantage of that enthusiasm while it was there. In a short period of time, we had nearly 300 volunteers assisting our law enforcement efforts. Background checks were run on these helpers, and they were given instruction and classroom courses.

There was also a beefing up of our School Resource Officer program. There were two such deputies when I started, and we expanded that to nearly twenty. These deputies were permanently assigned to a school to both build a positive relationship between students and police officers, and to teach and regulate behavior. So much of what children perceive about law enforcement comes from television or talk in the schoolyard. Learning to be lawful citizens starts in school, and I wanted to defuse any potential gap between the students and us. I wanted them to talk freely with the deputy and feel like they could go to one if they had a problem or to seek advice.

Another of my goals was to earn national accreditation for the department. There was a formal procedure to follow and it gave us a stamp of professionalism and respectability to those law enforcement agencies that conformed to a set of rigid, uniform policy standards. Ed Duff's department was so far removed from this recognition that it would take substantial time and effort to accomplish this objective. But I was confident we could do it. Nearly 1,000 standards would have to be met. I had the standards and knew what had to be done. Improving to these regulations would be beneficial not only to the department, but to the county residents, too.

Alice had done a fantastic job in our first year in the department. But there was something wrong and it would take a while to identify what it was. Alice had made me a quilt in her spare time that was made up of all the Sheriff's patches in the state of Florida. It was a tremendous gift and one both Jeannie and I deeply appreciated. I hung it up on the wall near my office where I could view it regularly. One day, she noticed it hanging askew and tried to right it. As she reached for the quilt, she fell. She didn't know why. She told no one about her accident.

A week later, as she was driving home, she inexplicably drove off the road, narrowly avoiding injury to both her and the vehicle. She felt fine and couldn't explain either mishap. She didn't want to alarm Parker, who was recovering from cancer surgery himself.

Two weeks after the car problem, Alice Jones suffered a massive stroke that robbed her of the ability to read, write or speak clearly. She retained her motor skills, but the rest was extremely difficult for her. She mixed up words and sentences and communication with her was an effort. Jeannie, Sheila and I were devastated at this turn of events. Alice and Parker both had contributed so much of their skills and time to us during that hectic and competitive campaign and she had continued to assist me in the Sheriff's Office. Not long after her stroke, Parker Jones died and shortly thereafter Alice passed away, too. Their passing was a great loss to us as we felt as if our own parents had just died. We were grateful that we were able to know them and learn from their vast experience.

Our hiring practices were more effective as we added new deputies and we established stricter qualifications. We rejected as many as 80 percent of the people who applied for work because of work history, past drug usage, fraudulent application statements, unverifiable past employment, and driving records. We didn't want any "John Wayne types" in the department. We needed deputies, not cowboys, and I was already stuck with some of the latter who should never have been hired in the first place.

I was unprepared for how limiting the county charter is for the Sheriff. My hands were tied on most hiring and administrative issues. Under Volusia County's unique charter arrangements, only the county manager had the ultimate authority to hire and fire. About the only people Tom Kelly couldn't fire were those elected to office—like me. It was no secret that Kelly favored an appointed Sheriff rather than one whom the people could elect (and un-elect). And now here I came, ready to make changes in a department that Kelly had practically run by himself. We were clearly on a collision course.

If we wanted to fill a personnel vacancy, we had to contact the county's Personnel officer. That office would send over a list of eligible hires who had already been tested, from which to select a replacement. Also, if we wanted to purchase any approved budgeted items, no matter how small, someone from the county Central Services unit would have to approve the order. This hampered and delayed effective daily operations.

Dr. Tom Kelly, originally from Maryland, held a Ph.D. in Public Administration. He was bright, articulate and difficult. He had a ruddy complexion that reflected his Irish heritage. He ran the county much as a dictator would run a country. He possessed solid manipulative skills and held the County Council and the *Daytona Beach News Journal* in his pocket. If a member of the Council questioned any policy or procedure, Kelly would load them down with the paperwork of county government to see if they could unravel it. He clearly called the shots.

He was immensely popular with the *Daytona Beach News Journal*, especially Josephine Davidson.

⁀ ⁀

THE CHARTER RULES

The Volusia County Charter is treated like an ancient scroll by those in power here. It gives a few the ability to control most of what happens in this area. Control is difficult to give up once it's in hand. Anyone that threatens this sacred document becomes a target. An elected Sheriff is an impediment to this power base. Making the position an appointed one would remove that problem. Tom Kelly was not interested in the checks and balances of an elected system.

A local state senator, Ed Dunn, had helped push through legislation so Volusia County could establish a charter back in 1970. Volusia County residents likely didn't realize it at the time, but they were giving power previously held by the citizens now to only a few. As I said, those few liked this control and it had been that way ever since. You oppose it at your own risk.

In a special election in June 1970, voters succumbed to a biased campaign and voted for the charter. Three elected non-partisan offices (county property appraiser, supervisor of elections and the sheriff) were changed from constitutional offices to department heads reporting to a county manager, making this charter government the only one of its kind anywhere in the country.

Under this system, the Sheriff is not autonomous over hiring, firing, the budget, or any other administrative function. I can set law enforcement policy, but if a deputy needs any disciplinary action, including firing, the county manager has the final say. I can only do so much in that regard. If I take action and the deputy appeals to the county manager who then disagrees with me, the deputy stays. Imagine running your own business that way!

All the changes I wanted to do were not embraced enthusiastically at the county level. Automation was needed. More deputies for the high crime area were needed. Modern police equipment to help solve crimes was needed. A better working environment for the communications center was needed. It was all destined to be a struggle.

Kelly was a staunch Democrat and I was a newly elected Republican. That didn't help, although what possible difference that made in law enforcement I couldn't say.

We battled over the budget, personnel decisions and equipment. Kelly would make changes to every budget I proposed to the county council. He said it was his job to submit a budget to the county council, therefore he had line item veto power and he exercised it every time, more as a demonstration of control than for any valid reasons. I had to fight to put back in many of Kelly's changes and it needlessly prolonged the debate over my budget every year. The end result was generally fine, but it was a struggle. The citizens would come in masses after a hurried telephone campaign on our part. They spoke on behalf of the agency and pleaded our case for budget approval. Every other county sheriff in Florida had the right to appeal the budget to the governor of the state, except this Sheriff.

My problems with the county manager brought the issues out front to the people of Volusia County. They could finally see the ties that bound the hands of the Sheriff. Before long, there was a movement afoot to put an amendment on a November ballot to restore the office of Sheriff to a constitutional one as it is everywhere else in the state.

A local attorney had drafted, pro bono, language to be used to put the Sheriff question on the ballot. The question called for an amendment of the charter and read, "Shall the Constitutional Office of Sheriff be restored in Volusia County, repealing all conflicting provisions of the Volusia County Charter with the exception of the functions of the Department of Corrections?"

The group trying to make this change came to me for support. What could I say? I agreed to publicly pursue the petition drive. The language proposed the change as an amendment that required 5 percent of registered voters to sign a petition to have the question placed on ballot. If the change were a repeal of the charter, that would require 15 percent of registered voter signatures. That was a significant difference in the number of names needed.

I spent as much extra time as I could trying to obtain signatures. Jeannie and Sheila were back on the campaign trail, setting up tables at all public events with help from our loyal supporters, to inform voters and obtain a signature. The signatures had to be turned in to the supervisor of elections to check the validity of the name and the person's voting status. It was amazing the number of people who did not realize the sheriff reported to the county manager and could not make the typical management decisions every CEO makes. Their signatures followed quickly after this revelation.

These actions ran afoul of the *Daytona Beach News Journal* and the *Orlando Sentinel* newspapers. The *News Journal* was especially protective of the Volusia charter, and they used the power of the pen to fight against any change to this "Holy Grail." I was somewhat surprised by the *Sentinel's* stance given that their home base, Orange County, didn't have any such provisions in their charter about the sheriff.

As we closed in on enough signatures to place the question on the ballot, the inevitable challenge to it came. The *News Journal's* own attorney, Jon Kaney, represented an individual, a staunch Democrat, who brought a suit stating that the petition's wording called for a repeal of the charter, not an amendment. The repeal, of course, would require 15 percent of voters' signatures and there wasn't time to accomplish that now. We had always set our sights on a higher number than 5 percent to offset any invalid signatures, but time was against us to personally see and obtain signatures from almost 10 percent more of the people who could legally vote in the county.

The challengers knew this, so rather than attack the increasingly popular public issue about the constitutionality of the Sheriff's office, their plan was to say it called for a repeal and disqualify it from the ballot due to a lack of enough signatures. No one involved in the petition drive anticipated this possibility. In retrospect, the language drafted should have been sent to the Attorney General's office for an opinion on its clarity, but it was late now for that strategy.

A retired circuit judge was drafted to listen to the arguments and rule. We, of course, argued that the intention of the petition drive was to amend this one portion of the charter regarding the Sheriff's office and that's how the question was worded that people signed. Jon Kaney argued that it wasn't clear from the petition what would happen to the Sheriff's office if this portion of the charter was overturned, and didn't fully explain the ramifications the amendment would have on the charter. It was, he said, a repeal of the charter's existing provisions and as such was not an amendment.

The judge eventually sided with Kaney. He ruled that the language was too ambiguous and not specific enough to be considered a simple amendment. He said the wording was too vague for voters to know what they were voting for or against. Then he further muddied the water by agreeing that this type of change was a repeal, not an amendment.

This murky decision left us without any options to put a proper question on the ballot. On one hand, the judge said this wording about restoring constitutionality of the Sheriff's office was too vague. This meant attempting to rewrite it with that wording in was doomed to fail. On the other hand, the judge had also called it a repeal, meaning that even if we came up with a better-worded question, we needed 15 percent of registered voters' signatures to even get it on the ballot. It was too late in the year for that to happen.

The only possible avenue for us was to challenge the judge's decision in total, but an appeal could take weeks, even months, and time was our enemy once again. We had been backed into a corner with no way out.

The county council seemed willing to work with me. The county manager was another story. I decided to put together a committee to look into recommending changes to the county council on several items, including budget approval that affected my office. Perhaps, we could loosen the tight rein held by the county manager in another way. I asked both Mel Stack and Jon Kaney to serve with others on this committee. It was actually Kaney's idea to create more independence through this route rather than challenging the charter. They went to work on the problem, and I continued my efforts to step up the evolution of the Sheriff's Office to a more professional law enforcement organization. Eventually, Tom Kelly retired and Larry Arrington was appointed as the new county manager. Arrington approved and implemented the committee's recommendation, making my life a whole lot easier. Larry Arrington was a breath of fresh air.

One of the ways I could use dollars other than tax revenue was to use funds confiscated from drug dealers. The state of Florida allows law enforcement to use those funds under statutory guidelines. Most of the sheriff's offices used the money to purchase new equipment, ironically enough, to better fight illegal drugs. The dealers' own money would be used to further crack down on their crimes.

Another of the areas I wanted to improve was in the deputies' standard uniform. Deputies here had never been issued uniform hats. I wanted a professional standard uniform which deputies would be proud to wear, including a Stetson hat. For medical reasons alone, a hat needed to be worn out in the hot Florida sun to avoid skin cancer. Rather than ask the county for more money, I requested the use of dollars from our confiscated funds account to pay for this apparel.

This infuriated one of the county council members, a man with the singular name of Big John. He was a long-time county councilman who frequently took pleasure in arguing against us in county council meetings. He was an overweight, bearded man. Big John routinely hired prisoners newly released from jail at a low wage to work in his tire and automotive shop. He wore black workman's boots and a blue work shirt with the name "Big" stenciled on the front of it.

He thought the hats were a tremendous waste of money. He even sent Tom Kelly to ask that I remove the hat request from the council agenda. My response was that the deputies need the hats, deserve them, and at no extra cost to the taxpayer.

Big John owned a garage that performed routine auto maintenance such as oil changes. One day, he complained on the radio about the money spent on the hats and that the deputies weren't even wearing them. He said if anyone had or took a picture of a deputy wearing a hat and brought it to his shop, he would give the person a free oil change.

Jeannie heard this over the airwaves, went to retrieve her scrapbook and found twelve recent pictures of deputies wearing their hats. She drove down to Big John's and asked for the free oil change, showing the picture to the attendant. She gave out several of the other pictures to waiting patrons so they, too, could participate in the free oil change.

Big John was furious, but he had no choice than to honor his public statement. It was free oil change day for a number of people there. Jeannie then called Captain Dale Anderson, who in turn contacted a number of off-duty deputies to dress in full uniform and take their patrol cars down to Big John's for a free oil change. She also called our Public Information Officer, Gary Davidson, so that the media could also be there. For the rest of the day, deputies came in for their free oil change. Big John said he had to check with the county attorney to see if he could give county cars a free oil change. The media was alerted and soon there were plenty of photo opportunities and television time for Big John and the parade of deputies in line for some free car maintenance. He finally went back on the radio to stop his free promotion, acknowledging reluctantly that perhaps the deputies did wear hats after all.

This was not my only battle over what I spent our confiscated funds on. At one point, Tom Kelly wanted to use the funds to make up for a million dollar budget shortfall. My department was not part of that shortfall problem—I had brought us under budget in my first year—and the confiscated funds were not intended for this purpose.

I personally thought it would be a bad precedent. Confiscated funds used this way one year would be an out for them every year into the future. That was not the purpose of this money, and I refused to allocate the funds in that manner. Deputies risked their lives to seize these dollars, therefore the money should be used for law enforcement.

Kelly and Big John, who was chairman of the county council, both felt they were entitled to the money and went after it. In a public meeting, I said this was against statutory law and suggested the county seek an opinion from State Attorney General Bob Butterworth. In September 1991, he backed us up with Florida statutes and an attorney's opinion, and Tom Kelly and Big John had to back down.

≈ ≈

ACCREDITATION

In addition to the lack of hats, our deputies were lacking cameras, fingerprint kits, standard issue firearms, and traffic vests (an accreditation requirement), among other items. Deputies were forced to buy their own sidearms. It was a significant cost to them. Standardizing the weapons would ensure that all deputies used the same weapon, and it would also save them money. In addition, they would have the same ammunition to share if needed during a shoot-out, a grim reminder of the FBI shoot-out in Miami in the 1980s when officers couldn't share because they carried different caliber weapons. Confiscated drug funds helped buy these necessary parts of the police officer's repertoire. If we wanted these officers to do a professional, thorough job and help to bring down the crime rate in the county, we had to give them the right tools with which to perform their tasks. We purchased better weapons and fingerprint kits. This upgrading was vital if we were ever to attain national accreditation.

We were forced to seek more money from the county council to accomplish some of this needed department facelift. I wanted to automate the communication center and the administrative areas. In order to accomplish this, we first had to buy computers. We had to fix the communications center environment, patching up leaks and acquiring sufficient seating and headsets to accommodate all those who worked there. It was built as part of a civil defense building, and while it could withstand a military bomb attack, it was not exactly conducive to a pleasant work environment. They had to adapt to our new decentralized offices, alerting officers in an area immediately to a call or a problem. Slowly, but surely, the improvements came and started to pay off. We also had gone to a non-smoking environment because of the computers, and it helped to bring sick time down considerably.

We upgraded to an 800-megahertz radio system that allowed everyone out in the field to be on a state-of-the-art two-way radio system. The agency needed the radio system and we thought we could bring the rest of the county along with us. We assembled all the public safety offices and municipal government leaders, most of who would be users to the system. An agreement was reached that everyone would utilize the upgraded system. We also wanted an emergency system that would be of critical importance, especially during hurricane season, a six-month period lasting from June 1 to November 30. A portion of a traffic fine was allocated to pay for this improved method of communication. The only people unhappy with this were those we stopped and ticketed.

In addition to raising the technical merits of the Sheriff's Office, I also wanted to improve personnel standards. Discipline had been lax in the latter years of the Duff regime, so I knew a step-up in this area was sure to draw grumbles from the ranks. But it had to be done. As law enforcement officers, we were expected to maintain the highest level of discipline and integrity, and my department was going to toe the line in this regard. I didn't mind an officer making a simple mistake. I did mind a repeat of that same error.

For the first several months after taking office, disciplinary actions were necessary on a regular basis. My concerns ranged from sloppy appearance to excessive use of force. I didn't make these decisions alone. Reprimands, suspensions, firings and other actions required input from division commanders, who were members of my staff. We met weekly to discuss these types of matters and other issues which affected the agency.

This policy had the desired effect. Deputies who performed at a substandard level were weeded out. I'm sure I made some enemies in the process. But it was for the general good of the Sheriff's Office and ultimately for the citizens of Volusia County. Fortunately, the majority of the people in the department were hard working, determined officers and support personnel. It wasn't all negative enforcement, either. I also stepped up the personal recognition for a job well done.

It took nearly three years, but the Volusia County Sheriff's Office became nationally accredited in late 1991. A three-member review team from the Commission of Law Enforcement Accreditation conducted a week-long inspection, reviewing the department from top to bottom. There were nearly 1,000 commission standards to meet, and we were told we had met over 95 percent of them, sufficient for accreditation. It was a tremendous step forward for the department and inspired confidence that we were on the right track to building a fundamentally sound law enforcement agency. These standards made our operations more efficient, reduced liability, made us eligible for more grant money, and ultimately would serve Volusia County more effectively. We were the 189th law enforcement agency nationwide to be awarded this distinction. It was a proud day for all of us.

Another inside battle to be won was to smooth relations with other police agencies within the county. In addition to the Sheriff's office, there were sixteen municipalities, thirteen of which had their own law enforcement agencies, with our office providing contractual services to the other three. There were two other county agencies: the Beach Rangers and the airport police. Daytona Beach had the largest municipal police force. The police chief, Paul Crow, had an enormous ego and did not want any of our deputies doing investigations of any kind in his city, without his knowledge or approval. He was later removed from office for telling his police officers to un-arrest a prominent attorney's son, who was legally apprehended for drunk driving. The lawyer, Kermit Coble, had successfully represented John Travolta in a problem John had with the Spruce Creek Homeowners Association, who had tried to prevent him from landing his jet airplane at the landing strip near his home.

Port Orange's agency was also a challenge to work with. Their police chief, Bob Ford (who was appointed to the job I had applied for in 1987) did not like his officers fraternizing with deputies. He was jealous of the Sheriff's office because of our jurisdictional abilities, and wanted to maintain the old line way of thinking that this was his turf and no one else should enter. His patrol officers were ordered not to talk to our deputies, making their task more difficult. He didn't contribute any manpower to our countywide task forces consisting of members from several area agencies. These turf battles were unnecessary and an impediment to consistent law enforcement throughout the area. But I concentrated on the areas where communication was solid.

Some of the smaller towns chose to pay us to handle their law enforcement duties. This often made more practical and economic sense, but it was amazing how few cities actually supported this outsourcing policy. Many community leaders still wanted their own police department regardless of cost or effectiveness. In our area, though, Deltona, DeBary and Pierson all contracted with us.

While we made many strides in my first term in office, the area of greatest achievement was in our drug and cash interdiction programs along the interstate. With the success came plenty of controversy, and it set the tone for the legal maelstrom that was to come after our initial achievements.

≈ ≈

Reversal of Fortune

I had made my success as a state trooper by successfully confiscating drugs from the mules who took them north up Interstate 95. As Sheriff of Volusia County, I could now assign a couple of deputies to that same type of criminal patrol. I had over 300 deputies under my supervision and took the Directed Patrol Team, consisting of a Sergeant and three deputies for this assignment.

Veteran Sergeant Dale Anderson was assigned to head up this team. He had been with the Volusia County Sheriff's Office since he was 21 and was a strong leader. Also assigned was Deputy Bobby Jones, who had been with the agency for two years. Other team members were J.W. Smith, a black deputy, and Ray Almodovar, a Hispanic deputy.

As head of the Patrol Division, Leonard Davis had the responsibility of overseeing this team. They reported directly to him for supervision. The team members attended a 40- hour Criminal Patrol School run by the Institute of Police Technology and Management School in Jacksonville. The classroom activity focused the officers on going beyond the traffic violation for which the people were stopped. It taught the deputies to look for other signs of criminal activity and to legally follow up on any contraband found. We also sent them to the DEA's Operation Pipeline school that concentrated on the latest developments in criminal patrol and taught some of the more recent ways to transport both drugs and the cash to buy the contraband.

Early activity resulted in the seizure of a substantial amount of drugs. There were frequent successes, but their results were less than those I had been making on a regular basis as a state trooper.

One tactic we used was to put up a road sign on Interstate 95 that read "Narcotics Inspection Ahead." Obviously, we were trying to warn the drug couriers that we were on the watch and vigilant about stopping them. There was no actual inspection point. We didn't want to stop traffic. We did, however, want mules to reveal themselves by making an illegal U-turn, a maneuver we could stop them for and then proceed with our normal conversation in pursuit of a written consent to search the vehicle.

We had the support of State Attorney John Tanner. The Department of Transportation (DOT) expressed concern about the plan, however, even though they acknowledged they thought it was legal to put up the signs. They wrote me a letter holding me personally liable if anybody was injured as a result of the sign. Attorney General Bob Butterworth personally went down to the Governor's office to protest, pointing out that a Florida Sheriff was trying to do something about the flow of drugs and instead of support, he was being discouraged in his efforts. The DOT letter writer was eventually terminated, although for a different reason.

The American Civil Liberties Union (ACLU) protested the idea as did my old nemesis criminal defense attorney Dan Warren, who called the signs "Checkpoint Charlie", a reference to the guarded border between East and West Berlin.

The DOT was concerned about motorist safety if too many vehicles were swinging into wild and illegal U-turns to avoid what they believed was an upcoming traffic stop. We certainly didn't want to create a road hazard, but I wasn't convinced that was going to be a problem. We had stopped some cars that had turned south illegally, and there had been no close calls where traffic was concerned.

The signs did attract international attention, appearing both in *Playboy* magazine and on a Japanese television show similar to the old TV game show, "What's My Line?" However, the ACLU claimed we were taking away people's freedom by putting them up, that we were in effect creating a police state. That was outlandish. The drug traffickers were actually infringing on the rights and freedom of others and we wanted that stopped. However, the intense publicity about the stops indicating that there wasn't really a narcotics inspection alerted drug couriers that there was nothing to worry about as long as they didn't commit a traffic violation. This reduced the program's effectiveness, and I stopped putting up the signs three months after the program had begun.

I thought back over my arrests as a state trooper and the successful drug stops that had been made in the 1980s. The interesting fact about these stops is that I found enormous amounts of illegal drugs and very little cash. This made a great deal of sense if the money had already been used to purchase the drugs or to front additional drugs. Fronted drugs are illegal drugs given until sold, then payment is made.

If drugs were being transported north, then the cash to buy the drugs would be coming south. Most of the major dealers knew that we were looking for their couriers in the northbound lanes of I-95, but we weren't stopping people going south. They could bring the cash down to make the buy and then return by a different route. Our next strategy was to concentrate on southbound traffic and watch for traffic violations.

It was very uncommon for the law-abiding citizen to be transporting large sums of cash on the highway. There might be legitimate explanations, and I cautioned the team to be open-minded about the money and listen to what the driver and passenger(s) had to say. We would also use the K-9 unit to indicate whether there were traces of drugs present on the cash, a process highly approved by the courts.

So the team went to work. They made their stops for traffic violations, and then asked questions and observed carefully to see if there were reasons to go further. Most of the cumulative similarities mentioned in Part Two were appropriate here, too. Most of the time, a written warning about the traffic violation was issued. The warning itself should dissipate much of the normal nervousness a person feels after being stopped by a police vehicle. If the person was still displaying signs of nervousness, this generally indicated there was more to the story than concern over the traffic violation.

That didn't mean someone was transporting drugs or cash to buy drugs. The person could be traveling with stolen property or guns. It could be a person with children trying to leave the state in the middle of a custody suit. It could be people wanted by the police in another jurisdiction. The person might be driving a stolen car. The team found plenty out there on the highways besides drugs or drug money.

To me and the team members, drug money was virtually the same as drugs. Cash was the beginning of the entire transaction. A drug dealer was not likely to front a buyer the drugs in exchange for the promise of cash at a later date, especially if the dealer didn't know the people well. Seize the cash and the transaction never happened. In addition, the person who fronted the money to buy the drugs was not likely to give a courier a second chance with some cash to try again. I heard later from the DEA that their wiretaps were picking up conversation about our cash seizures and how it was disrupting the drug organizations' business. That was music to my ears.

Deputy Bobby Jones turned out to be a natural at taking the stop further. Everything began with the traffic violation. Once that occurred, the wheels were set in motion. The stop had to be handled perfectly, using the methods that I perfected during my state trooper years which were now being taught all over the country. During the stop, the rest of the investigation was dependent on the deputy's power of observation. Deputy Jones was very adept at noticing little details out of place, indicators that there was something else going on in the car other than the violation. He would say, after the driver's documents were all returned and he or she was free to go, that there were a lot of drugs being transported in this part of the country and would the driver mind if he searched the car?

It was as easy-going and disarming as that. Once given permission, the deputies would search and often turned up large amounts of cash, for which the passenger(s) in the car had little viable explanation. The key follow-up questions then would be to determine the origin of the money. If the person (or people) in the car said it belonged to someone else, the deputies would try and contact that individual to verify where the money had come from. If the story was not provable, and we felt we had probable cause, we would contact the Sheriff's Office legal advisor, in this case Mel Stack, to obtain permission to confiscate the dollars. He would be told the location of the money, how it was packaged, and what had been said so far. Mel would then either OK the seizure, or not.

The deputy would typically ask the person or persons to sit in the back of the car while the investigation continued. In his car would be a tape recorder. It is legal to tape people in a police car without their consent. We heard some highly interesting and revealing conversations held in the back of those green and white cruisers.

In the meantime, the deputies (they always worked in pairs) would be photographing the money as evidence. Initially, we tried to count it out on the interstate so we could give the vehicle occupant(s) a receipt for the money right there, but it became too difficult, time-consuming and subject to human error. So we started transporting the dollars back to the Sheriff's Office where a counting machine could do an accurate job. In addition, we felt officer safety was an issue, not just from the vehicle occupants but from anyone driving along the highway that might be tempted by the sight of deputies counting drug money in plain sight.

Many times, people in the car did not even wait for a receipt or bother following the deputies back to the Sheriff's Office. All they wanted to do, if we weren't holding them on any specific charges, was drive away from Volusia County as fast as they could. However, they did accept Polaroid pictures of the seized cash. This way they could show the people who they were working for that the money had been seized by the police, and not been embezzled by the mules themselves.

The team's first seizure was $9,000 in cash. The seizures eventually averaged between $20,000 and $40,000. One weekend in April 1989 resulted in three stops and seizures totaling $140,000 in drug money. If there were no drugs in the car or evidence of other criminal violations, the deputies did not and could not legally detain the car's occupants. On this, we had full support from our State Attorney, John Tanner. I still had the guidance of Mel Stack, former State Attorney's office lawyer, who was now the legal advisor to the Sheriff's Office. Mel worked hard to make sure we did it right and stayed within all legal boundaries as they existed.

Defense attorneys and the ACLU naturally disagreed with us. They believed seizing money without making an actual arrest violated the individual's constitutional rights. But the real people being violated were the drug dealers who depended on these couriers to move both money and drugs. The drug war was not being won necessarily, but we could claim some victories and were definitely slowing down the criminal pace. Money was pouring down the southbound side. I was right about that. I felt though that our seizures were merely the tip of the iceberg; we weren't catching everyone.

The typical pattern was 1-2 males in a borrowed car, with a registration in a different name than the driver, and often a secret compartment where the money was hidden. It was essentially the same characteristic pattern that I had seen with drug stops. Clearly, the drug players were still in Florida. By using good law enforcement techniques and a Contraband Forfeiture statute, the team was having great successes.

Of the original team deputies, the only one I had to talk Sergeant Dale Anderson into assigning to the team was Deputy Frank Josenhanz. He had made some previous cases and I encouraged Dale to try him out. Josenhanz was not Anderson's type of cop. He was more of a cowboy (which I was unaware of) than anyone would have liked, but we gave him his opportunity.

And he fouled it up. Two months into the team's working efforts, Dale had reached an end with Josenhanz. The "cowboy" was a loner, out for himself and not a team player. Worse, he was not following established procedures. The first major problem we had was a deceptive call Josenhanz made during one of his stops. He had discovered $18,000 in cash and a convoluted story about where the money came from. At the stop, Josenhanz called the man's adult son in Virginia to find out why his father was in Florida. The deputy didn't identify where he was from and told the son that his father had been in a car accident. Josenhanz claimed he ultimately told the son why he had phoned, but still didn't say from where he was calling. He seized the cash and let the man go.

The son panicked and called his attorney to see if he could locate his father. The attorney called nearly every police jurisdiction from North Carolina southward in search of an answer.

Lying to relatives of a possible suspect was not an acceptable practice in the Sheriff's Office. I was concerned about this action by Josenhanz, more so than John Tanner was, who said that he felt the call was legal even if there were some moral problems with it. I had more trouble with it than that. Dale felt Josenhanz was not good for the team. He missed back-up assignments. He actually threw a small amount of marijuana away without making an arrest or turning it into our evidence section. I didn't need cowboys on the team and told Dale that if he didn't want Josenhanz, then designate him for reassignment. He did. Deputy Steve Rupert replaced Josenhanz.

Despite the successful seizures of cash going south and drugs going north, my operations still came under some local criticism. While the public support was clearly in my favor, local critics argued that our drug and cash interdiction was doing more to help other parts of the country where these people were from than to cut down on crime locally.

I really couldn't understand that attitude. I only had four people assigned (out of over 300 deputies) to this patrol. The rest of the deputies were concentrating on other parts of the county. So what if another part of the country benefited from our actions on Interstate 95? To me, if we saved some teenager from buying drugs in New Jersey because of a stop we made in Volusia County, that was worth it. Law enforcement success often depends on the team approach, not just within the department but from agency to agency across the country. We've arrested people here who were returned to their home jurisdiction to face charges and vice versa. Law enforcement depends on that kind of cooperation.

The stops revealed some interesting characters. Deputy Bobby Jones stopped a man one evening in a late 60s Ford pick-up truck whose tag light was out. This was not the type of vehicle you'd expect for drug couriers. The man was a Native American from a town near Lumberton, North Carolina. The deputy asked him casually where he was going. The man replied that he was heading south to see his lawyer because he was having trouble with the police. He told the deputy that he had been involved in illegal drug activity and his partner in this criminal enterprise had sold him out to law enforcement authorities.

Deputy Jones stopped in the middle of reading the man's license and registration. He had heard many and varied stories about the reasons people were heading south, but this was a first. After a few moments, Deputy Jones secured the man's written consent to search the car. The deputy asked the man if there was anything he should know about in the car. With frightening honesty, the man told him there was $115,000 concealed in the back of the seat.

Deputy Jones asked the man why he had so much cash. He figured it might be bond money for his lawyer to use at the man's upcoming arraignment. But that wasn't it. The man told Jones he was going to buy some cocaine that he hoped to sell so that he could set his girlfriend up with enough cash while he was in jail.

When you've been out on the road long enough, you hear some of the most incredible tales. This time, honesty was even stranger than any fictitious story the man could have told.

In another incident, Deputy Jones stopped a car that was speeding on the interstate at about 5:00 AM. When the car pulled over, he observed an elderly couple. The deputy walked to their car, thinking he would give them a warning to slow down. There wasn't a lot of traffic, but there would be shortly and their speed was well above normal. As he was walking to their car, he heard a "thump" sound. He wasn't sure what it was, but it bothered him. It was out of the ordinary and he didn't like things he couldn't easily explain.

The driver was a disabled retired military man whose wife sat in the passenger seat. Jones wrote up the warning, conversing with them as he did so. He asked the man if he had any weapons in the car. The man denied it. The officer suggested the couple get out of the car while he wrote up the warning. Eventually, Deputy Jones asked them for written permission to search the car. The "thump" still bothered him. They gave permission and he found a handgun on the floor on the driver's side.

He asked the man if he had any more weapons. The man said no and the deputy patted him down. He was not carrying anything else. The deputy suggested the couple wait in the back of the patrol car while he continued his search. In the trunk were 10 pounds of cocaine. From the back seat of the patrol car, a tape recorder captured the elderly couple's conversation. The first words the women said were, "Why didn't you shoot him?" The deputy was amazed at it all. These were not the kind of people you'd pull out of a drug trafficker line-up, but they were armed and dangerous and transporting drugs all the same. It was the thump sound that changed the face of this stop.

It was that stop that changed procedure for the team. They would ask the people to step out of the car right away and come back towards the patrol car, rather than spend a lot of time at their car where weapons could be only an arm's reach away. It was also easier to observe whether someone was carrying once they were clear from the car.

If there were two people (or more) in the car, separate conversations were held to determine if the travelers agreed on the same destination or if they even knew who the other person was with whom they were riding. The team was wary of kidnapping cases, in addition to the strong indication that conflicting stories generally meant that there was something else going on that needed to be followed up.

The team was re-named the Selective Enforcement Team, and while most of their work was on Interstate 95, I also had them working in troubled areas across the county.

Their investigative efforts resulted in the arrest of seven people involved in a string of burglaries in Deland.

During the early phase of our cash and drug interdiction policy, I received word on an appeals court ruling of a stop I had made while I was a state trooper. In December 1986 I had stopped a car with two men inside for following another car too closely on the interstate. It was an offense that generally warrants a warning, but the men inside and the circumstances at the time added up to something beyond a written warning. I eventually secured permission to search the car and turned up 37 pounds of cocaine. The men were tried and convicted and sent to jail. Their appeal was based on their lawyer's assertion that I had no probable cause for the search, that "following another car too closely" was not ample enough for asking permission to search.

The appeals court upheld my procedures and backed the conviction of the lower court. The ruling stated that I would have pulled over other drivers who were following too closely and that I hadn't singled these individuals out. They were right. I stopped a number of people for that offense, some of whom happened to be drug smugglers, others just over-aggressive drivers who needed to hear a warning. The court ruling simply underscored that we were following legal procedures in making inroads in the drug war.

The Selective Enforcement Team was patrolling both sides of the highway. Going north, they were finding narcotics, although less frequently than had been the case a couple of years earlier. These were criminal cases and the offenders more likely to be violent. Heading south, the team confiscated drug money, a civil case with less of a likelihood of running into a violent offender. People with drugs were more confrontational; the people with cash were just glad to be let go. We rarely heard from someone who had his or her cash seized.

Cash would be handled only at the Sheriff's Office. This was another mistake Deputy Josenhanz had made. He took the confiscated money home one night to count it, rather than bring it directly to the department. That's unacceptable procedure and contributed to his reassignment.

The dollars were counted and set aside. A report was written up and filed, and we waited to hear back from the people who had left the money behind. They could file for an immediate hearing to let a judge determine if the deputies had probable cause to seize the cash. If they didn't file for that, then there was a predetermination hearing held approximately three to four weeks after the seizure. At this time, the judge would rule on the probable cause issue. If it was determined that it was a proper seizure, then it went on to an actual hearing where the defendants would have the chance to prove the source of the money and its purpose. If the judge ruled we didn't have probable cause, we had to return the money to the individuals.

Quite often, we never heard from the people again. The money was designated as part of the Confiscated Funds account for the Sheriff's Office and it was used, instead of taxpayer money, to upgrade the equipment and crime-fighting tools in our antiquated agency. The drug dealers' contributions were used wisely and we were able to add the latest in technology to help us further fight crime.

Those that did call us generally did it through an attorney. The attorney would call, tell us the story about where the money originated and try to work out a deal for its return. The money seizure was a civil case and the majority of civil cases were settled out of court. If not, there would have been such a backlog in the justice system some cases might not be heard for years. The attorney would offer us a settlement for half the money, or 40% or 60% of the cash depending on how strong he or she thought the defendants' case to be. Our attorneys negotiated with the defendants' attorneys, and often a settlement was reached out of court, typical of civil cases.

The deputies on the team didn't like giving any drug money back, but often it became more expeditious for all concerned to handle it that way. We often notified the IRS of the seizure, especially when the amount was high, and there were times when we settled but turned the defendants' portion over to the IRS who had staked a claim to it. What happened beyond that was between the IRS and the defendant.

Much was made about our willingness to settle, but it was overblown. Plea-bargaining exists in all court cases and rather than endure a trial, an agreement is reached. This was no different. Our attorneys based their decision to settle on how strong they thought our case was, but also on the current caseload, the size of the seizure and the cost of trial versus the results. In addition, judges encouraged parties to settle cases amicably. These were prudent decisions made by people who knew how to negotiate these situations. Our function was to properly seize the cash and turn it over to the attorneys for handling. After that, we had little influence over what happened.

We were making a significant dent in the drug world. In 1991, while crime was up 1% across the state, the crime rate in Volusia County dropped 4% over the previous year. I was pleased with our effectiveness and confident that our methods could withstand even the closest inspection. At the time, I didn't realize how much scrutiny lay ahead of us.

Our interdiction work was turning up tens of thousands of dollars worth of cash, making you realize how big a business illegal drugs has become. Our deputies improved with every day of real experience they had.

Sergeant Dale Anderson was working with Deputy J.W. Smith, an African-American officer on the team, one night. They constantly sniped at each other good-naturedly and would make racial jokes back and forth, each one needling the other's origins. It was typical of both men and helped them bond as a team. One evening, a car ran off the road into the median on Interstate 95 and smacked into a couple of trees. The white male driver was despondent over the accident and Sergeant Anderson and Deputy Smith came over quickly to see if he was injured. After ascertaining that he was not, Dale took the opportunity to lampoon his partner by saying to the driver, "Could be worse. You could be black."

J.W. laughed at Anderson's poorly timed joke. But the recorder that had been switched on automatically when the deputies made the stop picked it up. It was an inappropriate comment to make, but Anderson said it and couldn't take it back. The media picked up this comment and went crazy.

This brought back up the question of our team singling out minorities for stops as part of a profile, and ignoring other people. None of this was true, but this incident had revived the issue and put it front and center again. Race was not part of any investigative follow-up that we did after a traffic stop. But it was difficult to convince some people of that. The allegation that we singled out African-Americans and Hispanics was ludicrous. I had both an African-American (J.W.) and a Hispanic officer (Ray Almodovar) on the team that was overseen by another African-American, Captain Leonard Davis. Race was not an issue with them. To them, there were two types of people—those breaking the law and those that were not. As Leonard Davis is quick to point out, it would be somewhat difficult to discern an African-American driver speeding by you on the interstate at over 70 mph and higher. It would be impossible to recognize that the person is Hispanic under the same conditions.

But Dale's comment had sent the whole issue back on the front page. Sergeant Anderson received a written reprimand for his inappropriate comments that became a permanent part of his personnel record. This was the normal disciplinary procedure taken in this situation. The team went on with their business of making cases.

On a February afternoon, Deputy Jones observed a vehicle swerving from lane to lane and pulled the car over. The driver, Levern Clements, was visibly nervous, hands shaking and whose voice shook while talking to the deputy. The passenger, Earl Fields, stated they were coming from South Carolina and were heading to Miami. Fields was the renter of the car. The deputy gave Clements a verbal warning about his erratic driving. After his paperwork was returned, the deputy asked Clements for permission to search the vehicle. He agreed. His nervousness had not subsided, generally an indicator that there was more going on here than a simple traffic warning.

In the trunk, Deputy Jones found a paper bag containing sizable bundles of U.S. Currency. Clements was evasive when asked about the origin of the money. A K-9 dog was marched to the bags and alerted to the presence of narcotic residue. Neither Clements nor Fields protested when they were told the money was being confiscated. Deputy Jones invited them to the station to witness the counting of the money and to obtain a receipt for that amount. They didn't hang around for a receipt. When the money was counted, it totaled $37,895.

Earl Fields came to the Operations Center the next day with a story. He told investigators that the money consisted of lottery winnings he had amassed over a period of time. He claimed to have won $213,000 after taxes on a Fantasy Five lottery ticket. He also claimed $27,000 on a Cash 3 game, a daily drawing where you select three numbers. He had also won $15,000, $25,000 and another $25,000 playing the Cash 3 game. He showed the officers seven tickets with the numbers 143 on them, and advised when and where he had bought them in Jacksonville.

The investigators wired the information to a representative of the Florida lottery, who advised that the winning tickets had, indeed, been sold in Jacksonville. There were 661 winning tickets sold across the state with the numbers 143 that day. The place in Jacksonville ended up paying out just under $1,300 in total for the winning tickets they sold, well short of the amounts Fields was claiming.

The Florida lottery representative went on to say that for Fields to say he had won $25,000 on a Cash 3 number was statistically near impossible and the representative did not recall one instance where the payout was ever that high for that drawing.

Fields ignored the suggestion that he likely could not have won the totals he was talking about in one Cash 3 drawing, let alone a number of times. He did say, however, that most of the money was spent on acquiring a piece of property in Miami to start a custom clothing business. He claimed a number of Miami Dolphins players as customers. He provided documentation of the property sale. He said the $37,000 or so that was seized by the officers was his left over lottery winnings.

He went on to tell the investigators that he occasionally stayed with a girlfriend in Jacksonville, and that's where he had previously kept this seized money.

He wouldn't say why he didn't use a bank. He told them that he kept the money in a stuffed frog in the girlfriend's bedroom.

It didn't turn out to be a stuffed frog, after all. His girlfriend, Bernie, told investigators it was a piece of furniture where you could take the top off. The top resembled more of a mushroom than anything else and when the investigators examined it, found that there was not nearly enough room to house $37,000 in the small bills that Fields possessed. The "mushroom/stuffed frog" had also not resided in Bernie's bedroom for quite some time. Instead, it was in the bedroom occupied by her 62-year-old mother.

Fields had a record and the investigators' inquiry in that regard brought a call from a joint federal/state Money Laundering Task Force, indicating that Fields was up to his neck in cocaine trafficking and innovative money laundering techniques. It was likely he was buying up winning lottery tickets at a percentage over their face value to put the drug money into legitimate circulation.

Another team stop involved several passengers in a car. The driver had been following another car too closely and was pulled over for a warning. The driver, whose name was Manley, said they were coming from Brunswick, Georgia and heading to Miami. The front seat passenger, a Victor Evans, produced the car documents. The car was rented and the renter, Mr. Sails, was not present. Victor assured the deputy that Sails knew where the car was and who was in it.

The deputy wrote up the warning, handed it to Manley and told him he was free to go. The deputy also asked if it would be OK if he searched the vehicle. Manley shrugged and said sure, go ahead. The deputy had the other passengers step out of the car. Evans' pockets were bulging and a quick glance by the officer told the man he had seen the lumps in his suit jacket pocket.

Evans took the money out. It took a little while. It was stuffed everywhere in his jacket. He said it was about $5,500 and he typically carried this much cash around. It was highly unusual for the average person to be carrying money this way, but more typical of a drug dealer.

Evans followed the deputy to the Operations Center where the money was counted by the money counter machine. The results were $5,000 exactly. A K-9 dog was brought in and Evans refused a receipt and left in a hurry after the dog reacted to the money, meaning some narcotic residue was present.

In another case, Deputy Ray Almodovar made a stop on a car that was following too closely. He pulled out behind the car and it continued following the other car too closely, so he pulled it over. The driver was a Francisco Muriel and the deputy asked him to exit the vehicle and bring his driver's license. It was a New Jersey license and Muriel said that he lived in Newark. The car belonged to a friend who had stayed in New Jersey and not made the trip.

There was a front seat passenger, Muriel said, who was a friend and the brother of the man who owned the car. They were coming to Florida to visit his friend's kids, one of whom was pregnant and suffering some complications. Muriel seemed nervous and could barely look at the deputy. Muriel added that he would only be in Florida a couple of days.

The deputy asked Muriel his specific destination. Muriel didn't know. He asked Muriel the name of his friend in the front seat. He didn't know that, either. The deputy was starting to get one of those feelings. He decided to talk to the other occupant of the car and advised Muriel to stay put.

The passenger's name was Jorge Nater and had a Puerto Rico driver's license. Nater confirmed that he was the brother of the man who owned the car. Nater had flown into Newark a few days before and was headed south to visit his brother's children. Deputy Almodovar asked him where these kids lived. Nater dug out a piece of paper that had several addresses on it and said Melbourne and Tampa. He said he was only going to stay a couple of days. He, too, was quite nervous.

The deputy returned Muriel's documents to him, gave him a verbal warning about following too closely and said he was free to go. As Muriel turned to leave, Ray Almodovar asked him if he was carrying anything illegal in the car such as weapons or narcotics. Muriel shook his head and when asked, gave permission for the vehicle to be searched.

The officer also asked Nater the same questions. Nater denied having anything illegal and granted permission to search, too. Underneath the rear passenger seat was a substantial amount of cash, thirty-six bundles in all, wrapped in different color rubber bands. There were various denominations of money in each packet, and they appeared to total about $1,000 each. Almodovar asked where the money came from.

Nater said it was his. He was going to buy a house in Pompano Beach with it. He said he was a seller of real estate and acquired the money through the sale of a three-story office building in Puerto Rico. He had just signed the papers for the sale three days ago in Newark. He did not have any of those documents with him.

Separately, Muriel told a different story. He said the money was for one of the children they were going to visit and they were supposed to deposit the money in a bank in Melbourne.

During the search, the deputy had the men sit in the back of his patrol car. When he listened to that conversation, Muriel said there was nothing to worry about, as there were no drugs in the car. The worst that could happen, Muriel told Nater, is that they could make him pay taxes on the money. Nater said they should have put the money in one of the tires instead.

The total money count was $36,990. Almodovar gave Nater a receipt for the money and confiscated it, believing it was to be used for some other purpose than the conflicting stories he had from each individual. Nater said he would have to return to Puerto Rico to obtain paperwork to prove the transaction. Almodovar listened carefully and nodded, but thought to himself, "didn't Nater say the deal was done in Newark?"

Muriel turned out to have a police record, reflecting that he was involved in a shooting incident in New Jersey four years earlier, with no further details available. He had recently been laid off from his job and had accepted $200 to drive Jorge Nater to Florida to visit relatives. He didn't expect to be stopped.

Deputy Almodovar had another case that turned up $265,000. He stopped a man driving a Ford Granada who had weaved out of his lane and into another, causing another car to swerve away to avoid him. The man had a Maryland driver's license that listed his name as Aubrey Marcus Duncan. The deputy asked the man if he had been drinking and how long he had been driving. Duncan said he did drink, but not that day, and that he had just had a colon operation and was looking for a place to urinate.

Duncan said he owned the car and had come south to go to Miami to play golf and he said that if he won he would stay there for a few days. Duncan had a passenger whom he described as a friend. The passenger was LaShon Mapp, from Washington D.C., who advised the deputy that they were going to Miami because it was her birthday and they were going to have a nice weekend together. Almodovar asked the woman to assist with the driving if Duncan got tired. She said he wasn't tired, he just had to urinate. She was extremely nervous.

Almodovar returned the documents to Duncan and told him he was getting off with a verbal warning this time. As Duncan turned to leave, the deputy asked Duncan if he was carrying anything illegal. Duncan said no and Almodovar asked if he could search his car. Duncan then told the deputy that he was a former police officer for five years in Washington, D.C. The deputy asked how long ago and Duncan said 1967. Duncan said he would rather the deputy not search the car. He said he was here under false pretenses, that he was engaged to be married, and the woman in the front seat was not his fiancée.

Duncan was extremely nervous now, saying he didn't want any trouble, he had told his fiancee he was going down to play golf alone. Agitated now, he told the deputy he owned a video store and his wife owned a funeral home. After a moment, he amended that statement to say his fiancée owned the funeral home.

Almodovar summoned a K-9 unit. The dog alerted and the search began. In the trunk was a brown paper bag and a gray duffel bag, which held a huge amount of currency wrapped in typical dealer fashion, with different colored rubber bands in varying denominations. They were in stacks of $1,000 and $5,000.

Duncan said the money was his, about $260,000 worth and it was to be used for gambling, which was illegal in Florida. The deputy asked him how much money did he declare on his income taxes. Duncan smirked and said he did owe the IRS some back taxes.

Almodovar confiscated the money and gave Duncan a receipt. There was $265,000 in the bag. Duncan eventually sued to get the money back. In the meantime, conversations with the DEA indicated Duncan to be a big-time drug dealer in Washington, D.C. He was not happy about the cash seizure and began hiding other assets such as cars from the Federal Government so they wouldn't be taken.

Judge Bill Johnson (AKA "Wild Bill") ruled that our office had to return the money, because there was no probable cause to seize it. He refused to allow the DEA to testify to Duncan's known dealer activities. It was virtually unheard of that a Federal DEA agent would testify in a state civil forfeiture case, but an agent was voluntarily here and, in accordance with Judge Johnson's ruling, not permitted to testify.

Duncan did not get the money. The IRS laid claim to it, having filed liens against him for over $400,000 in unpaid taxes. We had to comply with their order for the money. Duncan's lawyer, a man named Mobley, was knocking on the door to my administrative offices demanding immediate return of the money. He was expecting about $100,000 in attorney fees, so naturally he was anxious. But we had been told to send the money to the IRS.

The attorney was irate. He filed a motion with Judge Johnson to hold me in contempt of court. This occurred around Christmastime and I thought I might have to spend the holiday in jail. The Judge heard the motion from Mobley, but finally dismissed it. I spent the holidays with my family and did the American thing on behalf of Duncan—paid his taxes for him.

Duncan was not a happy man. That money loss cut significantly into his dealing. He had to hustle out on his own and was subsequently arrested in New Jersey on cocaine and heroin charges.

The team seized about $1.8 million in 1989 and $3.2 million in 1990. It was a successful law enforcement program that was squeezing drug dealers all the way up the eastern seaboard. We were operating within the parameters of the law and were accurate in our assessments as evidenced by the number of people who never pursued a claim to their money.

The defense attorneys didn't like it. The ACLU didn't like it. The citizens of Volusia County loved it. There were a few more enemies of the program out there who hadn't quite surfaced yet. Senator Bob Graham was running for re-election and asked for a briefing on the program, and we showed him the entire process. He felt that we were linking the money to a possible felony and thus justifying the seizures. He even posed for pictures next to the narcotic traffic stop sign. The team was proud of its success.

One other case involved three men, two from the country of Colombia and one individual from New York. They consented to a search and the deputy found $300,000 in three black canvas bags wrapped in thousand-dollar bundles, one hundred thousand in each bag. When asked where the money came from, the men said they found it in a McDonald's restaurant parking lot in Georgia.

They didn't wait around to see if the deputy believed their story. They not only didn't want a receipt for the money, they left the car as well. The deputies on the team all agreed that they were going to stop off at McDonald's on the way home to see if they had similar luck.

The Florida Supreme Court handed down decisions in 1990 regarding two stops I had made back in 1985. One case was based on a traffic stop; the other based on a profile stop where I relied on a set of cumulative similarities rather than a specific traffic violation. They upheld the conviction based on the traffic stop and overturned the one involving the use of a profile.

That was fine. In 1985, I was still experimenting within the parameters of the law to establish a procedure. We had been stopping solely based on traffic stops for years, so the decision didn't affect us, but simply verified that we were using the correct lawful procedure.

In 1991, our drug and cash interdiction efforts were given national television exposure on ABC-TV's "20/20" newsmagazine show. One of their reporters, Tom Jarrell, came down to Volusia County to interview us and watch the team at work. Jarrell asked us a lot of questions about the logistics of the stops. Once again, I emphasized to him that we were making traffic stops based on a traffic violation and would then assess the situation from there. It might only be a traffic warning or ticket or, if the given circumstances indicated something more might be going on, the deputy investigated further.

When the show aired in early 1991, it concentrated first on our team, what they did and their successes to date. Then it focused on one particular recent stop made in November 1989. Deputy Steve Rupert stopped the car Jerrod Davis and Sonia Hancock were driving for weaving, a traffic violation. After discussing this with them and determining there was more to this traffic stop than met the eye, Rupert asked for permission to search the vehicle after returning all of their documents to them and telling them they were free to go. This stop was being routinely recorded from Rupert's police vehicle, just as all the stops were for purposes of later review. The tape showed the two detainees stepping away from the car, but Davis kept getting up and moving towards the vehicle. After several warnings that Davis ignored, Rupert subdued Davis using force.

When you first watch the tape, the scene is gut wrenching as it is any time a police officer has to use force. I have never liked seeing this type of action and at first look, the single blow seemed severe. But Internal Affairs and the State Attorney's office investigated and found the use of force to subdue Davis to be acceptable since Davis repeatedly ignored verbal commands. Deputy Rupert became fearful for his life after Davis continued coming to the car and used the only means at his command to get Davis to obey the request to stay away from the vehicle. What the tape didn't show was that there was a gun in the car and Deputy Rupert discovered one kilo of cocaine.

One of the concerns for this team was that any individual stopped for a traffic violation could be a violent drug dealer determined to preserve their contraband at all costs. When you know there are dealers out there who would shoot their own son if it suited their needs, you exercise supreme caution in these situations. Had Davis not continuously ignored Rupert's request to stay away from the car, the arrests would have been uneventful. As it happened, the stop was now played out on national television.

Dan Warren was the attorney for Davis, an African-American, and Hancock, a young white female. He, too, was interviewed by Tom Jarrell, and he naturally took a dim view of the proceedings. He focused attention on the subduing of Davis to draw people away from the problems he could not defend—the cocaine and the gun. Warren was a former state attorney who had taken issue with my methods of drug interdiction for years. He would do anything he could to stop them. Our work on Interstate 95 was successful. If we weren't finding anything, Warren would have no crusade to prevent us from performing our duties. Because we were properly seizing drugs and drug money, he would try whatever method he could to discredit the program.

Rupert was eventually reassigned. But, in my view, he used a level of force that was reasonable based on the circumstances that existed at the time. It's hard to tell that all from one viewing of the tape, however, and I'm sure many other viewers held a different opinion about the case. I won't stand for brutality in any way, shape or form. But two independent investigators ruled the use of force was within acceptable limits and I concurred.

Among those with a different opinion was Circuit Judge Gayle Graziano, who lowered Davis' bond to $10,000 (from $75,000) and ruled that kilo of cocaine found was not admissible in court after viewing the tape. In her mind, there was no reason to ask for permission to search the vehicle. The traffic stop, she said, was warranted, but the search was not. Davis had admitted that there was a .25-caliber pistol under the seat of the car and Sonia Hancock was certainly carrying the kilo of cocaine. However, the circumstances as the Judge saw them did not warrant asking for the search. Our office did appeal the decision on the civil forfeiture, but after assessing all of the factors in trying this case, elected to finally drop the case.

It happens. Here, the Judge had dismissed the key evidence in the case— the kilo of cocaine. Without it, there was concealment of a handgun and resisting arrest, but it was the drug charges that the state attorneys wanted to prosecute and without them, the case was not worth pursuing in their mind.

In late July 1990, Mel Stack decided the time was right for him to pursue a career in private practice. This was his condition when joining the agency in December of 1988 and I knew this day would come at some point. I hated to see Mel go, but he had done a tremendous job for me, keeping us within all legal standards, especially pursuing the innovative drug and cash traffic stops on the interstate. Mel's legal expertise helped us successfully prosecute the majority of the cases we made on I-95. We wanted to do it right and Mel made sure we did. We had become extremely close over the last few years, but I was glad for him to realize his goal of a private legal practice.

Mel helped us hand-pick his replacement, Nancye Rogers Ege, a former legal advisor to the Daytona Beach Police Department and a native of Volusia County. She had graduated from the University of Florida and received her law degree at the University of South Carolina. She had been an assistant state attorney in the time leading up to her appointment as legal advisor to our county agency. She was a great addition to the Volusia County Sheriff's Office and her legal mind would be continually put to the test over the next few years.

By 1991, we had established the agency as a positive, professional force within the county. Despite the restrictions of working under the charter law, we were making great improvements in all areas of law enforcement since I took office. In mid–1991, though, a peculiar incident took place that should have served as a foreshadowing of what lay ahead for both myself and the Sheriff's Office.

➢ ➣

THE STRANGE LIFE AND DEATH OF HELEN MCCONNELL

Helen Lucille McConnell was late for dinner. A mainstay at the Oak Hill eatery called Pop's Bar B-Q, she was supposed to meet her date, Joel Frink, there around dinnertime. When the 61-year-old did not turn up, Frink called her house.

McConnell answered the phone in a foul mood. She screamed at Frink over the phone and reportedly told him that she no longer wanted to live and intended to take her own life that night.

Frink called the police.

This was not the Helen McConnell Oak Hill residents later said they knew. She had moved to the small Volusia County community of less than 1,000 people more than 20 years earlier, relocating from North Carolina with her husband Harold Hendry. She and her spouse were farmers, raising cattle on a 50-acre property some 10 miles from town. Her husband had died about ten years previous to this July night in 1991. She had continued to work the farm, and would drive her pickup into town for dinner three or four nights a week to Pop's Bar B-Q. She generally sat on the end stool at the counter, cigarette dangling from her mouth, willing to discuss the local news.

Not tonight. Oak Hill police officers responded to Frink's call and met with him at the restaurant. They asked him to call McConnell back and they would listen in on the conversation. They heard McConnell once again yell to Frink that she was going to kill herself. Alternately shouting and whispering, McConnell told Frink that she was upset over the possible loss of her property and being committed to a hospital because of her mental instability. She said she had a pistol in her lap and was going to "blow her brains out."

The Oak Hill police called Sheriff's Sergeant Russell Schaidt, who then called McConnell personally to talk to her. After a brief conversation, she told Schaidt she would talk to him if he came out to her property. She said she was armed and if he weren't who he said he was, she would be prepared to fire. Accompanied by another deputy, the sergeant drove to the McConnell residence. No lights were on in the house when they arrived. Schaidt called McConnell to come down from the house to unlock the gate. She refused. He turned on the blue flashing lights of the vehicle and called her using the loudspeaker in the patrol car. McConnell's response was to flash her own spotlights on the property.

She called 911 to report that there were men outside her home who had come to do her harm. She was told these were Sheriff's deputies, but she chose not to believe the dispatcher. Schaidt tried again to call, but McConnell didn't answer. Instead, as the two deputies discussed their next move, a shot rang out from the direction of the house. The deputies took cover and saw through the barbwire fence that McConnell was standing on the front porch, cradling a rifle. She turned on her heel and went back inside.

The two deputies exchanged confused glances. Ten minutes later, McConnell fired another shot in their direction, and they called for the SWAT Team to come out. The sergeant sent his deputy down the road to await their arrival, while he kept watch on the house.

Sergeant Schaidt continued his vigil to try and coax McConnell out of the house. She reappeared on the porch, but made no effort to come down and unlock the gate. She flashed her spotlights and called 911 again. The dispatcher tried in vain to convince her that the Sergeant was a legitimate Sheriff's deputy trying to help her.

The seven member mini SWAT Team arrived around 11:30 PM. They were advised of the general location of the house and property. The SWAT team surrounded the house and could see McConnell moving around inside, occasionally flickering the spotlights. They formed a perimeter around the house to keep McConnell contained and awaited the next move. Dispatchers were still unsuccessful at getting Helen McConnell to acknowledge the deputies with anything other than gunfire. At one point, she told the dispatcher that whoever was out there was provoking her and her dogs and that the person was going to break in and rape her. She said she was going "to shoot the goddamn son of a bitch."

Suddenly, the evening was shattered again by a barrage of bullets coming from the McConnell household. She was repeatedly firing a .410-gauge shotgun, moving back and forth from the front to the rear of her house. Sergeant Schaidt would later say he could hear the bullets zinging through the trees, whistling past branches where the SWAT team was in position. The officers took what little cover there was from the gunfire erupting from the McConnell household.

Just after midnight, Helen McConnell made her last assault on the SWAT team. She came out of her house carrying a revolver and began firing shots in the direction of her dog pen where several of the animals had kept up a steady crescendo of barking since the shotgun blasts had echoed throughout the yard. As officers again looked desperately for cover, one of the SWAT team members, Deputy George Tracy Hernlen, fired back as McConnell pointed her gun at him, his bullet hitting her in the chest.

The SWAT team called for emergency medical personnel, but when paramedics arrived McConnell was virtually gone and they were unable to revive her. Later tests would reveal her blood alcohol level to be three times the legal limit. The ordeal for Helen McConnell was over. For the Volusia County Sheriff's Office, it was just beginning.

Interviews with neighbors painted a picture of a woman who was hard–working, but prone to erratic behavior. Her personality could range from friendly to antagonistic within a short time span without anything seeming to set her off. McConnell had also called a friend on her final evening to say that there were people outside her house that were trying to get her. It had seemed to the friend that Helen had been drinking, not an infrequent occurrence. During those times, she would talk about rapists posing as police officers trying to get into her house to attack her. She had recently taken to firing on people that trespassed on her property. Several people said she was a good farmer and her property showed it. But it also seemed clear that she had recently adopted a self–destructive personality that finally achieved its goal.

Routine procedure following a shooting required that Deputy Hernlen be placed on paid leave while an internal investigation of the affair was conducted. Hernlen was an eight-year veteran of the Sheriff's Office and had been on the SWAT team for six of those years. He had consistently received excellent or better than average evaluations and his file was filled with a number of commendations.

In situations that call for deadly force, as this one apparently did, deputies were not required to fire warning shots or shoot to wound; they were to shoot to stop the aggressor. The plan that the SWAT team had quickly formulated was to either sneak into McConnell's house and subdue her if that was feasible, or possibly lob in some tear gas and rush in and disarm her. Their goal was to keep her from killing herself, but they were obviously unsuccessful.

Some friends of Helen McConnell took up a petition to protest the shooting as unwarranted. The media reported regularly on the incident, with both the *Daytona Beach News Journal* and the *Orlando Sentinel* keeping the story on the front page in the days that followed. One headline read "Deputy fires shot that shakes town." The two *Sentinel* reporters who primarily covered the story were Jeff Brazil and Steve Berry. I didn't know it yet, but I was only a few months away from crossing paths with these journalists again.

The SWAT team responded with negotiators that night, but were unable to be patched through because a telephone operator refused to place a call to McConnell's home, as the negotiators did not have a credit card with them to charge the call. Even after explaining the situation, the operator refused to connect them with McConnell. Perhaps she would have hung up on them as she had on the other officers who had called that night, but a negotiator was prepared to deal with distraught people and who knew what would have happened if she was able to talk with them. We'll never know.

I contacted the Florida Department of Law Enforcement (FDLE) and requested that they investigate the case in addition to Internal Affairs. There was enough public outcry from some residents of Oak Hill about whether the shooting was too hasty and not called for, given the circumstances, and I wanted an outside group of investigators to come in. I didn't want someone saying we were just protecting our own people, should our report come out as I thought it was going to—that deadly force was justified.

A few days after the incident, a Daytona Beach attorney took advantage of the publicity to try and help one of his clients, a drug dealer who had been arrested the previous December. He claimed now, eight months later, that his client had been harassed by Deputy Hernlen, who both beat his client and put a gun to his head, after his arrest. It was obvious what the attorney was doing. His client had been arrested several times over a nearly four year period and was now desperate to look for any defense he could find. Hernlen was an open target.

Our internal investigators concluded that use of deadly force was justified and Hernlen returned to work in September 1991. He was assigned to an administrative position while awaiting the outcome of the continuing FDLE investigation. He was already the target of a lawsuit (along with SWAT team head Lieutenant Robert Bosco) charging him with violating the constitutional rights of Helen McConnell. Shortly after that, another suit was filed by the same attorney on behalf of another individual who had been arrested by Hernlen a year earlier for impersonating a police officer. This suit claimed that Hernlen had maliciously kicked and beaten the individual after arresting him. The man had been convicted in January of the impersonation charge, but had waited until now to file this particular suit.

In late October, a coroner's inquest that reviewed the FDLE report and called and questioned witnesses ruled that the shooting death of Helen McConnell was justified. This vindicated Hernlen and Bosco. I had been reviewing SWAT team procedures in the weeks prior to the incident and after to bring them in line with what was necessary to have the department accredited. Accreditation procedures called for an incident manager on scene separate from the SWAT team commander. I instituted that change in the days before the verdict in the coroner's inquest was reached.

In the report released from the coroner's inquest, Deputy Steve Rupert, who was part of the SWAT team and also involved in the drug interdiction case featured on the *"20/20"* newsmagazine show on ABC-TV, testified that after the shooting Hernlen had walked around in tears and in a daze. "She aimed the gun right at me," Hernlen had told Rupert as the deputy comforted his fellow officer. The team members all testified that the incident had escalated quickly beyond any previous SWAT call they had made.

It was a sad, unfortunate incident and one that everyone in the department had wished never happened. But the question of whether force should have been used was answered in the investigation.

In January, Bosco and Hernlen resigned from the SWAT team. This team was an extra duty with additional pay for which deputies could volunteer. These resignations were voluntary and not sought by me, but my feeling was that these two individuals were concerned about whether the past publicity on the McConnell shooting would affect their judgment on future SWAT assignments and whether it would jeopardize other team members.

In February, the attorney who had filed a lawsuit on behalf of McConnell's sister, who lived in North Carolina, against Hernlen and Bosco for violating McConnell's constitutional rights dropped the case. The attorney said that McConnell's sister was emotionally exhausted and did not wish to pursue the suit.

The U.S Justice Department was the next agency to be involved in the case. Oak Hill resident Ray Goodrich had formed a group called Citizens Against Bad Law Officers and he called the FBI branch in Daytona Beach, the Florida Lieutenant Governor Buddy MacKay, Florida Senator Bob Graham and Congressman Craig James about the McConnell incident. The investigation was termed routine by the U.S. Justice Department and is done any time charges of police misconduct are brought to their attention. Their investigation brought them to the same conclusion as everyone else in law enforcement that had scrutinized this case – that there was justification of deadly force.

The formal matter of the Helen McConnell case was finally closed. But I would hear from her supporters again during the 1992 election race. I would also hear again in 1992 from the *Orlando Sentinel* reporters assigned to the McConnell case. Finally, on Thanksgiving Day 1991, I was entertaining family in my home when I received a call from a young reporter named John Holland of the *Daytona Beach News Journal*. He wanted to go into detail about the McConnell case and the results of the coroner's inquest. As it was a holiday and an issue that had been discussed for weeks in the newspaper, I told him "It's Thanksgiving, I have a house full of family and I have already made my statement about this case." He wasn't satisfied with that response and continued to press his questions. He persisted and I finally had to tell him I was hanging up and simply did so.

It would not be the last time I heard from this reporter, either.

⊃ ⊂

FAMOUS AND INFAMOUS CASES

The first term in office had been an eventful one. Between the drug and cash interdiction success and its international reputation, the department's successful accreditation as a professional law enforcement agency, the *"20/20"* report, and the Helen McConnell SWAT team shooting, the Volusia County Sheriff's Office had more than its fair share of publicity in these first four years.

But there were other cases going on that also attracted more than the usual public attention during this first term. From bikers to female killers, it was an unusual period of activity as my first term drew to a close.

Daytona Beach is host to one of the country's largest assembly of motorcyclists each March in an event called "Bike Week." Each year, tens of thousands of motorcycles come to the area for a week-long series of events, including motorcycle races at the Daytona International Speedway. In the 1980s and 90s, this gala was marred by a consistent commission of drug crimes and other felonies by a vocal minority of bikers.

Florida's largest motorcycle gang, the Outlaws, had dominated this minority (referred to as the 1%ers) for years. They were engaged in any number of crimes over the course of a given year and Bike Week gave them an opportunity for increased activity. During the 1980s, a rival group called the Warlocks had invaded on Outlaw turf and wrestled for control. There were frequent attacks by gang members against the others that culminated in the execution of the local Central Florida president of the Warlocks, 44-year-old Raymond "Bear" Chaffin.

Chaffin was found shot to death on February 22, 1991 in the garage of his home in Edgewater, a small town in the southern part of Volusia County. He had been shot four times in the back of the head with a small-caliber handgun. We suspected members of the Outlaws gang to be responsible.

We had long been running an undercover investigation into the Warlocks' criminal activities, which including drug dealing, gun running and other operations. The Warlocks were a local Central Florida group and we wanted their criminal deals stopped if we could. The investigation was nearing an end and the Chaffin murder sped up the timetable for the inevitable bust that had been in the planning stages for some time. We were concerned that Bike Week would bring in large followings of Outlaws and Warlocks and that a turf war might explode over the Chaffin killing. We didn't want Bike Week '91 remembered for acts of violence.

Chaffin was to be buried on March 2 and we planned the bust for that day. What better opportunity to have all the Warlocks' members in one place at one time for whom evidence had been compiled for the last several months?

Under a dark, threatening sky, dozens of Harley Davidson motorcycles made their way to the Bellevue-Cedar Hill funeral home as Volusia County Sheriff's deputies directed traffic. The service was held as nearly 100 SWAT team officers from three counties, FDLE, ATF and the Orlando Police Department prepared for the bust. After the service was completed, the group moved across the street to the Cedar Hill cemetery.

Members of the gang held posts as sentries, on the lookout for Outlaws.

When it was over, the bikers returned to their Harleys and prepared to ride away. The officers swept in as police vehicles blocked the roadway at both ends of the procession of bikes. Startled residents in the area looked on as the Warlock members dismounted their bikes and took up positions face down on the ground as ordered by the deputies. The Warlocks offered no resistance and the arrests, thirty-two in all, went on in an uneventful manner. All the officers from the various agencies represented handled their job perfectly and brought off this unprecedented mass arrest. We seized dozens of weapons, including submachine guns, explosive devices, silencers, and knives, and drugs were confiscated as well.

The Warlocks had been stockpiling arms for some time and most of those weapons including pipe bombs and machine guns, were also taken. The suspects were charged with a number of offenses and the Warlocks gang was effectively broken as a result.

Bike Week stayed uneventful that year and has been a different, more law abiding event since that funeral bust.

* * * * * *

A 51-year-old electronics repair shop owner named Richard Mallory from Clearwater had a liking for Volusia County nightlife. On a November day in 1989, he started up Interstate 4 towards Daytona Beach.

Along the way, he picked up a hitchhiker, a blonde prostitute carrying a .22 caliber pistol in her purse. What happened next isn't completely clear, but Mallory's bloodstained Cadillac was found abandoned in Daytona Beach a day later. In December, two men scavenging for scrap metal in a wooded area north of Daytona found a badly decomposed body underneath a piece of carpet. Richard Mallory, shot four times, pants pockets turned inside out, had been found.

It looked like a robbery-homicide and there were few clues to go on. Investigator Larry Horzepa of the Volusia County Sheriff's Office was assigned to the case. He was looking for a killer, but at the early stages of the investigation, there was nothing to indicate the killer was a woman.

Over the next several months, Horzepa began to see communications from other Florida counties of similar types of deaths: males, aged between 40 and 60, who liked to travel the highways and whose bodies were found shot and left in wooded areas off the highway. The similarities were too close to ignore. Someone was convincing these travelers to take them in their car for a ride and then robbing and killing them.

A break in the case came when onlookers saw two women crash a car through a fence on the 4th of July in Marion County, Florida. The two women got away on foot, but the car was traced to yet another male traveling on the roads, this time a 65-year-old who was en–route to visiting family in Arkansas when he disappeared.

Police were able to put sketches of the two women together and circulated them widely, hoping for identification. In September 1990, another man was found in the same county, shot and robbed. He was a retired Air Force major named Dick Humphreys who was a former Alabama police chief. He had a weakness for assisting female motorists in need, however, and it was this tendency that apparently got him killed.

It appeared now as though the murderer of Richard Mallory and these other men (at least six by this time) was a woman, possibly two women. The sketches continued to make the rounds, and were finally put on a nationally syndicated tabloid TV show. It paid off.

One woman was named several times, Tyria Moore, a hotel maid from Ohio. The other woman, a blonde, was identified by several different names. Our investigator Horzepa eventually learned that the two women liked to hang out in the bars of Volusia County. Their favorite spot was *The Last Resort*, a biker bar in Port Orange.

Undercover officers staked the place out. They spotted the blonde woman come into the place and watched her carefully. She was going by the name of Lee and spent the next couple of days drinking at the bar, playing country music on the jukebox and sleeping on the front porch in a car seat. She was chatting with another middle-aged man when the investigators went to arrest and take her into custody in January 1990.

Her name was Aileen Carol Wuornos and she was initially labeled as a rarity—a female serial killer. Later, federal investigators would tell us that she wasn't technically a serial killer since she had many opportunities to kill and didn't, lashing out in a deadly way only on seven occasions that they knew about. The 34-year-old was prone to hiking along the highways, pleading her ways into cars with a sob story or an offer of sex or both and she often robbed the victim that slowed down to take her in and sometimes, as Richard Mallory discovered, she killed. Moore was her lover and companion, but Wuornos insisted that she was the killer and that Moore was innocent of any wrongdoing.

The first trial was in Volusia County for the murder of Richard Mallory, the only killing that had happened within our borders and the first killing she would admit to in her statement. She told us where we could find her .22 caliber handgun—in a waterway south of Daytona. We did recover it and tests linked it to the Mallory killing.

Wuornos own life had been a nightmarish odyssey that included teen pregnancy, a father that was a convicted child molester who later committed suicide, and a life on her own by the age of 14, living off her earnings as a prostitute. The case made national headlines and Wournos was finally convicted of murder and sentenced to death row in 1992.

* * * * * * *

In March 1991, a masked gunman burst into the office of an Edgewater dentist named Norman Larzelere and shot him once in the chest with a shotgun. Larzelere, who worked in a house that had been converted into a dental office, had seen the short, stocky man with the gun enter the office that Friday afternoon and had fled into the waiting room area, closing the wooden door behind him. But the man fired right through the door and Larzelere took the hit in the chest. He was airlifted to Halifax Medical Center in Daytona Beach, but died in the air before reaching the facility.

His wife Virginia was on site that day, working there as the office manager, along with one other employee. He was the father of four children and had been practicing in Volusia County for some time.

The subsequent investigation revealed that Larzelere had a substantial amount of life insurance, about $2 million, and that his wife was the primary beneficiary. There was nothing unusual in that, except when murder occurs you often look to those closest to the victim first. There seemed no other apparent motive, as the dental office was not robbed. Someone came to Larzalere's office with the sole intent to kill him.

Slowly, witnesses accumulated that helped to build a case against Virginia Larzelere. There were two people that testified to having an affair with her and reported that she had asked them to help her kill her husband. Two other key witnesses said they overheard Virginia and one of her sons, Jason, talking about killing Larzelere, and that later she asked them for help in disposing of the shotgun evidence by putting the weapon in concrete and tossing it into a creek. She and her son were arrested for murder.

The latter two witnesses were granted immunity and they testified against Virginia Larzelere during her trial. Jason, who seemed to be the actual killer, was to be tried separately. Virginia masterminded the entire plan, directing it from behind the scenes. Even though she did not actually pull the trigger, she was convicted of murder in 1992 and sentenced to death.

Her son Jason had a different court result. He was acquitted of the crime, apparently a pawn of his mother's in the circumstances that led to killing his father. His mother appealed her decision on the basis that she was given death while everyone else involved walked away. In 1996, the Florida Supreme Court upheld her Volusia County conviction.

Larzelere and Wuornos served on death row together during this period of time. There were only six women in that capacity in Florida at the time and one-third of them had come courtesy of Volusia County. This was also a high-profile local case, although it did not quite grab the headlines that Wuornos claimed.

These cases all surfaced during my first term in office. They were unusual, attracted a substantial amount of publicity, and we brought them to successful conclusions.

By mid-1992, there were many accomplishments to be proud of in this first term. As it turned out, it was the calm before the storm as I was about to begin a series of battles that would test my family and I to the extreme.

Sgt. Dale Anderson at an I-95 cash seizure of over $300,000 drug dealers monies.

John Travolta and Sheriff Bob at Spruce Creek Fly-In.

Sgt. Bobby Jones with drug monies seizure.

Rocky Lawrence, songwriter; Jeff Cook, member of Alabama. Sheriff Bob presenting Jeff with Honorary Deputy Plaque in appreciation for his stand against drugs.

Kelly Preston, John Travolta and son Jett with Bob in front of their jet.

Sheriff Bob with Orlando Magic player Anthony Bowie.

Top left: 3rd term photo, 1996.

Top Right: Harlem Globetrotters star player, Curley Neal, with Sheriff Bob at the 10th annual 100 Deputies / 100 Kids Christmas Party.

Middle: Sheriff Bob with Flordia Attorney General Bob Butterworth.

At left: Sheriff Bob, Captain Leonard Davis and Sergeant Dale Anderson setting up inspection sign on I-95.

Right: Sheriff Bob with children on "Take Your Child to Work Day" at the Volusia County Sheriff's office.

Below: Family friends Robert Paulik, Jack Mitchell, Sheila Vogel, John Travolta, Jeannie and Bob at the set of the filming of The Generals Daughter.

Citizen Observer Program (C.O.P) led by Director Leonard Jansen with 200 volunteer members.

Right: Bob announcing his candidacy for Volusia County Sheriff at the I-95 Port Orange Rest Stop with Jeannie and Sheila at his side, 1987.

Below: Family Potrait by beloved friend and photographer, Jack Mitchell.

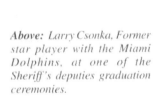

Above: Larry Csonka, Former star player with the Miami Dolphins, at one of the Sheriff's deputies graduation ceremonies.

Left: John Travolta and Kelly Preston with Sheriff Bob enjoying one of the many activities during Daytona Bike Week.

Some of many Vogel supporters ready to line the bridge Election Eve. From left: Howard Town, Buddy Ridgell, Sandi Core and Bob, 1996.

Above: Sheriff Bob delivering the Memorial Day Speech at the New Smyrna Beach Riverside Park before hundreds of veterans, 1994.

At right: Bob revisiting Parris Island, S.C. in March 1996, standing next to a memorial for the battle he fought at Hue City, Vietnam.

Sheriff Bob with country music star Jeff Cook of Alabama, filming an anti-drug message which was aired during the promotion of Alabama's concerts.

60 Minutes *star Harry Reasoner filming Trooper Bob on his successful drug indictions on I-95.*

Tom Cruise and Sheriff Bob during the filming of Days of Thunder. *The helicopter was used in the crash scene of the film.*

Above: Jeb Bush, candidate for Florida's governor, visiting Bob at the Sheriff's Office in Deland, 1994.

At right: Sheriff Bob visiting with Donald Trump at the Daytona 500 Race.

Florida Governor Lawton Chiles meeting Jeannie and Sheriff Bob at a reception hosted by friend Bill Crotty, 1994.

U.S. Supreme Court Justice Clarence Thomas with Sheriff Bob. (Later they both ate three hotdogs each.) Daytona 500 Race, 1999.

Golfer Greg Norman flanked by Deputy Bill White and Sheriff Bob.

Above: *Jeannie and Bob renew acquaintances with Donald Trump and his girlfriend, 2000.*

At right: *Trooper Bob, 1980 photo.*

Florida Senator Bob Graham with Bob and Jeannie at the home of Hawaiian Tropic Founder Ron Rice.

Above: *Jeb Bush campaigning for Governor with an endorsement from Sheriff Bob, flanked by friend John Thomson, Jeannie and Veteran Don O'Lore in the background, 1998.*

At right: *Sheriff Bob with 20/20 anchor and friend Tom Jarrell.*

At left: USMC Pvt. Bob Vogel, 1966, boot camp.

Below: Setting up a camp near An Hoa, Vietnam.

Above: "Ace" Hendricks, a fellow Marine and Bob standing next to a 5th Marines sign in Phu Bai.

At right: USMC Corporal Bob in 1968 upon arrival in Vietnam near Hue City.

ELECTION NIGHT, 1996

The phone in the back room rang regularly for the next hour. The news was not any brighter, and for the first time I started to think about my future. What would I do next if I wasn't re-elected Sheriff? What would the next few years bring for my family and I? Sheila had her heart set on going to Stetson University, a fine local school in Deland. She wanted to study law, and yet our financial situation was somewhat cloudy based on the election results tabulated to this minute.

Very few public servants, Sheriffs included, were in it for the money. These were not high paying jobs compared to those of equal responsibility in corporate America. Yet these were duties that most of us served gladly for other than monetary reasons.

The very act of doing something that benefits the community as a whole is a reward in itself. Certainly the act of policing is one critical to the successful and pleasurable lifestyle of any area. Law enforcement is a great equalizer, without which the country would return to the days of the Wild West.

I wanted to finish what I had started. I wasn't through yet. It had been an uphill battle bringing the Volusia County Sheriff's Office into the late 20th Century in both personnel and technology. Volusia County's local charter rule added further barriers, handcuffing the Sheriff in terms of decision-making in the Office, but we were making progress on that front.

We were looking at the numbers again in the back room, studying Ron's chart, trying to predict what would come in next. Several large precincts had yet to report, and I hoped that these later numbers would turn the tide.

As we talked quietly among ourselves, the doors to the back room opened and muscling his way in was Bo Portner, the Volusia County editor for the Orlando Sentinel newspaper. We were astonished at the interruption, surprised that he would try to force his way in when we clearly weren't making any public statements yet.

Several sets of eyes stared at him as he announced that he had come to interview the Sheriff about the results. Jeannie recovered first, and jumped up and took Portner by the arm, escorting him outside. She told him he could talk to the Sheriff when the race was over. She came back in, took a look around the gloomy room and her eyes rested on Leonard Davis, wondering why the big man didn't handle that chore instead of the smallest person in the room.

We had all been struck so dumb by the suddenness of the attack that only Jeannie had the presence of mind to move. It was always that way with the media, it seemed. Swift, vicious attacks seemed to be their offensive plan against the Sheriff's Office. I thought back to their largest strike of all—by the Orlando Sentinel in June of 1992—in a series of articles that changed everything from then on for me, my family, and the Sheriff's Office....

CHAPTER FOUR:
WHEN A PULITZER
ISN'T ENOUGH

ALL THE NEWS THAT'S UNFIT TO PRINT

It began with a public records request.

The *Orlando Sentinel*, a Central Florida newspaper that was primarily aimed at residents in counties south of us, wanted some reporters to look at cases related to cash seizures made on Interstate 95. They had a lengthy list of files to be reviewed and it would take our staff some time to pull them, but as always, we complied in a timely manner.

Little did we know what this request would precipitate. Nor did we fully understand the newspaper war that was being conducted on our home turf. The *Sentinel* wanted to make inroads into the Volusia County population, who primarily subscribed to the *Daytona Beach News Journal*. This would all become clear later on.

At this point toward the end of my first term in office, we were taking stock of our accomplishments to date, developing strategy for further positive effects on our community, and gearing up for a re-election campaign. We had made some significant progress in my estimation, from our interdiction program on Interstate 95, to professionalizing the Sheriff's Office, to formal accreditation.

Now the *Sentinel* wanted their turn at reviewing our Special Enforcement Team's successful cash seizure program. I was proud of this team and what they were doing to thwart drug dealers at their own personal risk. The best way to hurt a drug dealer is in the pocketbook. Take away their cash and the drug deals don't happen, cutting down on the subsequent crimes that can stem from a drug buy. You can't buy cocaine with a credit card. It's cash on the line and that's where we wanted to legally intervene.

Using court–tested measures on how to legally ask for permission to search a vehicle if suspicions warranted, we had seized nearly $8 million dollars in suspected drug money in the three years before the *Sentinel* reporters showed up in early 1992. We were putting a dent in the drug trade by lifting one of its key commodities—money.

These reporters were not the first to be curious about the program. In addition to the television feature news show *20/20*, we had talked not only to the press about this law enforcement undertaking but to other police agencies who were looking for advice on how to curb their jurisdiction's drug problem.

As an organization that many law enforcement agencies were now looking to for help with their own drug problem, we continued to fine-tune our program to stay within the boundaries of the law. We put in as many safeguards as possible to ensure we were getting it right. If there was someone on the team like Frank Josenhanz, who we felt was not performing properly, disciplinary action including removal from the team followed.

We were training law officers from Arizona to Georgia on our drug and cash interdiction program. I had even done some training of my old unit—the Florida Highway Patrol—in the proper way to handle a stop.

Now it looked as if a local newspaper had taken an interest. The *Orlando Sentinel* had acquired a piece of property on the western side of my county. Volusia County was widespread in area, stretching 1200 square miles and divided east and west by two major interstates – I-4 east/west and I-95 north/south. The bulk of the population resided in the eastern section – in Daytona Beach, Ormond Beach and New Smyrna. But the west was rising with Deltona (in the southwest part of the county) and even DeBary and Deland (a few miles north of Deltona) serving as bedroom communities to the larger metropolitan area of Orlando.

These western areas, particularly Deltona, considered itself more a part of Orlando than Daytona Beach, the largest city in Volusia County. As such, there was greater interest in the *Sentinel* as a newspaper than the *Daytona Beach News Journal*. The *News Journal* also catered (at that time) more to the eastern side of the county, so it left a wide-open opportunity for the *Sentinel* to begin entrenchment there.

They sent two reporters to follow up on their public records request. Jeff Brazil and Steve Berry were two young journalists assigned to reviewing the records and apparently write a story from both that research and a few interviews. Brazil was small, wiry, and a bit mousy actually, with a fast-talking way about him. Berry was more laid back, quieter than his partner, and similarly small in appearance. We were to see these two men around the Sheriff's Office regularly for the next several weeks.

They began innocently enough. They initially talked to the Sheriff's Office legal advisor, Nancye Jones, about their assignment. We had no problem giving them complete access to the files, space to review them and the availability of a copy machine. We were also completely comfortable with our efforts in cash and drug interdiction. We were locking up drug dealers and disrupting the drug flow.

We knew we had established a solid program that was producing results and doing well within the stated bounds of the law.

When Brazil and Berry first spoke with us, they admitted up front that they didn't like or agree with the forfeiture laws as they currently existed on the books and which we were enforcing on the streets. They also said they knew our program was within the law and wanted to give us a chance to tell our side of the story.

Perhaps we were naïve to believe that. What newspaper would commit the money and resources for two reporters to spend several weeks in a county they had little circulation in just to get our side of the story? Later, it was clear they had a specific agenda and it didn't involve telling our side of anything. We should have realized that no newspaper had two people spend six weeks on one story that had a favorable conclusion for law enforcement.

I saw very little of them personally during this time. There were many things to do between finishing up the Sheriff's Office accreditation process, to implementing new policies and procedures, to upgrading some of the antiquated equipment, to meeting with citizens in various parts of the county to address their specific crime concerns.

They requested an interview with me toward the end of their research time. I wasn't sure what to expect, but it didn't take long for me to see what their point of view on this story was going to be. Brazil started early, hurling questions like, "Why are you a racist?" and "Does your team target blacks?"

I couldn't believe their tone. These were absurd, uncomfortable questions put forth in an accusatory manner, looking for a reaction. Berry said little, maintaining his low profile, but he would occasionally throw in a question that seemed all the more vicious because it was unexpected coming from him. Maybe these guys considered themselves the 1990's version of Woodward and Bernstein, but they had chosen the wrong program for a conspiracy theory. Both men appeared to be quite intelligent, but it was clear they had their story written before they called on me. All they wanted to do was use quotes that they could make fit their article.

It was obvious they felt the interdiction program to be racially motivated. During the O.J. Simpson trial, this would be called "playing the race card." A respected Pulitzer Prize winning journalist would later tell me that the *Sentinel* was relying on what had become the "new McCarthyism" of American journalism. This was the charge that law enforcement policies are predominantly racist and victimizes blacks and other minorities. In this atmosphere, the simple fact that law enforcement affects minorities at all is proof that racism is alive and well and the motivating cause for such policy.

My impression during this interview was that Brazil and Berry were going to hammer us in their newspaper. There seemed little we could do to convince them that race was not a part of any law enforcement policy in my department. I asked them to go see the individual in charge of the drug and cash interdiction squads, Leonard Davis, an African-American who had become indispensable to me. He was a Florida State graduate, a career law enforcement officer and hardly one who would foster racist policies among our deputies.

They never made any attempt to talk to him.

If they had, they'd have heard about the legally approved measures used by our interdiction teams on the forty miles along I-95 inside Volusia County's borders. They would have heard that there are only five deputies out of more than 300 in the Sheriff's Office that patrol this area and stop cars for traffic violations.

Nothing in what we did was based on the person's race. We stopped people who committed a traffic violation. A substantial number of whites were stopped, as were blacks, Hispanics and other minorities. We didn't know who it would be when we pulled the car over. The *Sentinel* reporters, regardless of what they initially said, chose not to listen to our side of the story at all.

I had always been very up front with the media. I conversed frequently with reporters during the 1988 campaign for Sheriff and continued that practice after I took office. I never sought a reporter out, but would continuously answer their questions when they came to me. We were never selective about who was given information from our office—everyone received the same details from us about a media-worthy event. One reporter had actually commented on how much better the situation was now than under former Sheriff Ed Duff, who simply refused to talk to the media. I was quickly beginning to see why he'd adopted that policy.

Their series of articles began appearing on June 14, 1992, three weeks before qualifying for re-election. Not only was it a feature story, but a front page one at that. Entitled, "Tainted Cash or Easy Money?" the stories predictably attacked me and my deputies for our cash interdiction program. They were brutal, unsparing and totally inaccurate. Even though we knew the story would not be favorable to us, nothing really prepared me for the slanted and incorrect information that was portrayed as truth. For people reading this story, I'm sure there was shock and outrage. I would have felt the same except for one salient point—I knew the truth.

The first day's articles gave a general overview of the stops we made, complete with statistics and a side story about a young woman named Selena Washington, who had $19,000 in her car in two Crown Royal bags (a favorite of drug dealers). She was portrayed as an innocent victim who was taking the money to Miami to buy building supplies for her Charleston, South Carolina home to make repairs caused by the damage made by Hurricane Hugo.

The next day, June 15, the reporters played their "race card." The subtitle of this story was, "Blacks, Hispanics big losers in cash seizures". Another headline ran, "Sheriff Vogel says whites are less likely to transport drug money". The *Sentinel* repeatedly made the statement that 90% of the 262 cases they reviewed involved minorities. They also said that 199 of the 262 cases didn't even involve an arrest, just a seizure. There was a side article about a Hersel Lawson, who was transporting $31,000 that the newspaper said was the proceeds from a bank loan to be used to open a bar with a friend in Fort Lauderdale. Another side article depicted the story of Edwin Johnson, a self-employed businessman who had his life savings of $38,000 seized by deputies.

On June 16, the article talked about Earl Fields, a lottery winner whose winnings of more than $37,000 was confiscated by our interdiction team. There was also an extensive analysis of the amount of confiscated cash we kept and how that money was used to "bankroll the fight against drugs".

The June 17 article that ran revolved around a tape that an Orlando-area attorney had given to the *Sentinel*. The tape was said to have shown more than 30 traffic stops over 4 days by Sergeant Bobby Jones of the interdiction team. The article alleged it was proof that we mostly stopped blacks and Hispanics. The attorney represented a woman whom was stopped and ultimately convicted by a Federal jury on charges brought as a result of that stop. The attorney's comment? "If you stop enough blacks and Hispanics on I-95, you're bound to find some with drugs and money."

That day the *Sentinel* also ran a reaction from me on the series of articles. I told them what I thought, that the articles were sleazy and misleading and cited two examples which they refuted in the bulk of the article.

Finally, on June 18, an editorial appeared in the *Sentinel* entitled, "Cash seizures gone amok". The opinions expressed accused me of setting up an ambush to specifically take money from innocent motorists, people against whom there was no criminal evidence. The editorial said we rarely took people to court; that we simply cut deals and kept some of the money in a clear case of abuse of power.

After two decades in law enforcement, I had felt comfortable dealing with the criminal world. I knew what to expect. I understood what legal boundaries I had to act within to apprehend this element. But nothing had prepared me for this vicious assault. Nor were my deputies ready for this written onslaught. The power of the pen was said to be mighty and these stories showed how influential the written word could be.

We knew the reporters didn't like the state law that allowed confiscation of cash believed to be used in a crime. They had stated that up front. What we didn't anticipate was their selection of just a few cases to try and make the leap to a portrayal of our team as racist. They had reviewed nearly 300 files; there were many more they didn't review and yet they selected the ones that best fit a story that had obviously been written before they ever arrived at the Volusia County Sheriff's Office.

I asked Nancye Jones, our legal advisor (who had recently wed Sergeant Bobby Jones, under criticism himself for the seizures), to review every one of the cases mentioned in the *Sentinel* articles to be sure our officers had committed no wrongdoing in their confiscation. The cases cited had taken place over a couple of years, and it was difficult to remember all of the details on each situation without a re-reading of the files. I knew that there were incorrect statements made in the article about Selena Washington, the woman who claimed she was going to Miami to buy building supplies for her Charleston, South Carolina home which was severely damaged by Hurricane Hugo, but I wanted to check over the facts again before responding to the *Sentinel* pieces.

The first thing we did was to go back over the same 262 cases. The *Sentinel* had stated in virtually every article that 90 percent of the stops were of minorities. Actually, reviewing the same 262 cases, the percentage of stops of minorities was 74 percent, a significant difference. It was certainly more accurate than the figure of 90 percent the reporters kept tossing around, a number that outraged readers. This was the first of many inaccuracies that slanted this article unfairly.

Truthfully, the 74 percent figure also seemed high. The *Sentinel* only looked at 262 cases. There were more they didn't review and adding in those numbers brought the overall percentage of minority stops down even further. In any event, statewide statistics showed that more than half of the people arrested in the state for drug offenses were blacks. This didn't accurately portray the African-American community, either, the majority of whom were law-abiding with the same low tolerance of drugs and violent crime.

Our office did not indiscriminately search any vehicle. Permission was secured in all but a handful of cases where a K-9 dog sensed drugs in the car and an individual's consent was no longer necessary. It didn't matter what race, creed or color the person was; they were either committing an illegal act or they weren't.

The *Sentinel* also repeatedly made the point that only 63 arrests were made as a result of these 262 stops. In reviewing these same 262 cases, we counted 107 arrests, again a substantial difference in what the *Sentinel* reported as fact. In addition, seizure information was routinely given to the Drug Enforcement Agency and the individual had sometimes turned out to be part of a DEA case elsewhere. We may not have made the immediate arrest, but apprehension was made later by another agency on the basis of some of our information. We had testified in cases held in Virginia, Maryland, Georgia and elsewhere to help bring some of these people to justice.

Obviously, the *Sentinel*'s math was well off the mark. But they had the podium and there seemed little we could do to except point out the inaccuracies and hope that they printed a retraction.

The individual cases were even more interesting in reviewing what parts of each story the reporters chose to tell and what they omitted. In each case, the omissions were significant enough to give a reader an entirely different perspective of the "victim" of the cash seizure team.

The first day's articles included a story about a 21 year-old Navy reservist named Joseph Kea who told us he was on his way to Miami for school. He was stopped on March 13, 1992 for speeding, and Sergeant Jones asked permission to search and he subsequently found $3,989 in a nylon bag. The money was folded in $100 rolls. He had no luggage and his Navy uniform was wrinkled with a pair of scuffed shoes. The newspaper said that Kea's attorney had provided Navy pay stubs to show the source of the money and a resume detailing his steady salary and work history. He had no criminal record and eventually reached a settlement with the Sheriff's Office whereby $2,989 of the money was returned to him.

The file showed that Kea was with a passenger, both of who verified that he was in the Navy reserve and ordered to go to Miami, but neither of them specified exactly where they were going. The newspaper later indicated in a subsequent article that there was a Reserve Readiness Center in South Florida for both the Navy and the Marine Corps. However, Kea had no idea what school it was or its location. Further, and more important, Kea carried no formal orders regarding the trip to Miami, which was required and must be carried by any Navy personnel. That alone made the destination suspicious.

Neither Kea nor his passenger had any luggage save for Kea's uniform that was rolled into a ball and stuffed in the corner of the trunk. His shoes were scratched and scuffed. This again did not indicate an individual traveling as a Navy Reservist. The uniform and shoes were typically in excellent order, take it from someone who served in the Marine Corps.

Kea had said the $3,989 was savings from the Navy. It was packaged in various $100 rolls, which was more indicative of how money is presented in a drug deal, rather than how someone would keep their savings.

We had an order from a judge finding probable cause for seizure based on these circumstances.

The documents provided by Kea included Naval Reserve earnings statements of $98.01 for January 1990 and $90.76 for July 1989. There was a pay voucher for June 30, 1989 of $1,406.15. There was a 1988 Wage & Tax Statement of $391.80. There were various withdrawal and deposit receipts for a period running from August 15, 1988 to December 7, 1989 totaling $1,050 deposited and $2,059 withdrawn. He also sent us a fall 1989 registration for Armstrong State College with tuition at $455. The most recent documented evidence was the January 1990 earnings statement, more than two years prior to the stop.

Kea had handwritten a note giving his employment history since 1986. He claimed he had an income tax refund of $800 in 1987, although his documented earnings the next year in 1988 were only $391.80, which would represent a huge drop in pay. He further claimed a $2,500 enlistment bonus for joining the Naval Reserve, plus June 1989 pay for active duty of $1406.15 and November 1989 totals of $232.48. No documentation accompanied any of these claims.

We eventually agreed to settle the case, retaining $1,000 and returning the rest of the money. These cases are not unlike a criminal case that is plea-bargained and settled.

If this legal procedure did not occur, the court system would be completely bogged down. Our attorneys weighed the costs of prosecuting versus the seizure amounts and chose when to take a defense attorney's offer (or suggest a settlement) and when to pursue in court. In this case, we settled and Kea agreed. There were a lot of questions surrounding his situation for which he did not provide adequate answers and documentation. His lawyer received 25 percent of the $2,989 returned.

The next case listed in the June 14 article was that of Jose Raposa, the 29 year-old owner of Tri-Star Paint Shop in Massachusetts, who had cash in the amount of $19,000 seized on May 2, 1991. The article said that Sergeant Bobby Jones did not believe Raposa's story that he was headed to Miami to look for antique cars or that he had just obtained a home-equity loan because these antique car dealers required cash. The newspaper said Volusia County investigator Paul Page investigated Raposa but could find nothing on him. Eventually the case was settled with 75 percent of the money returned, from which Raposa paid his lawyer $1,000.

The case file revealed that there were two people in the car—Raposa and Farias Simao. Initially, Simao told Sergeant Jones that he was going to Miami to look for work. Raposa had told Jones separately that Simao was going to Miami to see the man's mother-in-law. Conflicting stories like that generally indicate the two people in the car don't know each other that well, another potential character-istic of people involved in transporting illegal contraband that our deputies are trained to spot.

When the $19,000 was discovered, Raposa first said it was his savings. The money was bound in rubber bands and wrapped in tin foil. He added later that he was a self-employed painter and had saved the money over a year. He agreed to come to the Operations Center so we could issue him a receipt for the money. There he added that he had taken the money out over a five-month period. Later still, he called Paul Page, the investigator, to say he had 1990 income of $70,000 from a painting business he ran out of his home and had taken out an equity loan four months prior for several thousand dollars.

The only documents provided to us by Raposa and his attorney were a savings account statement showing a $41.93 balance in October 30, 1990 down from the highest balance of $32,125 on October 10. There were no records of withdrawal slips provided nor did Raposa indicate who had withdrawn that money. The attorney's letter indicated that Raposa took an equity loan out on October 2, 1990 for $32,118.50, but no valid documentation was ever sent to back that up. There were only documents signed by Raposa, no bank officer signatures or bank seal or the usual indicators of a valid transaction. This information, if true, should be readily available, but it was not provided.

Again, we decided to settle the case and retained $4,750.

This first article also carried a quote from Chief Circuit Judge McFerrin Smith who was said to be dismayed by the *Sentinel's* findings and questioned whether the Sheriff's Office was more interested in collecting cash rather than curbing crime. "At best, it looks borderline, doesn't it?" he was quoted as saying.

Later, a reporter from a publication called *Accuracy in Media* re-interviewed Judge Smith about his comment. The Judge replied that what he actually said to reporter Jeff Brazil was "if the situation was as you described, it would be deplorable, but you are not telling the whole story." The Judge pointed out that a state court must give final approval to all forfeitures, whether contested or not. The Sheriff's Office could not keep any money unless signed off by the court. *Accuracy in Media* later printed a rebuttal to the *Sentinel's* stories based on their own investigation of its allegations.

The last case mentioned in detail in the first article was about Selena Washington, the South Carolina woman heading for Miami to pick up building supplies to repair her house, damaged by a hurricane.

The reporters wrote that the 43 year-old woman wanted to go to Miami to hunt bargains for these needed supplies. She was traveling with her cousin John Washington and was stopped for driving 72 mph in a 65-mph zone. She gave permission to search the car. When the search turned up the $19,000, Selena Washington said she had to go to Miami for the supplies because there was price gouging going on in Charleston during the Hurricane Hugo clean up. She insisted that the deputies could call back to her father in South Carolina or her son who was a probation judge. She told deputies that she was a Realtor instructor and owned several pieces of property. She said she had never been arrested.

The *Sentinel* reported that they verified she had no criminal record and had provided documentation about the money. They also reported extensively on our use of a tape recording device inside the police car. As noted by the television show *20/20*, when a search was being conducted the passengers were seated in the patrol car until we had finished. The law states that you can record conversations in the police car without having to advise the individuals that this is happening. In this situation, one of the statements Selena Washington made to her cousin was, "You ain't got nothing stupid in there, have you?" John Washington denied it.

Finally, the *Sentinel* reported that she wanted to fight in court to get her money back, but her attorney convinced her to settle for a return of $15,000 (of which he received $1,000). He advised that it would be too costly to fight it in court.

A review of our files and investigation revealed that, contrary to both her assertion and that of the newspaper, she did have a prior arrest and conviction in 1982 for illegally transporting liquor.

When she was stopped, she initially said she was going to Florida to her cousin John's house. John said he lived in Miami and was going home to visit his relatives. Selena gave no other reason for the trip other than to let John spend time with his family.

It was only after the search turned up $12,000 in flash rolls in a Crown Royal bag and another $7,000 in a second Crown Royal bag in Selena Washington's purse that she said she was going to Miami to buy building supplies. She initially said the money was an insurance payoff on her damaged home in South Carolina. Later, she told us her father had actually given her the money.

The deputy had a right to be suspicious. The Crown Royal bags and the money folded in $100 rolls was typical of cash packaged for a drug deal. That she withheld the information about going to Miami to buy building supplies for her home until after the money was found simply added to those suspicions. The deputy was thinking, "why not buy the supplies closer to home? If the prices were high in Charleston, why not go to Savannah, Georgia instead? How was she going to transport any lumber or supplies home? The car she was driving in was too small to hold any adequate building materials. And why Miami? Building supply costs in South Florida were probably the highest in the entire southeast. And why now? Hurricane Hugo had hit South Carolina six months earlier. Why wait that long and then go to buy the highest cost supplies in this part of the country?" It just didn't sound right.

A later investigation of her South Carolina home showed that it had been unoccupied for some time. Neighbors said that it was a rental property and it had sustained minimal damage compared to other houses in the same area. Selena Washington had not even been compensated by the federal agency for disaster relief.

A local judge had signed an order authorizing the cash seizure.

The documentation she provided was an undated, unnotarized note from her father saying he had loaned his daughter $6,800 to help her repair her house to be paid back ultimately by insurance money. The total documented receipts from her father to her amounted to $5,650 in the weeks immediately preceding her trip to Miami. There was a notarized statement from her niece saying she had lent her aunt $4,000 ($2,000 in cash, $2,000 in cashier's checks) for repairs. Her attorney sent a letter stating that Selena Washington had applied for disaster relief, especially since the roof was badly damaged. He also stated the loans from her father and niece totaled $12,800, well above what the documentation she provided had indicated. The attorney also said Selena Washington was on her way to Miami to meet with a roofer that she had contracted to repair her home. This was the first time we had heard that, and neither Selena nor John had mentioned anything about a roofer.

The last case mentioned on this first day of stories was that of Jorge Nater and Francisco Muriel, stopped on February 4, 1991 for following another car too closely, a cash-seizure discussed previously in this book. The reporters wrote that Nater and family friend Muriel were traveling to South Florida, Nater to buy a house in Pompano Beach. Deputies found $36,990 in the car which Nater said was from selling an apartment complex in Puerto Rico three days earlier. The story said Nater provided documentation regarding the sale, a sworn affidavit from the buyer and testimonial letters from the mayor, police chief and a priest in his hometown in Puerto Rico. Nater had no criminal history. The Sheriff's Office eventually returned all but $6,000 of the money.

During the search, Nater and Muriel waited in the patrol car, during which time they were recorded with Nater saying that if they were allowed to leave maybe they could hide the money in a tire.

The case file showed that the driver Muriel was from New Jersey and that he was going to visit children of a friend because one was about to give birth and there were complications. He didn't know the address of his destination. He also said that Nater was his friend, although he didn't know Nater's name, first or last.

Nater told our deputy that he had flown to New Jersey three days earlier to see his brother. He was going first to Melbourne, Florida and then Tampa to see his brother's kids.

The money was found in wrapped $1,000 bundles with different color rubber bands. After the money was found, Nater said he was going to use it to buy a home in Pompano Beach. He said he had signed papers in New Jersey when he was there to sell a building in Puerto Rico and had received the money then. He had no documents with him regarding the sale just made in New Jersey. However, he said he'd get them later in Puerto Rico.

Separately, Muriel told our deputy the money belonged to Nater's daughter and was to be deposited in a bank in Melbourne. Later, Muriel told investigators that he'd been offered a couple of hundred dollars to drive Nater to visit relatives in South Florida.

The conversation in the patrol car started with Muriel telling Nater there were no drugs in the car and that neither of them had a criminal record. Nater responded by saying they should have put the money inside a tire. Muriel told Nater not to worry because all they could do was make him pay taxes on the money.

Nater's attorney in Orlando sent certain documents regarding the sale of the property. The documents lacked attorney seals and a Puerto Rican license number, both of which were legally required in that country. Contracts were post-dated to the time of the seizure and the paperwork was signed in Puerto Rico, not New Jersey as Nater claimed. The property in question was appraised upwards of $300,000 yet Nater had said he'd sold it for $60,000. Several sources in Puerto Rico told investigators it was easy to get character references from officials there, as they all did favors for one another. Other sources indicated a high level of corruption within both the government and police department. The entire story was inconsistent and suspicious.

So, the *Sentinel*'s first article had been full of inaccurate statements and material omissions. Apparently, if a fact didn't fit a particular story's slant, it wasn't mentioned. But a look at all of the facts from this file review showed our deputies using reasonable suspicion along with a probable cause concurring ruling from a judge to seize the money. That some cases were settled is just part of the legal process today. Attorneys make deals and the case is over. This is definitely not the preference of law enforcement officers, but we accept it as a matter of course.

The more I reviewed our files, the more frustrated I became with the haphazard reporting of Brazil and Berry. These guys were on a mission and if it meant running over this law enforcement agency to get there, they would do it. I had never been taken to task for doing my job before. But that's what this was all about. We were enforcing the law as we knew it and for which we had legal guidelines to assist us. State attorneys and court judges backed our methods on each and every one of these cases, and yet the articles would lead you to believe the Volusia County Sheriff's Office was targeting innocent minority motorists to raise cash for the department and the people were powerless to defend against it.

This was equally frustrating for the deputies on the team. They were out on the highway nearly every day, risking their lives to stop the flow of both drugs and drug money. They knew drug dealers had become a lot smarter today, hiring people to do the transporting of contraband and cash for them. Drug dealing is a secretive business and dealers generally withhold most of the information about the transaction from their mules, telling them only enough to arrive at a pre-arranged place to transport their illegal goods. Many of the mules didn't know who was in the car with them, a circumstance that the team turned to their advantage when coming across conflicting stories and people driving together who were unfamiliar with each other. The cases the *Sentinel* was describing predominantly fit the classic "mule." It just wasn't portrayed that way or readers would have a different opinion of the same story.

The second day's article featured more individual stories. Hersel Lawson was stopped on April 15, 1991 and deputies seized $31,000. The story stated Lawson was a Virginia businessman with a used motorcycle shop in Roanoke. He told deputies the money was the proceeds of a bank loan and that he was taking it to a friend in Fort Lauderdale to open up a bar. He was carrying cash because he had previously declared bankruptcy and didn't want the courts to know about the money. The money was found in a Crown Royal bag and there were marijuana joints in the car that Lawson attributed to a hitchhiker he had picked up in Jacksonville. The reporters said he provided bank records of the $25,000 loan to police and that a friend corroborated his story about them opening up a bar in Fort Lauderdale. The article concluded by stating that a mediator ordered the Volusia County Sheriff's Office to return 88 percent of the money to Lawson.

A review of the official file told a different story. There were no bank records or corroborating information about the bar. What Lawson actually said at first was that he was going to visit a buddy in Fort Lauderdale who owned a bar. According to Lawson, the friend wanted Lawson to sell his motorcycle shop in Roanoke and invest in this bar.

After the money was found, Lawson changed his story. He said he was going to meet a Suzette Johnson who had a site picked out for building a bar. He told the deputy to call Johnson, but didn't know her name or address. He said he would have her call us when he got to Miami, but we never heard from her.

Lawson first said the money total was $25,000. He then amended that estimate to $31,000. He said he had saved the money from a motorcycle shop owned by Lawson and his father. He told us neither his father nor his wife knew about the money. He said he had not filed taxes in 1990. He gave his 1989 income as $24,000. He admitted he was hiding funds from a bankruptcy judge.

A local judge found probable cause to seize the money.

An investigator visited the motorcycle shop in Virginia and met with Lawson's father. The father said he gave money to his son to buy motorcycles in Florida to increase the shop inventory. He didn't know where Hersel was going to buy them or what type they were. He admitted not knowing much about motorcycles at all and referred any questions to his son. The shop didn't appear to have space for any new inventory.

The father then said his son was going to buy a greenhouse in Florida after the senior Lawson had seen an advertisement in the Wall Street Journal. He didn't know the location of this greenhouse, though.

The father then said the money came from business proceeds plus a bank loan of $25,000 taken six months earlier. He showed the investigator paperwork for a $14,000 (not $25,000) loan. The father also said the business filed bankruptcy in 1987 and his son had just personally filed a short time ago.

Mediation is a settlement proposal and not an order as the newspaper emphasized. Either party can reject the mediator's proposed settlement. Both parties chose to accept it and $27,250 was returned to Lawson. The mediation report signed by Lawson required that the settlement be kept confidential.

The *Orlando Sentinel* violated this confidentiality.

The other case reported in detail in the second day's series of articles was that of Edwin Johnson, a man who had his life savings of $38,923 seized by Volusia deputies. He was returning from Georgia to Florida when he was pulled over for not signaling a lane change. He told deputies that the money they found in a bag in the trunk was profit from his businesses, Ed's Lawn Service in Miami and Thirst Quenchers, Inc., a discount beverage service he had previously owned for eight years. He said he carried cash because he didn't trust banks after a wage garnishment as a result of a 1985 lawsuit. He had very little luggage for the trip and appeared nervous talking to the deputy. He had one old misdemeanor on his record that the paper quoted then Volusia County Sheriff's legal advisor Mel Stack as saying was insignificant. Johnson fought for six months to get his money back but eventually settled for $28,923, about 75 percent of it.

The file showed that Johnson was riding with a woman who he claimed to be his girlfriend and that they had been in Georgia visiting her relatives. The woman told the deputy separately that Johnson was her cousin, not her boyfriend. The money was found in a Crown Royal bag, in rolls wrapped in different colored rubber bands. Johnson first said he didn't know how much, then guessed at $32,000 (it was $38,923). Johnson said the money was solely from the lawn service business, an assertion amended later by his attorney to include the prior business Thirst Quenchers as well.

When asked about what he paid in income taxes the prior year, Johnson told the deputy, "That's the problem with this money and that's between me and the IRS." He declined a receipt for the money when it was seized.

He had a record, which was sealed in 1977.

He did provide documentation on the wage garnishment. His 1989 tax return showed a $12,116 income from Thirst Quenchers. He received a tax refund check in September 1989 of $4,057. His attorney's letter stated that Johnson had never been arrested nor the subject of any criminal investigation (not true). He further said that the 1985 garnishment turned Johnson against banks. Johnson, the letter went on, sold off equipment at Thirst Quenchers to start the lawn service and that the money he had was from the sale of equipment from the lawn service (something he hadn't told the deputy) and some profits. Lastly, the attorney asserted that Johnson had closed out Thirst Quenchers in 1990 with $24,617 in cash and $13,500 for sold equipment.

The balance sheet for Thirst Quenchers, however, did not support either of those figures.

The remainder of the stories published by the *Sentinel* on June 15, 1992 had to do with 90 percent of our stops being minorities, a figure we know to be inaccurate. Their contention was that we use a drug courier profile to stop motorists and these characteristics include race.

That simply wasn't true. I had ceased using a profile to stop cars back in my state trooper days based on a state court ruling and had certainly not brought that outmoded concept to the Sheriff's Office, but how do you get that message out to the public? The *Sentinel* had a ready-made forum, but law enforcement agencies do not have the same readership or public following. Brazil and Berry had refused to interview the head of the team, Leonard Davis, an African-American. Nor did they interview one of the team members, Deputy Raymond Almodovar, a Hispanic-American whose parents were born in Puerto Rico. Ray would have told them that he moved from New York City to Florida to raise his family away from a drug-plagued community. Both Leonard and Ray would have told the *Sentinel* they would never use or endorse the use of race as an indicator that a car should be stopped. They would have said we never used any race profiling in our training.

But their stories would have interfered with the theme of the *Sentinel*'s articles.

The primary story in the third day of articles dealt with a man who claimed to be a Florida lottery winner. Earl Fields, the *Sentinel* reported, was stopped for a traffic violation on February 4, 1991 and had $37,970 seized as a result. A Miami clothing maker, he told Deputy Bobby Jones that the money was lottery winnings. He detailed his winning more than $400,000 in lottery money over an 18-month period. The money was wrapped in various rolls and Fields appeared nervous during the entire stop. Fields' attorney demanded the money back, the story went on, providing a canceled check in the amount of $213,698.48 signed by then State Lottery commissioner Rebecca Paul. The Lottery Department confirmed the winnings. Volusia deputies were convinced Fields was operating a money-laundering scheme buying valid ticket winners for more than their value to "wash" it. No proof of this was offered and no investigation was done. Fields demanded a trial that the Sheriff's Office pursued. However, Fields got cold feet when he saw it was to be an all-white jury and settled, getting back $23,000 of the money and paying $8,000 of it to his lawyer.

According to Fields' case file, he was traveling from South Carolina to Jacksonville and then Miami. The money was found in a paper bag, wrapped in rolls. Fields was evasive about the origin of the money and left the scene without waiting for a receipt. He had a passenger who had a 1982 possession of cocaine arrest. Fields himself had two prior convictions—for cocaine possession in 1973 and gambling in 1974.

A judge found probable cause and authorized seizure of the money.

Fields' attorney provided a lottery check in the amount of $213,698. The attorney also alleged by letter that we had seized $50,000; it was actually $37,970. Fields provided seven lottery tickets dated August 30, 1990, all with the same numbers. John Fraiser of Florida Lottery security said that for Fields to claim, as he had, that he won $50,000 from these seven tickets was highly improbable and statistically nearly impossible. He also said it was common for drug dealers to purchase winning lottery tickets to conceal contraband funds.

It was one method of laundering money and it was worth the extra paid to the person holding the winning number, as anyone who knowingly agreed to launder money would only do it for a fee.

Fields backed out of the trial and agreed to a settlement.

The *Sentinel* ran an editorial June 18 that was the summary document for the series of articles the newspaper had run. It accused me specifically of targeting southbound traffic to confiscate funds that the department later used to purchase fancy equipment like computers and radios that our regular budget did not allow. The editorial charged that my deputies targeted innocent black and Hispanic motorists and subjected them to questionable stops, interrogations, vehicle searches, cash confiscations and out-of-court settlements. The article said my priorities were skewed towards cash seizures and, again, 90 percent of the stops made were of minorities.

By now, nothing that appeared in the *Sentinel* surprised us. They had accused me of abuse of power when in truth the only entity that had abused its power was this newspaper through false reporting and omission of the complete facts about these cases. Using their daily paper as a forum, they had the first and last words on any discussion they wish to print. They weren't interested in facts. They weren't interested in truth. They weren't interested in anyone's opinions but their own. They weren't interested in law and order, reduced crime rates, or halting the tremendous drug problem in our state. Their interest was in pushing ahead their own agenda, and in this case I was their target.

The *Sentinel* would have you believe that we had stopped our drug interdiction northbound on I-95 to concentrate on cash seizures. We hadn't. Cash seizures southbound generated more activity because we had more cases of people driving south to make their drug purchase. Thanks first to my successful work as a state trooper and then to our team's results, Volusia County already had a reputation for drug interdiction northbound and drug dealers were giving instructions to detour around our county. That was the result of good police work and it wouldn't be long before the same orders were given to those coming south.

My office was holding its own in the war against drugs. Stopping any deal is important. Small-time dealers become larger players if they are successful early on. People who use drugs as a result of these transactions tend to commit other crimes themselves as a means of getting money to pay for their habits. It's a vicious cycle in which we were putting a serious dent. It would have made a good story.

But it was not the tale the readers of the *Sentinel* read.

Readers did not learn that:

- 85 percent of those people stopped in the cases the *Sentinel* reviewed had either a prior or subsequent felony or narcotics arrest;
- 43 percent of all these cases resulted in an arrest of one or more individuals;
- 25 percent of these cases also involved possession of drugs;
- 26 percent of the cases involving cash seizures involved white motorists;
- 27 percent of both drug and cash seizure cases involved white motorists;
- A judge must agree and sign an order to make a cash seizure;
- In not one case covered in detail by the *Sentinel* did the individual whose cash was seized provide valid documentation that matched the story told in the paper;
- Settlements were as much a part of this process as they are with other arrests;
- The Special Enforcement Team was headed by an African-American and two of the five deputies patrolling the interstates were minorities: one Hispanic and one African-American.

These facts were left out of this supposed landmark series of articles about law enforcement violating people's civil rights. These facts didn't support this general theme and that meant they never saw the publishing light of day.

The truth was that this team was doing an excellent job of enforcing the law and attempting to turn the tide of the drug war. Instead of being hailed for our actions, we were being railed against by a print media without an adequate forum for response. Deputies that we had singled out for their stellar performance were now labeled in print as racist and harassers of innocent people.

The editorial on June 18, 1992 was not the last we would hear from the *Orlando Sentinel*.

It was also not the last we would hear from Selena Washington and Jorge Nater.

My job was to keep the morale of the department and specifically the Special Enforcement Team up to its usual standards. I knew there were some things that I could control and others I could not. The print media was not an element I could control. I was secure in how we were handling our law enforcement procedures and content to let anyone look into my office's activities. It was important to keep our deputies and staff on the same positive track we had been on since taking office in 1989.

I had spent many years perfecting the art of drug and cash interdiction along the highways and refined the measures to be taken to make this program successful. This was done within the framework of the law and with the able assistance of attorneys along the way. Over the years we had developed a keen sense of knowing when someone who was stopped for a traffic violation had much more to hide.

I had never dreamed in all the years that our work in this type of law enforcement and the process I helped to create would become controversial enough to warrant the type of blatant attack that decorated the headlines for a week in June 1992.

I was wrong.

I was upset about the articles, but it was not in our department's best interests to dwell on them. We had truth on our side and for now that would have to be enough. As a public figure, I needed to put personal feelings aside and simply get on with the job. So I turned the other cheek and went forward.

≈ ≈

Let's Go To The Videotape

Berry and Brazil were back in our offices shortly after their articles appeared that June, this time demanding to see the videotapes we made of the cash interdiction stops.

It was a slightly different atmosphere in our offices now and the reception toward the reporters was about what you'd expect after the first articles twisting the truth had appeared. But they have every right to request the tapes and naturally we made them available, as we are required to do.

I could see more trouble on the horizon. The team taped every stop. But after a time, Mel Stack advised that we didn't need to save the stops for which no suspicions were aroused, no evidence searched for and no case was made. At this point, the tapes contained mostly stops that we made that were successful. It was not going to be representative of all the stops the team made. It was not going to show all of the people who were let go with a traffic warning. The statistics were going to be even more skewed than the falsehoods already printed in the first series of articles.

The team had already seen what videotapes could show that is easily subject to misinterpretation following the "20/20" news broadcast two years earlier. I had no idea what to expect from these reporters' view of the tapes, but it was easy to forecast that they would place us in the worst possible situation.

The mood was edgy around the office and I tried my best to keep people up, relaxed, and focused on their tasks at hand. We had plenty to do without worrying about the next series of articles from these so-called reporters. The team was working a number of different assignments, since drug and cash trafficking generally slowed down in the summer months.

The *Sentinel* ran the stories in August and they were predictably slanted. Their "race" theme had created a furor the first time around, so they stayed with it through this next batch of stories. One headline ran, "Color of driver is key to stops in I-95 videos." They ran charts and graphs showing the number of Black and Hispanic drivers stopped versus White drivers. Once again, the tapes did not reflect all of the stops because we taped over the ones where no cases were made.

If anything, our department did its best to avoid any appearance that we are biased towards anyone. We treated every individual the same way. Color or ethnic background has no place in law enforcement operations. Our interdiction team consisted of individuals with varied backgrounds. When they made a stop, they were on the lookout for cumulative similarities that indicated the individual was carrying drugs or cash to buy drugs. Race or ethnic background was not one of those factors. We took each case as it came. We didn't put the drugs or cash in anyone's hands. The person was either breaking the law or not. Those were the statistics that were most vital.

The people we stopped sometimes didn't even know exactly what they had in the car. What they did know was that someone had paid them money to drive a car from point A to point B and that the trip involved transporting illegal goods of some kind. These couriers were usually just in it for the money and when they were stopped, just hoped the team wouldn't find whatever was in the car. This was not about race. It was about money, pure and simple.

But the *Sentinel* had too much at stake now to let up or change the type of reporting they were doing. For whatever reason, they had singled out the Volusia County Sheriff's office as their target, and were not going to rest until some action had been taken against us.

$\approx \approx$

SEARCHING FOR PLAINTIFFS

The articles simply weren't enough for the *Sentinel*. Certainly they knew that they had twisted the facts around to suit their story and now they wanted to take this story to a higher level to justify the validity of what they'd written. They'd driven their opinions down the throat of their readership in hopes of attracting more subscribers in Volusia County.

It wasn't happening. While their stories had outraged people who normally read their paper, it wasn't bringing new Volusia County readers in. The *Daytona Beach News Journal* generally ignored the *Sentinel*'s efforts to pull readers away from them. They weren't about to give another newspaper credit for breaking a story on their own turf. I'd like to think the *News Journal* believed the stories were slanted and untrue, but I had become quickly jaded about the motivations of the media.

Facing difficulty in Volusia, the *Sentinel* took their stories on the road. They began with editorials accusing us of civil rights violations. Typical language for these opinion pieces read, "The person who deserves most of the blame is Volusia County Sheriff Bob Vogel, whose Interstate 95 drug squad unfairly targeted mostly minorities to be stopped and searched." Desperate to involve the highest authorities in the state, they dared Governor Lawton Chiles to act, writing in their newspaper, "Governor Lawton Chiles also deserves a good dose of the blame for his weak response to the actions of Mr. Vogel's drug squad."

They went even higher, "Members of Congress should pressure the federal Justice Department to change its guidelines for seizing cash and other property and to guard against abuse. Such federal changes would strongly influence changes in the Florida seizure law, which Mr. Vogel has abused."

The Governor's office, Congress and the Justice Department were lofty targets. They began lobbying these entities to take action against us. They went to Congressman Jim Bacchus of Brevard County, an area on the East Coast of Florida directly south of Volusia County, to ask him to open a congressional investigation into the matter. He had been previously affiliated with the *Sentinel*, so he was a willing audience. The *Sentinel* tried to aid its cause further by contacting other Congressman. They ran into a dead stop when they called on Congressman John Mica of Orange County. They told him that every other congressional representative in the state had signed an open letter asking Congress to begin investigating the Volusia County Sheriff's office. Mica asked them to wait and called Representative Tillie Fowler who replied, "what letter?" to Mica's inquiry. He thanked her and told the *Sentinel* he wouldn't be signing any letter, taking them to task for attempting to deceive him about who had signed this supposed letter.

This was a newspaper so desperate to justify their stories that they would lie to a Congressman to move the chances of a congressional investigation closer to reality. I had never heard or seen anything like this campaign they were conducting.

Their efforts in Tallahassee met with immediate reward. They lobbied the Governor's press secretary Julie Anbender to have the Governor look into the activities of my drug and cash interdiction team. Less than a week after the first series of articles appeared in the *Sentinel*, Anbender announced that Governor Chiles was creating an informal panel to look into seizures of cash from motorists. She did note that while they would be looking into specific cases opened up by the Volusia County Sheriff's office, they would also be reviewing the "general workings across the state of the law allowing such seizures."

Chiles was working with Commissioner Tim Moore of the Florida Department of Law Enforcement to look into the seizure process, particularly focused on the settlements. Moore would be on the panel, as would J. Hardin Peterson, Chiles' general counsel. They would be selecting others in the near future.

This panel investigation was fine with me. It couldn't be any more biased than the *Sentinel*'s efforts and once they reviewed our tight-knit procedures and saw how we actually conducted our stops, I was certain we would be exonerated from the newspaper's blatant accusations.

We had tinkered with the team's method of operation over the three and a half years they had been at work. In June, I announced two procedural changes. The first would be to record in writing the conversations between drug squad supervisor Bobby Jones and the deputies on the team, so there would be no question as to what was said and the reasonable suspicions these officers might have. The second change was that the top staff in the department (that consisted of seven commanders and myself) would be personally reviewing any settlements made in the cash seizure program. For most of the early years of the team's activities, Mel Stack had taken on that responsibility. His successor, Nancye Ege, would still be negotiating any settlement. The difference now was that my staff would review also to see if we found the terms acceptable. Up to this point, we had stayed out of the settlement process. Since it had raised so much negative response, we felt a second check of what the settlement's terms were was valid.

The Governor completed the panel appointments in July. In addition to Moore and Peterson, he selected Jacksonville Sheriff Jim McMillan, Miami Police Chief Calvin Ross, George Aylesworth, legal advisor for the Metro-Dade Police Department, Ed Dunn, an attorney and former State Senator from Volusia County who had been defeated by Bob Butterworth in the State Attorney General's race in the 1986 election, and Wayne Evans, a lawyer with the Florida Highway Patrol. Ross was the only African-American on the panel, a point the *Sentinel* was quick to point out in a searing editorial. They appealed to the Governor to put more minorities on the panel. The *Sentinel* was no longer content to report news; they had become the story.

Chiles responded to the *Sentinel*'s protests by adding two Hispanic members to the panel in July. They were Jorge Hernandez-Torano of Miami and Maria DeJesus-Fernandez, both trial attorneys. This may have appeased the *Sentinel*, but the NAACP was vocally unhappy about the final panel make-up. The state president, Tom Poole, stated that since blacks were the primary targets, black members of the panel should total 50 percent. Of the two trial attorneys added, only Hernandez-Torano had ever handled seizure cases. The *Sentinel* ran an editorial criticizing the panel before it had even begun, entitled "Hammer or Rubber Stamp?" They had their panel, but nothing short of my removal from office was going to make them happy.

The *Sentinel* was not yet through influencing the course of action. In an attempt to solicit witnesses for the panel to interview, the newspaper ran a boxed advertisement repeatedly that ran as follows:

"For three years, a special drug squad at the Volusia County Sheriff's Office has been stopping motorists on Interstate 95 and searching their cars for contraband. In hundreds of cases, the officers seized money. And it appears that thousands of drivers have been stopped, the majority of whom were black and Hispanic. If you have been detained while driving through Volusia County, we'd like to review your case."

The ad listed two *Sentinel* telephone numbers that people could call.

The newspaper was clearly on a mission. But I wasn't that worried about motorists coming forward, because I knew that the people we stopped and ultimately searched almost always had something to hide. They put up little or no protest when the cash was seized and were relieved to be released. I was sure the *Sentinel* would not be hearing from these people.

The *Sentinel* had the ball rolling. They had the state of Florida looking into our efforts. In September 1992, Congressman John Conyers of Michigan would start a congressional investigation into the forfeiture laws the *Sentinel* accused us of using to abuse people's civil rights.

I had spent countless hours reviewing and re-reviewing the work the drug and cash interdiction team had done on the Interstate. I was confident we were doing it right, that we were not violating anyone's rights, that we had stopped the people who were moving drugs or cash to buy drugs through our county. I was convinced the panels would see that this was the case.

By July 1992, I had to officially declare my re-election candidacy by formally filing to run for Sheriff of Volusia County again. Actually, I hadn't given the re-election much thought with all the hype created by the *Sentinel* articles, the accreditation process, upgrading our office technological support, professionalizing the office and simply trying to bring down the crime rate. I was unaware of any candidates that were to run against me. If there were none, I would run unopposed and would continue to focus all efforts on the Sheriff's Office without diverting attention to a campaign.

I filed my candidacy officially on Monday, the first day of the qualifying week. I had raised no money yet for the campaign, since it didn't appear there would be one. But on Friday, the last day of qualifying, a candidate finally surfaced to file his forms. It was Ralph Henshaw.

JUST THE FACTS

Ralph was one of the original Seven Dwarfs (Dopey) from the 1988 campaign. He had finished a distant fifth in the voting during the September 1988 election that created the run-off between Noel Ouelette and I in November. Ralph had been a deputy who former Sheriff Duff had fired (with concurrence from the County Manager) for marijuana use among other problems. He had run against Sheriff Duff, lost and was currently a used truck salesman and now a candidate for the Sheriff's Office for the third time.

Alice and Parker Jones, my previous campaign managers, were now deceased. The principal at the school where Jeannie taught had retired and was looking for something to keep her active. A political campaign seemed to fit the bill, so Marcee Osteen agreed to come help and coordinate the re-election effort. Jeannie would do a lot of the work as in 1988. We decided to decentralize the campaign this time and had area coordinators to drum up local support. It was likely going to be much lower key than the first campaign. We had to take Ralph Henshaw seriously, but this time I had the advantage of being the incumbent Sheriff with a record to run on. I wasn't worried about the *Sentinel's* influence. They had made very little impact in Volusia County and during the campaign, I would have the advantage of being able to show people what we were actually doing night after night on the Interstate and throughout the county.

This campaign wouldn't last as long as the 1988 effort did. There would be no primary since there were only two candidates. We would go right to the ballot in November, so the early months (August, September) would be devoted more to fund raising and setting up area coordinators. I would run as a proven leader on our office's accomplishments. The charge in 1988 that I had no administrative experience was not going to be used this time. Instead, Henshaw would concentrate on the *Sentinel* stories and the Helen McConnell shooting.

No one expected an easy campaign, even though we didn't think the *Sentinel* stories would be much of a factor, and there was no comparison from a law enforcement experience standpoint between Henshaw and I. But we weren't taking the campaign lightly, and it would give me a chance to get out amongst the citizens of our county and take their pulse as to the job we were doing for them in the Sheriff's Office.

What we could not predict was how nasty this campaign would eventually become. I'm a positive campaigner. I like to run on my accomplishments and ideas and not simply spend the time pointing out the weaknesses of my opponent. Henshaw took the opposite approach. Not having much to run on, it was easier for him to try and run down my campaign and divert attention away from his own lack of ability as a strategy to take the top law enforcement position in the county.

He played up the *Sentinel* stories and editorials as much as he could. He also used the Helen McConnell shooting to portray what he termed a lack of leadership at the top. This was the extent of his campaign planning aside from a concerted effort by someone to tear down as many of our campaign signs as possible during the last two months before the election.

As the campaign moved on towards November, a disturbing trend was unfolding. I had, as previously noted, instituted a progressive discipline structure within the Sheriff's Office. There was some fallout from that procedural change. One deputy had been fired for falsifying time cards and becoming involved with stolen equipment. Another had been terminated for beating a suspect held in his custody. Others had received letters of reprimand for their files. In my determination to make the Sheriff's Office a professional law enforcement agency, there had been a few deputies that didn't measure up to these standards, and they were not thriving in the new atmosphere. Almost all of those deputies who had been fired or received significant discipline sided with Henshaw during the campaign. They were generally present at the campaign rallies and proved to be an intimidating force to some of our loyal supporters.

In addition to wayward deputies, Henshaw also received support from some individuals who had been arrested, including a bar owner who was arrested for drugs. Henshaw drew support from a motorcycle group when he told them he wouldn't arrest them for not wearing a helmet, even though this was a Florida law he would be sworn in to uphold.

Candidate forums showed a profound difference between those that stood for Henshaw and those that rallied behind me. It was a fascinating and scary contrast.

Our supporters would often complain of being tailgated by motorcycle riders because they had "Vote Vogel" bumper stickers on their cars. Others thought they were being followed. Jeannie, teaching at a local elementary school, was being stalked. Sheila, attending high school, had the same problem. Signs that read, "Dump Vogel" or, "Remember Helen McConnell" were carried outside our rallies like picketers on strike. With or without Henshaw's knowledge, his intimidation campaign was beginning to have an effect on us all. My staff wanted a deputy with me at all times in the event that Henshaw's people tried something. I had been through Vietnam and years on the interstate late at night arresting drug dealers, and it was absurd to me that I now might need a bodyguard during an election campaign. But I occasionally agreed to the extra security, depending on the situation. I was more concerned for Jeannie and Sheila. Sheila was met by her school's resource officer each day and a number of people watched her car throughout the time while she was in school. Jeannie was under a similar watchful eye.

This extracurricular activity during the campaign would have been enough. But there was an additional unrelated twist that unraveled during this time period, adding to what was already a strange election run.

A local businessman named C.R. "Dick" Powell had been having a long-standing feud with a rancher named Clyde Hart over a piece of land called the

Cape Atlantic Estates, located between Oak Hill and Maytown in Volusia County. This land had been marked for development, and about 5,000 people had bought some property here by phone or mail over a five-year period from 1967 to 1972. Neither roads nor utilities had been put in at the time, as is now required to sell property today. The landowners were stuck with their land when the developer folded in the early 1970s. Poachers, timber thieves and others started in on this vacant property, and there seemed little the absentee owners could do about it.

Dick Powell offered these 5,000 owners a management service in 1981. He started the Cape Atlantic Landowners Association and collected hundreds of thousands in fees to maintain the vast property and protect it from others. Powell also bought some of the property from owners who just wanted out of the deal.

Hart also acquired some of the property through an auction to satisfy tax liens on the bankrupt developer. Hart now became the largest landowner in the Cape Atlantic Estates. It was the beginning of a long-standing battle between the two men that involved Hart pulling a gun on Powell and Powell cutting a fence on Hart's property. Both men had sued the other and significant time in civil court had been spent trying to work out a suitable agreement between the two. It was a re-birth of the old Hatfield-McCoy feud.

Some of Powell's friends left his side to join Hart in the legal battle. One of those was Bruce Best. His testimony and others stated that Powell, acting alone or as an agent for the Cape Atlantic Landowners Association, cut fences, started fires, put out spikes in the road, defrauded association members, forged documents and aided drug dealers. Powell claimed that Best was retaliating against him because he was foreclosing on some property he was selling to Best.

This mess stretched into the early 1990s and became a factor in my campaign when Volusia County deputies arrested Dick Powell and seized his helicopter in May 1992. The arrest was sparked by Powell's helicopter buzzing Best and his girlfriend because Powell believed Best's trailer was parked on his land. Powell said he was just getting close enough to photograph the trailer to prove its location was within Powell property.

He got a little too close. Best was trying to ward off the helicopter with a rake. Best's hog was killed running head on into a tree to escape the helicopter's swirling presence. His girlfriend was knocked down by the gusts of wind generated by the helicopter's blades, injuring her back in the process. Best put his girlfriend in his station wagon to drive her to the hospital and Powell's helicopter buzzed the car while it was traveling down Maytown Road. Two tree-trimmers, working on Maytown Road, witnessed this action and were nearly hit themselves. Our deputies arrested Powell, seized his helicopter under the forfeiture law and charged him with operating an aircraft in a careless and unsafe manner, a third-degree felony.

Powell claimed we damaged his aircraft after we seized it. We eventually returned the aircraft and the county gave him a check for $20,000 to cover the cost of any repairs. Powell penned a lengthy letter to members of the local Volusia County Pilots Association, alleging that the Sheriff abused both his rights and his helicopter and was a threat to all pilots in the county. His introductory sentence read, "Sheriff Vogel's disregard for your rights and his ignorance of the Federal Aviation Regulations can land you in jail!" He included some of the *Sentinel's* editorials, including the editorial entitled, "Vogel—Volusia's Shame."

I ultimately responded with a letter to all of these same association members assuring them that our deputies arrested Powell and seized his helicopter because he threatened the safety of several people. I pointed out he could have caused harm to himself, his pilot and his aircraft in an effort to chase Bruce Best away from what he felt was his land. If Best was squatting, there were many legal ways to have him removed that didn't include trying to re-enact the famous plane scene from Alfred Hitchcock's film, "North by Northwest."

But Powell wasn't done. At the Adam's Mark Hotel on Daytona Beach during a candidates' reception, a plane flew over with a "Vote for Ted Doran" sign, indicating its support for Doran in his run for the state attorney's office against John Tanner. A second plane financed by Powell flew over with a sign three times larger than Doran's that read "Dump Vogel." After a momentary silence, I said, "The difference here, Ted, is that you paid for your sign and I didn't."

That plane flew over Volusia County a number of times in the days leading up to the election. At one point, Jeannie had her elementary school class outside for recess and the plane appeared with its, "Dump Vogel" sign. That was not easy to explain to a group of school children. There was also a billboard on Route 1, a heavily traveled road leading into New Smyrna Beach where Powell bought billboard space and put up a sign that read, "Volusia's Shame—Dump Vogel." I had to admit it was a little disheartening riding by and seeing that sign up every day. Whether Powell even knew Henshaw was immaterial. He had become Henshaw's biggest supporter.

One morning as Jeannie drove to campaign headquarters, she noticed the billboard had been altered to, "Volusia's Fame—Pump Vogel." She was surprised and immediately began calling around to find out if anyone in our campaign had marked up the sign. No one admitted to it, even though Powell claimed it had to have been someone in the Vogel campaign. We found out after the election that Clyde Hart, the colorful local character who owned the New Smyrna Beach Speedway and significant amounts of land and cattle, was responsible for the alteration of the billboard. He was not one of our supporters, but there was no love lost between he and Dick Powell, prompting his action to change the billboard. We were glad it was not anyone in our campaign, since we had spoken outwardly and forcibly against doing anything in retaliation even though Henshaw's people were ripping down our signs repeatedly.

We had a safe lead in the polls as October wound down. I thought I'd win, but the edge of intimidation around the campaign and the nastiness of it were disturbing. During the last week, Sheila received a death threat. Concerned for her safety, Jeannie and I took her to stay with Jeannie's sister until the election was over. The year had seen an unprecedented number of attacks on my family and I, from the slanted stories of the *Sentinel* to stalkers from the Henshaw campaign to planes flying overhead and billboards with derogatory messages. But death threats! These were desperate acts and all the scarier because it seemed Henshaw's supporters could see the end result was not going to go their way. Jeannie took a leave of absence from her school during this last couple of campaign weeks to maintain a low profile as much as she could.

Not surprisingly, the *Orlando Sentinel* came out in favor of Henshaw in a Sunday, October 11 editorial that read, "Henshaw deserves a chance." The *News Journal*, eager to be contradictory to its competitor, endorsed me this time. They had opted for Ouellette in 1988. In their article, the *Sentinel* portrayed themselves as the local conscience of the area who came in to Volusia County to ensure the safe passage of innocent motorists through our county. I was beginning to think they actually believed that.

While Volusia County residents didn't read the *Sentinel*, listeners to WNDB radio in Daytona Beach had a chance to hear Ralph Henshaw personally on a daily afternoon talk show hosted by local resident Marc Bernier. Marc conducted an interview with the candidate and was astonished at Henshaw's lack of knowledge and inability to give a straight answer to any meaningful question. Clearly, listeners to the show heard what they would be getting for Sheriff if they voted for Henshaw and it was not a pretty sound. Bernier could only shake his head at the *Sentinel* endorsement of Henshaw for Sheriff and he told me later that it made the entire endorsement process by newspapers a joke. It would no longer carry the same meaning for him in the future.

Henshaw continued his campaign of intimidation to the end. At a fundraising event for me, Henshaw supporters handed out a flyer that took "nasty" to another level. On one side of the flyer was a diatribe against me and an encouragement to any reader of the piece to boycott the sponsors of the event whose names appeared on the reverse side of the flyer. All of the fine people who had contributed money to hold the fundraiser were listed from individuals to local businesses. Words in the flyer referred to me as a Nazi and even featured a picture of Adolf Hitler with my name inscribed below it, flanked by two other members of the Third Reich labeled as "Butterworth" and "Anderson", for Bob Butterworth and Dale Anderson. At the bottom of the page was this postscript: "Please, no Jews, Blacks, Hispanics or Old White People are invited to my reception."

I felt badly for my supporters who were named on the flyer and called, "closet racists, Ku Klux Klan members, Nazis and Hatemongers." Actually, the flyer called them "closeted racists", and while grammar was not the point of this hateful piece, it portrayed the ignorance that permeated throughout the message.

At this fundraiser, *Sentinel* reporter Jeff Brazil sneaked through a side door into this invitation-only event. As noted earlier, he was a small, mousy sort and was able to keep a low profile, surreptitiously pulling over people to ask them about me. That the *Sentinel* would resort to this kind of reporting practice was no longer surprising in the wake of the June and August articles they had printed.

I had made every effort to keep the campaign at as high a level as possible and avoid the mudraking that Henshaw apparently reveled in. But my supporters and residents of the county deserved an explanation as to who Ralph Henshaw was and what he stood for. My campaign followed up his flyer with a brochure of our own called, "Just the Facts."

In it, we took all of the known public records about Ralph Henshaw—proven facts —and put them beside my own records. We began at formal education, where I was a college graduate and Henshaw had received a GED (General Equivalency Diploma). My military service and awards showed my Vietnam veteran's status and ten military medals and citations I received. Henshaw was discharged after serving 19 months of a three-year enlistment with the label "unfit for further military service" due to tampering with an ID card, failure to obey an order and poor character. My law enforcement career and honors were well documented and numerous. Henshaw had been fired by Sheriff Duff in 1979, an action that was upheld by the Fifth District Court of Appeals of Florida who stated, "It is clear that but for Henshaw's position as a sheriff's lieutenant, he would have been arrested as the result of his conduct." He had been cited for smoking marijuana, witnessing drug transactions without taking proper action, warning a friend to get rid of stolen items before a raid, acts of gross profanity and indecency in a Deland barroom, firing into a fleeing vehicle even though he knew it contained two police informants, and interfering in a murder case by providing the defense with documents and vital information prior to the prosecutor's review, among many other violations. For this stellar career, he had earned the endorsement of the *Orlando Sentinel*.

The flyer concluded with a quiz:

"Which candidate was labeled "unfit for military service" and given a general discharge from the U.S. Air Force after serving just 19 months of a three-year enlistment?"

"Which candidate was fired as a deputy from the Volusia County Sheriff's Department?"

"Which sheriff candidate promised to remove derogatory information from a defendant's case file before a court appearance?"

"Which candidate tipped off a friend to dispose of stolen property prior to a planned Sheriff's department raid?"

Naturally the answer to all four questions was Ralph Henshaw. The brochure concluded with the question, "As a resident of Volusia County, which of the candidates, Vogel or Henshaw, would you want to serve as your Sheriff?"

It bothered me that I had to use the flyer. But residents of the county were getting skewed information from Henshaw, and I simply put public records down on paper for all to see who the real Ralph Henshaw was and what it would mean to Volusia County to put him in charge of the Sheriff's office.

Despite the intimidation, Henshaw was not making up any ground in the polls. He continued to trail me by a wide percentage. His tactics were starting to blow up around him. At a local election candidates forum, our campaign manager Marcee Osteen asked Henshaw a pointed question, "Isn't it illegal to promise jobs to people during a campaign?" Henshaw replied that he knew that and wouldn't do it. Jeannie made it a point to look directly at a couple of the deputies fired by our office and saw their faces pale at Henshaw's reply. An ex-deputy's wife left the room at that point, tears streaming down her face. In Jeannie's mind, these men had been promised their jobs back by Henshaw, and he was publicly refuting it now because he had no choice in this forum.

I won on Election Tuesday. Henshaw didn't get much support and, in the end, I received 70 percent of the votes cast. Local residents were not thrown by the stories in the *Sentinel* and the feeling I'd carried away from talking to people of Volusia County during the campaign was that they were pleased with the results we were getting. They didn't want Volusia County to be a pathway for drug trafficking any more than I did and were glad to see us making some inroads in the war against drugs.

We had watched the election results at the Pelican Bay Country Club. In 1988, we had viewed them from inside our tiny campaign headquarters where supporters jammed in and few people could actually see a screen. This time we rented three televisions and the race was over early. Our attentions turned to the presidential race, and I was frankly surprised that George Bush was losing to Bill Clinton. Little did I realize how the results of that election would affect my next term as Sheriff. With the election of Clinton came a host of new appointments to oversee law enforcement in this country. Some of them would wield a great deal of influence over the interdiction work we were doing on Interstate 95.

The *Orlando Sentinel* was disappointed. They ran a story that headlined, "Vogel: Voters ignored cash seizure stories." The article went on to quote Dick Powell, who called Henshaw an "out of the ozone" candidate with little chance of winning. The consensus was that a candidate who was less vulnerable to criticism could have had more of an impact. For all I knew, the search for my 1996 opponent had already begun. Perhaps the *Sentinel* would run a boxed advertisement as they were currently doing to find witnesses for the Governor's Panel. The 1992 election was history and my attention turned back to the Governor's Panel, who had held a few meetings but now stepped up their work since I won re-election and would be Volusia County's Sheriff for the next four years.

My first term involved bringing the department up to professional standards. This second term was going to be devoted to defending its honor.

≈ ≈

The Panel Review

While the re-election campaign was accelerating towards its November conclusion, there was plenty of activity with the Governor's Panel. It was formed after Governor Chiles was sent the June articles from the *Orlando Sentinel* and he had spent the summer appointing people to be on this review board.

The *Sentinel* continued to play a major role in the affair, well beyond their supposed duty to report news fairly and without bias. First, the articles that spawned the committee were slanted, misleading and incorrect. Second, they strongly encouraged the Governor to take some action. Third, they disagreed with the make-up of the panel and lobbied vigorously and successfully for additional minority members. Fourth, they launched a search via their newspaper for anyone who felt their rights had been violated on Interstate 95, encouraging them to come forward and tell their story.

The panel's charge was to look into forfeiture law actions across the state, but it was clear to us early on that the only law enforcement agency they were going to investigate was ours. Apparently, there wasn't as much concern for the tactics used by other police departments in the state. From the minute those articles appeared in June, this was a "Get Vogel" crusade.

Well, I was ready. I was confident in the process we used and knew that it would stand up under any scrutiny. At this point all I wanted was a chance to tell our side of the story, as the *Sentinel* articles were the only public word to date on our drug and cash interdiction program.

There was just one problem. The panel didn't tell us when their first hearing was being held. We called the Governor's office after the fact, was told it was an oversight, received an apology and were assured that we would be told of the second session.

Again, we were not notified. Ironically, we heard about it from a reporter and Nancye (Ege) Jones, our agency's legal attorney and I simply showed up.

The individual appointed as chairman of the panel was Ed Dunn, a lawyer, and a former Democratic legislator from Volusia County. His politics were important to him and he typically didn't see beyond that. I was a Republican, and Governor Chiles was a Democrat, so I knew that the political odds were stacked against me on this panel. I'd always tried to look past the party affiliation and simply voted for the best possible candidate. As a result, I'd voted both Republican and Democrat in recent elections. The chances of Ed Dunn voting for a Republican were so small as to not be measurable.

Dunn had run against Bob Butterworth for Attorney General in 1986 and lost. During this campaign, he actually rode with me one night while I was a state trooper making I-95 stops by myself. That could be a positive for me on this panel. At least Dunn had seen the procedures I used.

But I'd long been a strong supporter of Butterworth. He had served as a role model for me when I was a state trooper, and I liked working with him now as Attorney General. He always tried to do what he knew was the right thing for individuals and crime victims. This didn't always win him any popularity contests. He tried to recognize the bigger picture, not just the law enforcement side, and acted with the public's best interests at heart. Without a doubt, he's had the varied experience to help him with his decision-making. He's been a legal advisor to the Sheriff's office, a county and circuit judge, mayor, Sheriff himself (of Broward County), head of the Department of Highway Safety and Motor Vehicles, and now Attorney General. Dunn had been overmatched in his race against Butterworth.

But Dunn was running this show, in name anyway. The panelist frequently quoted in the *Sentinel* was Chiles' general counsel, J. Hardin Peterson, weighing in early on his feelings about our team's efforts on I-95. He told reporters he had heard complaints from all over the state and that while he didn't want to pre-judge the panel's conclusion, he felt that our office had gone too far in following the state forfeiture law. Of course, he hadn't talked to anyone in our office about our procedures for cash and drug seizure. Didn't want to prejudge? Right.

One of the first people to testify before the panel was the chairman of the state House Criminal Justice Committee, a Democrat from Tampa named Elvin Martinez. So, too, did Susan Somers, an attorney for the Florida Department of Law Enforcement who would be giving the panel an overview of the state forfeiture law. We were scheduled to testify some time later in the year.

They did at least hear some of my comments that the *Sentinel* articles were way off base. The panel decided to independently review both the cases and the videotapes that the *Sentinel* had reported on. I thought that was a positive move in the right direction. At least they could see that what the newspaper had reported bore little resemblance to the facts. All it had done was rile people up for the wrong reasons. I was also interested in Chiles' counsel's statement that complaints were coming in from all over the state. What did that mean exactly? Complaints about our agency? If so, apparently those who lodged their gripes with the state weren't interested in testifying because, to the best of our knowledge, the only individuals scheduled to testify so far in addition to me were attorneys.

It took them some time to review the information. In addition, they prepared a list of questions for me to answer about our program. I was given a deadline and met it, despite being in the middle of a reelection campaign and running the Sheriff's office.

But the *Sentinel* took another shot at me prior to my testimony. I faxed our responses to the panel's extensive questions on the day it was due. The *Sentinel*, however, reported otherwise. In an editorial entitled, "Vogel's shameful lack of regard", they wrote that I didn't respond in time because some of my employees were on leave. They said it was "scandalous that I was showing little regard for the state panel charged with looking into this mess."

I shouldn't have been surprised. This newspaper had already shown a consistent disregard for the truth. Why would this be any different? Our office did call to advise that, once again, they were wrong, and the list of responses had been faxed to the panel. The editor said they would print a retraction. They did. It was in small print, tucked away on the inside of the newspaper. They had already accomplished what they wanted.

The newspaper did have some concern that their information might be disputed. They attempted to short-circuit the effort to get at the truth of their reporting by writing in another editorial that "the danger" of this review "is that panel members may get swept up in a debate over inconsequential data and lose sight of the big picture." Inconsequential data? It was these incorrect statistics upon which their entire story was based. These were desperate words now. It was published the week after I had trounced Ralph Henshaw in the Sheriff's race, and these latest comments could be a result of their disappointment in that outcome.

In November, we finally testified before the panel. Nancye Jones (who had married one of our Special Enforcement Team deputies, Bobby Jones) took the panel through the process by which we determine probable cause to seize cash under the state forfeiture laws. It wasn't as simple as the *Sentinel* made it sound and we were careful not to confiscate money where some doubt might exist as to its origins. We only acted on the forfeiture law if we felt there was overwhelming evidence that the money was earmarked for an illegal transaction. Nancye receives calls at all hours from deputies in the middle of an investigation to inquire about whether probable cause existed to make a seizure.

During her testimony, Peterson, the Governors' counsel, asked Nancye if her husband minded that she received all these calls from strange men in the middle of the night. That sexist remark had no place in these proceedings and said more about Peterson than anything else. I was not pleased with the comment, but Nancye brushed it off like the true professional she was.

Nancye's husband, Deputy Bobby Jones, testified as did Leonard Davis. The *Sentinel* wouldn't talk to the big-framed man, but this panel interviewed him. Leonard reiterated that the team did not stop anyone based on race and told the panel that he resented any implication that it did. "Under no circumstances," he said, "do we tolerate bigotry from anyone in the department." He also advised that the videotapes were periodically reviewed to be sure rights weren't being violated.

It felt good to tell our side of it. There were panel members whose minds were made up before we spoke, and it was doubtful we changed any of their thinking. Those with an open mind, though, were doubtlessly swayed by the honesty and integrity of what we were trying to do, within the legal constraints, in the fight against drugs. Naturally, the *Sentinel* took issue with our comments to the panel and headlined their latest editorial the next day with, "Vogel is out of step, out of line." But the only one out of control was the newspaper itself, and they couldn't see that they had stopped reporting the news and had begun trying to create it.

The panel continued to hear testimony, but only from other attorneys. One Daytona Beach attorney, Paul Dubelled, testified and he said he was aware of the inner workings of the interdiction team. He was unfamiliar to us and Nancye felt certain he had never defended anyone in a forfeiture case. Later, she checked and verified this. He had never represented anyone stopped on I-95, but he was allowed to weigh in with his testimony on the process.

The panel review dragged on into December. Interestingly, one person called in to testify was Cary Copeland, head of the U.S. Justice Department's asset forfeiture program in Washington, D.C. He told the panel that forfeiture took the profits out of crime and was a key ingredient to waging a successful war on drugs. He also cautioned the panel not to rely on the distorted statistics provided by the *Sentinel*. He illustrated a case that he was personally involved in where the *Sentinel* had misconstrued information and published erroneous data. He had called the newspaper's editors to tell them their facts weren't accurate and would mislead the reading public, but they were indifferent to his protests. It was compelling testimony here, though, and substantiated a lot of the comments that we at the Sheriff's Office had made.

Copeland also pointed out the sad fact that a disproportionate number of minorities were engaged in the illegal drug trade here in the United States. That, he told the panel, was a sociological reality. He felt a lack of higher education and poverty pushed more minorities into a life of crime. He said that you couldn't criticize a law enforcement program that arrested more minorities than whites if the minorities were more involved in the criminal process. It would be more suspicious if the arrest numbers were higher for whites than minorities.

This was similar to comments that Leonard Davis had made. He had often said if the person you happen to catch transporting drugs or cash to buy drugs was a minority, that didn't get him or her a free pass.

The panel continued to hear testimony from lawyers, but not people actually stopped on I-95. After the *Sentinel* ran their plea for plaintiffs day after day in their newspaper, no one who had been stopped on I-95 had come forward to testify before the panel. If our program was targeting innocent people and violating civil rights on a regular basis, you would think it would be easy to find people willing to speak out against our team. But, to this point, there was only silence.

The panel finally came up with a series of reform recommendations. They planned to send to the Governor several ideas that could be drafted into legislation to amend the current state forfeiture law. These reforms included:

- requiring law enforcement agencies to pay attorney fees if they lost a court battle over a seizure;
- require agencies to make seizures a natural outgrowth of law enforcement work rather than the primary purpose of any operation;
- outlaw the hiring of lawyers to handle seizure cases for the law enforcement agency on a contingency fee basis (apparently about 10 percent of the state's agencies do this—ours does not);
- prohibit out-of-court settlements without judicial review;
- require agencies to establish in-house review panels to investigate complaints;
- require that agencies adopt FDLE standards as guidelines for seizing money (although these were similar to current law).

They rejected some ideas individual panel members proposed, such as requiring the deposit of the seized money into a state trust fund and outlawing seizures not related to an arrest or specific felony.

That they hadn't made any specific recommendations about our department's procedures infuriated the *Sentinel*. In an editorial published before specifics of these reforms were decided, the editors wrote that the panel needed to "propose major changes in the law." They said that I was a "zealot who uses racist practices to collect money" and that the only way to "stop my abuses of the law was to have a grand jury investigate them when the panel finishes its work." The article was called, "Hammer or rubber stamp" and the *Sentinel* was obviously upset that only a few reform recommendations would be coming out of the panel, even though the task force had not finished meeting yet. I guess they had a pipeline into the group and knew what lay ahead and they didn't like it.

The newspaper wasn't giving up. In a long article published just before Christmas 1992, they wrote a profile of me calling for a state, Congressional and legal investigation into our agency's activities. They even published my high school grades that were admittedly lacking in some areas. In typical selective fashion, they withheld my college grades that were far better. They were out, as they had been all year, to create an impression of me and no facts to the contrary were going to get in the way of their misleading profile.

When the panel released its recommendations publicly, the *Sentinel* was further angered. They even disparaged the strongest reform suggestion, that of requiring agencies that lose a seizure case in court to pay the plaintiff's court fees. They felt that would actually discourage people from taking the agency to court since if the individual lost that person would have to pay the agency's court fees. Naturally there was the usual chance to call me someone who "tramples people's rights and unfairly seizes property from people who haven't been charged with a crime."

Cash seizures had slowed dramatically since the *Sentinel* articles were published. The resulting widespread publicity had caused drug dealers to shift their routes. It certainly didn't make sense for them to bring their drugs and cash through Interstate 95 if there was a good chance they were going to lose it. They weren't dumb. We were on the Interstate conducting our usual law enforcement activity, but the illegal activity had simply slowed down. This was the whole point of our efforts. To win the war on drugs, you had to discourage the deals. We were doing that, hurting the dealer in the best possible way by lightening their pocketbook.

I also wanted our deputies to document the illegal stop by writing up the warning or ticket more frequently when the stop was made. We would also try to catch the traffic violation on tape rather than start the video after the stop is made. I also intended to have a weekly review of videotapes and seizures to continually evaluate our effectiveness. I advised Ed Dunn of these intended changes. He felt these modifications addressed most of the panel's concerns.

Even as the panel was publishing its final recommendations, the Florida House Criminal Justice chairman was already rejecting them out of hand. Elvin Martinez, who had testified at an earlier panel meeting, said he wasn't interested in passing legislation requiring the loser in a seizure case to pay all court proceedings. He was in favor, though, of having all seized money go directly into the state treasury. Of course, that would take the forfeiture funds away from law enforcement use and require taxpayers to pay more to financially support their local agency. Seized money has meant that drug dealers are ironically helping to pay the local costs to fight crime. Martinez wanted to end that.

The panel's final comments were anti-climatic after all of the *Sentinel* buildup. The panel lauded our agency for our commitment against the war on drugs and for making some modifications to our interdiction procedures. They said nothing about racial bias or civil rights violations or any investigation into our department. There was nothing to find on any of those scores, so these results didn't surprise us. But I'm sure the newspaper was disappointed, although they had already written the panel off a few weeks earlier.

Peterson, the Governor's counsel, said a few things at the final panel press conference that shocked us. He said there was not enough here to remove the Sheriff from office. That was a stunning revelation of Peterson's belief in what the panel was all about. Set up to review statewide forfeiture law practices, the panel concentrated only on my agency. I guess they didn't find what they wanted! We had prided ourselves on being the most successful agency enforcing the forfeiture law to put a dent in the drug trade and we looked at our program as an example of what was being done right in this area, not wrong.

The Governor's panel was through. Their review had resulted in the testimony of five criminal defense attorneys, one civil attorney, three law enforcement agency attorneys, and one citizen whose property (an airplane) was seized for forfeiture without any connection to Interstate 95. No one who had property seized on I-95 appeared before the committee to complain despite a concerted effort to encourage the attendance of any and all who felt wronged by the law or the Volusia County Sheriff's office.

The panel's report had given our program a clean bill of health and congratulated us on our fine-tuning of the program to put it on even more solid ground. This report essentially rejected the *Sentinel's* public claims of racism and violations of civil rights. Did the *Sentinel* print that?

Of course not. Their headline read, "Vogel Panel Disbands: He's Cleaned Up His Act." That comment was Peterson's and the *Sentinel* used it to show in print that they were right all along. Newspapers have the last word in any public discussion and they exercised it here, claiming credit for bringing this situation to light. That there was never anything to bring to light in the first place was something that would likely never find it's way into print.

Two of the twenty-four short paragraphs the *Sentinel* devoted to the panel's findings restated the original charges the newspaper had made. Nowhere did they say that the panel did not substantiate these charges. Nearly half the article covered a separate event, that of the showing to a Florida legislative committee a three-hour videotape of our traffic stops. The committee watched two stops and members were quoted in the *Sentinel* as saying that they were disgusted and outraged. These were carefully edited tapes that did not show the entire procedure nor did they show all of the stops made, all of which would have made for a less biased viewing.

The tapes were edited by the Reverend George Crossley, a local Christian radio and TV host who was publicly campaigning to have me removed from office. He was a close friend of one of the *Orlando Sentinel's* editors, and had been able to obtain copies of the videotapes. His editing of the tapes matched the *Sentinel's* interpretation of the stops. When the facts didn't suit your story, you altered the evidence. Crossley was likely motivated by the great opportunity the tapes provided to boost the ratings of his shows.

We were no strangers to Crossley. Back during the 1992 campaign, he attended a candidate's forum held at a local church. Jeannie was there and after the event she was standing in the parking lot talking to some of our supporters. Crossley came out, got in his black sedan, and drove straight towards Jeannie. Only Charlie Griffy's saving hand pulled Jeannie out of the car's way. Since Jeannie was not in the path that Crossley needed to drive to exit the parking lot, we could only assume the act was deliberate. Now, he was trying to run us over on the airwaves.

The local Volusia paper, the *Daytona Beach News Journal,* was more objective about the results. Their headline read, "Cash Seizure Policy Gets Panel OK". One panel member was quoted as saying that there wasn't any evidence of or any ongoing systematic abuse of minorities. They even quoted Peterson as saying, "I really don't see any basis at this point in time for the governor to chastise Sheriff Vogel for what he's done." Naturally, this newspaper was probably secretly pleased that the *Sentinel* articles had been invalidated.

The panel may have been through, but the *Sentinel* was not. There were still plenty of sympathetic ears to pour their story out to and to continue to try and give their reporting credibility through some type of legal action.

∼ ∼

WORKING ON ALL FRONTS

Back in June, the *Sentinel* had made every effort to get Congress to look at the national forfeiture laws. The Governor's panel had heard from Cary Copeland, the head of the U.S. Justice Department's asset forfeiture program, who had pointed out that taking the profit out of crime is one of the best ways to deter illegal activity. It was hard to argue that point, thus the *Sentinel* concentration on racism as a motivation for interdiction teams like ours. That would be more likely to get Congress' attention. Congressman Jim Bacchus of Florida was doing his best to try and bring the *Sentinel* story to national prominence.

Shortly after Copeland's testimony before the Governor's Panel, I called him in his Washington, D.C. office to offer my thanks for his remarks. I was stunned to find him packing up. Cary said he had just been informed that his position had been eliminated and that the federal government was doing away with the asset forfeiture program. He told me he had been assigned to an entirely new position within the Department of Justice. He seemed to be shocked by the news and I wondered if his testimony at the panel had anything to do with this sudden reassignment.

In August 1992, Jeff Brazil had written a lengthy article entitled "Forfeiture laws seize national scorn." In the piece, he talked about Volusia County and also cited examples of seizure abuses across the country. He reiterated his charge of racism against us and stated that Congress was expected to hold hearings soon to review if blacks, Hispanics and other minorities were being targeted, if innocent people were victimized, and if police put more emphasis on seizing cash than on fighting crime.

They had found a willing listener in Michigan Democratic Congressman John Conyers. At this time Conyers, an African-American, was upset that nearly $30 million in U.S. Justice Department expenditures was paid to informants over the previous two years. He was quoted as saying that "the idea of the forfeiture fund was to make the dealers pay for the war on drugs, not to provide a windfall for profiteering middlemen who may well be using the money for additional criminal activities." He vowed to start hearings into the forfeiture laws as soon as possible.

By the time he did convene hearings in late September 1992, he was a well-read *Sentinel* reader. After the first day of hearings, he was quoted in the *Sentinel* as saying that the Volusia County Sheriff's Office was an example of priorities gone awry. He said getting cash off the streets instead of drugs was not the way to fight this war. He also stated that he would probably be contacting Governor Chiles about it. Whether he ever did or not, the Congressional hearings gave way to re-election campaigns that fall of 1992. Critics of the forfeiture laws were concerned that their constituents might view them as being soft on crime, so there was no hurry to investigate.

On the state side, the Florida legislature now had some recommendations from the Governor's panel. In a late February 1993 editorial, the *Sentinel* called the panel "spineless and disappointing." They also said the panel's recommendations were "wimpy" and looked to Representative Elvin Martinez for leadership now on this issue.

In late March, Martinez' committee turned out a bill that adopted some of the panel's recommendations. These included the payment of attorney fees by either the law enforcement agency or the individual depending on the outcome, and requiring development of consistent, statewide policy guidelines and training on how to enforce the forfeiture laws.

The Florida House was looking at a bill proposed by Democratic representative Jimmy Charles of Ormond Beach. His bill incorporated most of the panel's suggestions except allowing the county or circuit court to handle seizures under $15,000 and the abolishment of attorneys being able to work for law enforcement agencies on these cases on a contingency fee basis.

Charles' bill passed the House and a similar bill that was sponsored by Locke Burt, a Republican from Ormond Beach was passed by the Senate. There were some technical differences to work out, however, to have a final bill that could be voted on by both houses and sent to Governor Chiles. But these differences were not worked out to the satisfaction of Florida Senate lawmakers and nothing came out of all that effort in the spring.

The U.S. Supreme Court itself acted in June 1993 on the forfeiture law issue. In a unanimous decision, the Court ruled that cash and property forfeitures were limited by the constitutional prohibition on excessive punishments. Seizures would be legal if they did not exceed the amount of a potential fine had the owner been convicted. Forfeiture was part of the punishment for a wrong, the Justices said. The Supreme Court ruling was the result of a South Dakota case where a man entered a guilty plea for a single count of possession of cocaine with intent to sell. In a civil proceeding after the criminal trial, the man's house and auto repair business was seized.

This would have some effect on our I-95 interdiction team cash seizures. The state of Florida, however, would have to publish guidelines on the amounts that would be considered excessive punishment to the crime.

In April 1993, the *Sentinel* finally received some recognition for their reporting efforts. Their stories on our team's activities had been originally filed for Pulitzer Prize consideration under the "human interest" category in 1992. But that was the year Hurricane Andrew roared through South Florida and the series of stories that followed by the *Miami Herald* seemed to have a lock on that award. So the *Sentinel* submission was moved to a different category—investigative reporting—and Jeff Brazil and Steve Berry won the Pulitzer Prize for their stories in that classification.

It gave the newspaper a chance to run their headlines again, "Tainted cash or easy money" and to say that the Sheriff had "all but" stopped his interdiction practice after their reports. "All but" of course is a clever term, disguising the truth that the slanted reports hadn't altered anything, but cost taxpayers a substantial amount of time investigating a department that was making an extraordinary impact in the war on drugs.

How could the Pulitzer Prize be awarded to a story that was largely contrived? Facts were altered, errors printed, and there were material omissions that would have changed the reader's perspective. For this, a newspaper won the top journalism award? Like Governor Chiles, apparently the judges simply read the articles and didn't bother looking into the validity of them. Of course, one of the judges was the *Chicago Tribune*, the owner of the *Orlando Sentinel*. You can be sure that didn't hurt their chances.

You would think the Pulitzer committee would be a little more cautious about bestowing this award after the *Washington Post* voluntarily returned its prize given to reporter Janet Cooke for her story on an 8 year-old heroin addict that she eventually confessed was made up. The *Sentinel* didn't make up their story, but they used their own pre-determined conclusion and attempted to twist facts into shape to fit that premise, even though their "investigative reporting" should have shown them it was false. They should have received the Pulitzer Prize for fiction.

I would no longer have the same feeling for this "prestigious" award.

We hadn't "all but" changed anything in our interdiction efforts. Deputies were documenting better and we were reviewing tapes and seizures more regularly, but these were all a part of fine-tuning the team's work. The essential procedures stayed the same and were still resulting in successes.

In separate seizures on I-95 in 1993, we had found $35,000 in suspected drug money after suspicions were alerted following the stop of a car without a visible license tag. $20,000 of the money was concealed inside a panel in the car and another $15,000 was in a passenger's purse. In another case, a police K-9 dog alerted to the presence of drug residue on nearly $25,000 in a tan leather bag in a North Carolina car stopped for an improper lane change. Another stop for an expired license tag resulted in a crack cocaine arrest as the driver attempted to hide a bag under his car after the stop.

These were the types of cases we were making in our efforts to battle drugs in our county. We had made our area safer for residents and drug dealers were instructing their mules to avoid our county at all costs. These were efforts we were making before, during and after the *Sentinel* stories.

The newspaper celebrated its award, but wasn't through trying to bring credibility outside of journalistic circles to their stories. In 1993, at long last, they found two people willing to pursue legal action against our office for I-95 stops: Selena Washington and Jorge Nater.

≈ ≈

A CIVIL ACTION

After the Governor's Panel, Jeannie and I had decided to take a long overdue vacation. I had taken hardly any time off at all during my first term, as there was so much to do in the pursuit of professionalizing the Sheriff's Office. The year 1992 had added the *Sentinel* attack plus re-election and Chile's task force. The latter inquiry went right on into 1993 and when it was over, I needed a break.

We were not going far. Tampa was only a couple of hours away, and I would be in reach for any problem or crisis in the Sheriff's Office that should arise. We arrived, checked into our hotel and I called the office to see if anything was up. I had only been away a few hours, but in that time frame the NAACP had filed suit against our office over the traffic stops. The vacation ended before it began. We checked out within a short time of checking in and returned to Volusia County.

The NAACP had recently held their annual meeting in Orlando and, unbeknownst to me, I was on their agenda. This organization had been briefed by the *Sentinel* following publication of their stories last year and apparently had been mulling over some type of action. A Public Records request had come in to our office a few weeks earlier from an attorney in Tampa, asking for copies of the I-95 stops, and this lawyer turned out to be the one representing the NAACP and any plaintiffs they had.

"Plaintiffs" would be a tall order for them. The NAACP had filed a class-action suit, meaning that a large number of plaintiffs could be represented in this legal action against our office. The Governor's Panel was unable to find anyone that wanted to testify, and class-action suits usually have dozens of plaintiffs listed under it. The typical class action suit is one where a group of people wronged by one entity join together to take up a legal battle. A plane crash generally results in a class action suit by survivors and/or beneficiaries of victims of the mishap. I didn't know how many people were to be represented under the NAACP's suit, but I would have been surprised if they could find enough people willing to testify. These were people who were involved in illegal drug transactions, and they were more likely to avoid calling attention to themselves than to go public under this suit.

The NAACP was also in a critical membership situation. Interest had waned in their activities and their numbers were down. This lawsuit was a chance for them to drum up interest in their organization again and to remind African-Americans that the NAACP was there to fight racial bias on all fronts. This gave them an extra motivation to follow through with their civil action.

They had one woman willing to list her name on the suit. That hardly represented a "class", but it was a start. The suit was filed on behalf of Selena Washington of Charleston, South Carolina and all other blacks and Hispanics who were not arrested when their cash was seized by Volusia deputies while traveling I-95 between 1989 and 1992.

Selena Washington was the woman from South Carolina who was stopped with her son and agreed to a search that eventually turned up about $19,000 that was wrapped in $100 flash rolls and stuffed into two Crown Royal bags. She offered a couple of stories about where she was going and where she got the money. She finally said she was going to Miami to buy building supplies for her home in Charleston, even though she did not have a good explanation as to why she didn't buy these supplies closer to home. She had said that prices in Charleston were too high, but Savannah, Georgia and Jacksonville, Florida were far closer than Miami to purchase these materials. Investigators found that her home did not appear to have significant damage to it, and she had not received any federal money for damages as yet, although other homes in her area that were badly damaged by Hurricane Hugo several months earlier did get some federal dollars.

We eventually agreed to settle the currency forfeiture case and returned $15,000 of the money. But to us there was more than probable cause that this cash was intended for some type of illegal transaction and I felt we could defend ourselves in this new class action suit. The Tampa attorney, Charles Burr, called her "the perfect plaintiff." There were apparently no other plaintiffs yet. The suit called for our office to return the rest of her money and pay an unspecified amount in punitive damages.

Burr would be assisted by the chairman of the National Association of Criminal Defense Lawyers' task force on forfeiture reform, a Tennessee attorney named Bo Edwards. Two other attorneys were also listed as assisting in the trial preparation.

This suit was not all that was happening that early summer of 1993. Congressional hearings were beginning again with re-election campaigns well out of the way. Selena Washington was slated to testify before a panel looking into abuses of the forfeiture laws. Governor Chiles had also alerted his former press secretary Julie Anbender, who was now serving in the same position with newly appointed Attorney General Janet Reno (a Floridian and friend of the Governor). He advised that the panel had disbanded, but that the Attorney General might want to look into the practices by the Volusia County Sheriff's Office.

Many of the allegations appearing in the news stories now referred to race-based profiling as our reason to stop a car on I-95. Governor Chiles was quoted as saying it, as well as several other Florida state and congressional representatives.

That would be easy for us to defend, since we did not and had not ever used any race-based profiling to make traffic stops. All stops were made for a specific traffic violation. After that, deputies were trained to look for signs that pointed towards an illegal transaction. Race was not one of those signs.

I was confident this would all come out again during the civil trial. I held no animosity towards the NAACP for the lawsuit. They were a fine organization and our office had supported them in the past and would continue to support them. We had made significant strides in minority hiring since I had taken office in January 1989 and were proud of our record. Still, there was a long way to go, but Captain Leonard Davis, who oversaw the drug and cash interdiction programs, was doing his best, along with recruiting deputy Cliff Williams, another African-American, to bring in new officers from the minority communities.

The Special Enforcement Team continued their work as usual, which included the I-95 stops. We were making a difference out there in the drug war, and even though drug dealers had given instructions to stay out of Volusia County, there would be those that didn't want to go the long way around our county to get out of or into the state of Florida, and we needed to continue our law enforcement efforts on the highways.

Congressman John Conyers reconvened his hearings during late June 1993. He had an interesting ally in Representative Henry Hyde from Illinois, who would later go on to head the impeachment inquiry into President Clinton. Selena Washington gave the primary testimony on its first day. She said she would never drive through Volusia County, certainly not at night and that keeping some of her money when she wasn't charged with a crime was wrong. Her testimony about the stop and her responses given to deputy inquiries was not accurate. She told the panel that she and her son committed no driving infraction to be pulled over. Our office did not testify due to the NAACP suit. After hearing only one side of the story, the reaction was predictably negative. Representative Alfred McCandless of California said that her story reminded him of movies about Southern sheriffs and that the NAACP lawsuit was going to cost Volusia County dearly. Florida representative Corinne Brown said that what happened to Selena Washington was unconstitutional and un-American.

I anxiously awaited the opportunity to tell our side of this story in court. Virtually everyone involved in the so-called investigation into our office's practices continued to quote from and rely on the statistics published by the *Sentinel*. These statistics were clearly wrong and manipulated and changed to substantiate their findings. That everyone from the Governor's office to congressional representatives to the attorneys preparing the NAACP lawsuit continued to rely on them without separately verifying their accuracy was amazing to me.

We had very little support for our side of the story. We were able to quote the proper statistics on a local Volusia talk radio show hosted by Marc Bernier. He asked good questions and let us recite the proper numbers that anyone else could find if they simply spent the time looking it up. Marc's show was a port in the storm for us and we appreciated the chance to get the word out to local residents that I (and my deputies) were doing the job they elected me to do.

We had additional support from the publication *Accuracy in Media*, co-written and run by a former Pulitzer Prize winning journalist himself, Joe Goulden. Joe did his own research, and found the inaccuracy of the *Sentinel* reporting to be beyond the realm of a simple numbers mistake. The discrepancies were so wide, Joe had to believe the report was deliberately falsified to support the claims the reporters made.

That issue of *Accuracy in Media* was published and sent to all of Congress and every major media outlet. One of the *Sentinel*'s editors was furious and called Joe Goulden and ranted about his reporting on the articles. Joe simply replied, "show me anything in my report that is inaccurate." The *Sentinel* editor could not do this, of course, but continued his tirade against Joe for a few more minutes before abruptly hanging up. It felt good to see the truth begin to come out, even if in a limited way.

The Volusia County Council began reacting to the publicity and the pending law suit in July 1993, perhaps taking Congressman McCandless' statements seriously, that this legal action would cost the county dearly. However, money that had been earmarked for illegal transactions and seized by our Special Enforcement Team had paid the costs to date of the lawsuit. While a couple of county council members expressed some concern over the potential costs, I had their backing and there was money in the confiscated funds account, saving taxpayers the expense. I was certain we'd win, in which case the NAACP might have to pick up our legal tab. We certainly wouldn't have to pay their fees, so I wasn't concerned about estimating legal and punitive damages costs on their side. Their attorney Charles Burr was quoted as saying NAACP legal costs might run around $200-300,000.

Towards the end of July, Selena Washington could not be found. She was last seen in Charleston, South Carolina. Incredibly, there was some media speculation that our office had something to do with her vanishing act. The county had sent two of our investigators to South Carolina, but that was to accumulate information we might need for the eventual trial. This is routine procedure in a lawsuit.

Washington's attorney Burr implied that Selena had told him recently that she thought the Volusia County deputies were following her and harassing their neighbors. But the investigators were handling their job in their usual professional manner. They were accompanied on all of their interviews by a deputy from the Charleston County Sheriff's Office. I was concerned that she had disappeared, but knew our investigators had nothing to do with it.

Selena turned up in Miami a few days later, ending further speculation. Her attorney played it up for all that it was worth, liking the image that was being portrayed in the press of my deputies bullying witnesses. It was just legal posturing by Burr, and who knew how long it would be before this case ever came to court?

In that same month of July, Attorney General Janet Reno finally reacted to Governor Chiles' plea to look into our office's activities. Despite her having publicly defended the forfeiture laws and cautioning people against blaming police or generalizing about causes, she agreed to investigate the Volusia County Sheriff's Office.

There were others in Congress that had reportedly forced Reno's hand, including Senator (and former Florida Governor) Bob Graham, who had earlier praised our team's efforts and taken pictures with them. Congressional representative Corinne Brown, an African-American whose district included part of Volusia County, said she didn't see why she had to justify, "why I have cash money in my possession. It is not uncommon for the people I come in contact with to deal in cash money. It's a cultural thing, and if you're not in that culture, you may not understand it." Of course, she didn't see the money as we found it, wrapped in flash rolls, covered in drug residue and stored in Crown Royal bags.

Once again, though surprised, I was still confident our team's activities could stand up to any scrutiny, even from the highest law enforcement office in the country. This would bring the I-95 stops full circle, having been vindicated already by the state and currently awaiting the chance at the civil trial. If the Attorney General's office wanted to investigate, they were welcome in our offices.

The Department of Justice sent in a Jacksonville FBI man to investigate. His name was Mark Wood, and I put him in touch with Leonard Davis to set up the interviews he wanted. I suggested that the deputies and other witnesses interview with Mark on neutral ground, so there wouldn't be any concern that they weren't allowed to speak freely. But Wood didn't feel that was necessary and chose to talk to everyone at the Operations Center.

He spent some time here, talking to people, reviewing all the files and watching the tapes. He looked at everything in its entirety and I appreciated the thoroughness of his effort. What other way could you judge the Special Enforcement Team unless you went over the complete operation?

When he was finished, he gave us a clean bill of health. Again, I expected that result, but it was a relief to hear it. Wood wrote his report to the Department of Justice (DOJ), telling them that there was nothing here to investigate, that the team had done its job properly and well within accepted law enforcement standards and legal constraints.

But apparently the AG did not like this result. The DOJ sent another FBI investigator into our offices. He also took about a month and came to the same conclusion that Mark Wood did, and gave the DOJ the identical result: "there's nothing here to find." Again, I was satisfied. Here were two independent corroborations of our team's efforts by the FBI, who had no motivation to take a stand either way.

When the DOJ sent a third investigator down, a retiring agent from Washington, D.C., I realized they were not going to quit until they had a different investigative result. Two of the Justice Department's attorneys, Wendy Olson and Tom Perez, had actually taken control of the investigation personally and accompanied this third investigator to Volusia County. They began conducting their own interviews and covering the same ground, seemingly determined to find something. For the first time, I felt like our office was under siege. That the DOJ had brought these feelings to the surface was totally unexpected. I had always looked at the nation's highest law enforcement agency as the standard bearer for what we all do, every day, every week, every year. That they had focused so much attention on our operation, all but ignoring two positive investigative results, meant there had to be something else going on. Why would the DOJ spend so much time, effort and money looking into our practices? I could almost understand the first investigation, prompted by the Governor and the *Sentinel* articles. But after two different people independently satisfy themselves that these reports were inaccurate and our files and tapes told a different story, you would think this would be the result they'd hoped for. They wouldn't want a renegade Sheriff's Office loose in this country that would give law enforcement and, by implication, the DOJ a bad name. But somehow it seemed that this was exactly what someone at DOJ wanted, and they weren't going to quit until they had exposed some wrongdoing here.

I was shaken, but still felt that no matter whom they sent, our office would be exonerated.

The Congressional hearings had ended with a whimper, not a bang. Despite a lot of negative press initiated by Conyers, a couple of bills proposed in Congress languished and never saw the light of day. The national forfeiture law was already being fine-tuned by the DOJ, just as we did that with our own operations, and the Supreme Court had also ruled on their validity, within limits.

Closer to home, the Reverend George Crossley was taking his carefully edited videotape of the I-95 stops to the local college campuses. He showed his version of the tapes in public forums on the local campuses of Bethune Cookman, Stetson and the University of Central Florida. Crossley, a Henshaw for Sheriff supporter in 1992, continued to try and discredit me. Naturally, he was showing the "Crossley version" and *not* the full-length tapes of the complete stops that the Governor's Panel, the state attorney's office and the FBI had reviewed and pronounced satisfactory. Crossley went on a one-man campaign, but failed to whip up the kind of fury and outrage he wanted.

He even took his show to a delegation of local legislators. The Reverend Crossley portrayed himself as a conservative on his own Christian radio network and his Central Florida TV show, and brought every bit of fire and brimstone to his pleas for the Florida legislature to change the state seizure laws. Earlier efforts following the Governor's panel recommendations had failed, but Crossley let this delegation know, in no uncertain terms, that the time for change had come.

It did come—but for Crossley, not the state seizure laws. He was later charged with hiring a hitman to kill his former mistress' husband and to firebomb the man's house. One hitman turned out to be a snitch and the other an undercover federal agent. He was later convicted in court, with a substantial part of the evidence captured, ironically, on videotape. He gave the federal agent a .357 magnum and this exchange was shown over the Central Florida airwaves during the trial. Crossley blamed me for setting him up when he was arrested. I suppose I was fortunate that Crossley's threats against me now were only verbal.

The *Sentinel*, content that they had got the ball rolling against our office on several fronts now, continued in their efforts behind the scenes. State Attorney General Bob Butterworth, campaigning for re-election in 1994, was being interviewed by the *Sentinel* in their offices. Questioning had hardly begun when one of the editors asked him if he was a friend of Sheriff Vogel. He immediately said yes. They then asked why he wouldn't investigate my office. Butterworth drew the line then, saying that he would only answer their questions about what he had done as Attorney General. But they continued to press him about my office's activities and he eventually simply got up and left. Apparently, he didn't care whether the *Sentinel* endorsed him or not. He retained his Attorney General position easily in the 1994 election.

The class action suit had taken on another plaintiff by 1994. Jorge Nater, who had claimed that cash wrapped in flash rolls was the proceeds from a building sale in Puerto Rico, had joined Selena Washington in the civil action.

Nater had been a passenger in a car driven by Francisco Muriel who told deputies that he didn't know Nater's full name, but he had been given $200 to drive Nater to Florida. Nater had told deputies that he was on his way to visit relatives, and later when over $36,000 was found, said that he was going to South Florida to buy a house and that this money was the result of a building sale in Puerto Rico that he had concluded in New Jersey. While sitting in the back seat of the deputy's car, Nater said they should have put the money in a tire. The documents his attorney ultimately provided were not official and showed the building in Puerto Rico valued at $300,000. Nater had said he'd sold it for $60,000. We later settled out of court and returned $30,000 of the money.

I was also confident we could defend this case, too.

In June 1994, a federal judge finally took some action against the "class-action." Despite lengthy advertising from the *Sentinel* and an intense campaign to find plaintiffs for their suit, the NAACP had only Selena Washington and Jorge Nater to come and testify. U.S. District Judge Anne Conway dismissed the NAACP as part of the suit. They didn't have a class of plaintiffs and therefore were not entitled to class-action status. That left the suit as being Washington and Nater against the Sheriff's Office. The NAACP had originally filed on behalf of an estimated 315 black and Hispanic motorists whose cash was seized and an estimated 10,000 who were stopped and searched from 1989 to 1993. Only two had come forward.

The NAACP had sought an injunction against further stops by our Special Enforcement Team. But Judge Conway denied the injunction request and said that the NAACP had not demonstrated nor alleged any harm by the team. The NAACP's law team tried to play down this action by saying that the organization was never in the lawsuit for money.

By now, both sides had accumulated numerous depositions and I gave mine on the last day of discovery in July 1994. You don't really get to tell your side of the story in a deposition. You merely respond to the specific questions of the attorneys doing the asking. Word had leaked out that the deputy we threw off the team, Frank Josenhanz, had testified in his deposition that we were stopping people based on race. How he could say that was especially ironic, since his actions while on the team were of the type the team tried to avoid, thus prompting his removal. His testimony would certainly be discredited if this case ever came to trial.

There were overtones made to the NAACP to settle this case out of court early on, before the case dragged on, accumulating hefty lawyer fees. But the attorneys representing their case wanted to see it all the way through, visions of a multimillion dollar settlement dancing in their heads.

The DOJ continued to investigate our office. The U.S. attorneys from Washington, D.C. apparently gave them the thumbs-up that there really was something going on here. It was almost surreal. We were notified that the Civil Rights division of the DOJ was now officially investigating our office. It felt as if my back was to the wall, surrounded on all sides, but I was determined to fight to win on every front and prove our office was simply good at what we do, and well within legal boundaries.

The DOJ's attorneys, Wendy Olson and Tom Perez, were still in the interview process, covering a lot of the same turf that the NAACP civil suit had. This time, though, it was a criminal investigation, not a civil one, that they were prosecuting. This was not a lawsuit. They were on the search for indictable activities and were determined to lock me and several of the team deputies up on some charge. I had never imagined the DOJ (or any law enforcement office) on full throttle trying to bring charges against me. My role had reversed, from pursuing the criminal to being pursued myself.

Throughout this ongoing ordeal, I maintained my public composure. We carried on the work of the Sheriff's Office. We were not going to back down on law enforcement in any way. That would be tantamount to surrender. We continually evaluated our practices and procedures to be sure they stayed within the guidelines we'd set, but we continued to enforce them every day. I went home every night and reassured my family that everything was going to be fine, that we were going to get through this and that justice ultimately would prevail. I had nothing to hide, nothing to feel concerned about, and this attitude helped me get through the difficult days under the legal microscope.

As the civil trial drew near, the DOJ lawyers filed a request to delay it until they could complete their criminal investigation. They told Judge Anne Conway that the stay was needed to prevent witness intimidation and to protect the integrity of their grand jury probe. The civil suit was scheduled to begin January 5, 1995, but the DOJ asked that it be put off to the end of February to give them time to complete their investigation. They said that some of the witnesses would be the same in both trials and that their testimony in the civil suit would expose the strategy and potential targets of the grand jury investigation.

I wasn't sure how the judge would react. She had already tossed out the NAACP. I was willing to bet that she would have some comment on the fact that, as 1994 drew to a close, there was still nothing that the DOJ had found to publicize, despite an 18–month investigation that was both disruptive to our office and fruitless to date.

In mid–December, Judge Conway agreed to stop further depositions and hear what the DOJ lawyers had to say about their investigation and why the civil trial would interfere with it. She gave them time to bring forward all that they had against the Volusia County Sheriff's Office and explain the effect on the civil trial. The DOJ lawyers, Perez and Olson, asked that they be allowed to demonstrate their case confidentially. Judge Conway agreed.

Despite eighteen months of work, countless dollars spent, two FBI investigative efforts that exonerated the Sheriff's Office, and a substantial number of depositions, the DOJ didn't have anything. There were no indictments ready for the team's work on I-95, and they weren't close to compiling any evidence that any criminal wrongdoing existed in our agency. Perez argued that he didn't have time to prepare an adequate explanation, as there was no way he could know that the federal grand jury investigation formed several months ago would overlap with this civil trial.

Judge Conway was less than impressed. She said she saw no reason to hold up the civil trial based on the arguments the DOJ had made, and failed to see how civil trial testimony could hamper the federal grand jury probe. It was her second ruling that gave our side a boost and I was grateful for her straightforward, no nonsense approach to this entire affair. Enough was enough, she seemed to be saying, let's get on with the trial and see what everybody had to say.

Jury selection in the Washington/Nater civil trial began the first week in January 1995. Testimony was expected to last a couple of weeks. Judge Conway allowed a study of the videotapes to be used in evidence. She disallowed the plaintiffs' request to bring in a statistics expert to testify about the stops.

The expected testimony of Frank Josenhanz occurred in the first week. He testified that he and the rest of the team was instructed by me to stop blacks and Hispanics for traffic stops and search them for drugs and cash. I had thought many things of Josenhanz, but I had never attributed this type of outrageous lie to him. He was motivated by something, perhaps his dismissal from the team, but his story was pure fabrication. Leonard Davis and team member Ray Almodovar would certainly discredit Frank and his testimony with the truth.

The plaintiffs tried to discredit Leonard by saying he was a low-key supervisor and not really in touch with what went on with the interdiction team. Leonard did an admirable job in testifying, and spoke of the honor and integrity of the members of the team who he never doubted for an instant.

Selena Washington took the stand herself and repeatedly stumbled over the details of her stop, even contradicting part of the story she had told the Congressional committee over 18 months earlier. One of the details was the identity of the person traveling with her, who she had identified to deputies as Jonathan Washington, her son, but who turned out now to be someone named Gus Henley who was driving the vehicle without a proper driver's license. She apologized for lying, but it was symptomatic of her whole story which she had changed a couple of times during and then after the stop.

Jorge Nater had the opportunity to tell his story again. He insisted that the money was part of a real estate transaction in Puerto Rico that he had bought for $60,000. Luis Riviera, the individual who had purchased the property from Nater, wrote that he had paid $20,000 down and the balance with a personal check. That contradicted what Nater had told us, that he had received the proceeds from the sale in cash. Nater said Riviera was mistaken. Even letters meant to assist the plaintiff were at odds with his story.

He said he hid the money to protect it from robbers. He was even distrustful of his traveling companion, Muriel, whom he had met only a couple of days before their Florida excursion.

Another witness meant to help their cause, a Daytona Beach police lieutenant, unintentionally aided ours when he said that the percentage of blacks pulled over on the Interstate by Volusia County Sheriff's Office deputies mirrored the same numbers that the Daytona Beach department pulled over. Since some of attorney Burr's case depended on our department operating differently than others in terms of targeting minorities, this testimony seemed to hurt his cause.

Our attorneys, David Kornreich and Jeff Mandel, had done an outstanding job in their cross-examination of the plaintiffs' witnesses. There was little there that hadn't always been there and in our files and what new came out actually served to further substantiate the suspicions we had of the money all along.

Judge Anne Conway agreed. Not only did she think little of their case, but she tossed it out as a directed verdict without our side ever having to present evidence and letting it go to a jury. Judge Conway told the attorneys, Burr and his partner Melanie Locklear, that they hadn't even come close to proving the plaintiffs were stopped on I-95 because of their race. Selena Washington even admitted on the stand that her car was going at least 70 mph, a valid traffic stop under any circumstances. Judge Conway also felt that the Nater/Muriel traffic violation of following too closely was also a valid traffic stop, having nothing to do with intentionally pulling over minorities. She said there was no evidence that a reasonable officer wouldn't have stopped cars driven by white people under similar circumstances. The $3.3 million lawsuit had just been dismissed. Her ruling came on Friday, January 13, just a week after the trial opened.

Not only did the team members feel vindicated, but also once again the credibility of the *Sentinel* stories was undermined. The Special Enforcement Team had been and would continue to be color-blind. They were out looking for drug dealers after making a legitimate traffic stop. That's all it was and all it ever will be.

While I was confident of the outcome, the results were nonetheless pleasing. Coupled with Judge Conway's apparent disdain for the DOJ case, it gave me a lot of confidence going on into 1995. We had spent more than two years answering for the inaccurate, slanted reporting of a newspaper that had been validated by only one entity—the Pulitzer Prize committee. Everywhere in the real world where it counts, their stories could not hold up. Only the truth can sustain itself indefinitely and that's what we had going for us on our side. One more time, that had been sufficient.

The attorneys for both plaintiffs said they would appeal. They were buoyed by comments from the NAACP who said that a lot of minorities don't expect fairness from the judicial process. It didn't seem to bother them that a court official who tends to the jury members said that the jury had agreed with Judge Conway's decision.

The *Sentinel* said the trial did not go to the heart of what the Special Enforcement Team was doing out on I-95. That their articles accused us of racial profiling to make traffic stops and that Judge Conway had pointed out that in the only two cases where people were willing to come in and testify that this just wasn't true, appeared not to dawn on the newspaper. They published articles saying they were concerned this would mean that I would not be indicted by the federal grand jury set up by the DOJ, since proving criminal cases required substantially more evidence than do civil cases.

Burr and Locklear did appeal the case and it was finally ruled on in January 1997, two years later. In Atlanta, the U.S. Court of Appeals for the 11th Circuit upheld Judge Conway's ruling, stating that she had acted properly when she dismissed the suit after the plaintiffs had presented their case due to a lack of evidence. This case was now officially over.

But there remained the federal grand jury probe as they continued to depose witnesses and look for anything they could to indict someone in the Volusia County Sheriff's Office. Nineteen months now and still counting, and they had not filed one indictment. However, there was no mistaking their intensity and their unswerving commitment to their cause, as we were about to see.

INTERLUDE:
ELECTION NIGHT, 1996

The evening was getting late. At this time in the previous two elections, the celebrations would have been almost complete and many people on their way home.

Not tonight. If anything, the main room was getting louder, filling up with individuals who had heard that I was losing and had come down to try and change the night's fortunes. Even individuals who simply lived in the county and had not worked on the campaign got in their cars and drove to offer their support.

I asked Jeannie to find Nancye Jones, the Sheriff's Department legal advisor, out there in the craziness of the main room revelers. Dilys Harris was still leading cheers and camera crews hoping for a postmortem on the Sheriff Vogel campaign, had just turned off their cameras for now.

Ron Johnston's father Clyde had come in the back to check on us. When the silver-haired, good-natured man laid eyes on this gathering, he yelled out, "What are you all upset about? The returns? Gosh, I've never lost a Sheriff before and I'm not going to lose one now!"

He clapped his son Ron on the back and looked at me, saying, "Keep your spirits up, Sheriff! It's not over!" I nodded to him and said thank you, looking brighter and more confident than Ron did, although that wasn't saying much.

I was fighting a running battle with my insides. Outwardly, I showed little, but my stomach was dancing around inside me. I told myself that Vietnam and other early life experiences had steeled me for this kind of thing, that an election wasn't nearly as traumatic by comparison. I kept up this steady inner dialogue and knew Jeannie was doing the same.

During this time, I saw Dale Anderson sitting quietly, his at-times mischievous manner docile at the moment. Dale was tough, a survivor, and it pained me to see him looking down and depressed. He'd been through plenty already in the war to run me out of the Sheriff's Office by any possible method.

Nancye Jones came in with Jeannie and I showed her the numbers. Nancye, a native of Volusia County herself, was still upbeat. "There's time yet, Sheriff," she assured.

She was as positive at that very minute as she was during the most incredible fight of my life. As she turned to leave, she passed by Dale Anderson's chair, and I remembered how hard they had fought a U.S. Justice Department bent on destroying a few careers in the Volusia County Sheriff's Office....

CHAPTER FIVE:
FIGHTING TO WIN

GRAND JURY

For an entire Sheriff's term, our office had battled the allegations against it. Over the course of many months, we had won at both the ballot box and the courtroom and had thoroughly repudiated the original charges leveled by the *Orlando Sentinel*. By now, it should have been time to get on with our duties and our lives.

But no one was prepared for what came next.

Following the directed verdict in the civil trial, Lieutenant Dale Anderson, Sergeant Bobby Jones and I all individually received a specific targeted letter from the U.S. Justice Department, notifying us that we were now the actual focus of their years-long probe. This was not rumor or innuendo. This was an official document letting us know we were personally under investigation.

In a word, I was stunned. All my life, I'd been fighting for our country in one way or the other. From Vietnam to being a state trooper and then a Sheriff, I'd always charged ahead, knowing that our Justice Department was watching my back. I had always strongly believed in what I was doing and that we were making a difference in people's lives by enforcing this country's laws. I took it on faith that the Justice Department was behind every positive move our office made.

Suddenly, with one short letter, that belief had been shattered. After months of being told by their own FBI operatives that there was nothing here to find, two Department of Justice (DOJ) attorneys had just informed us that they were aggressively pursuing actions that could lead to the arrest of Jones, Anderson and I. Within a few moments in time, I had mentally reclassified the DOJ I had long worked on behalf of as the Department of Injustice.

Why us? Why was the full power of the federal government turned on against three people who had so honestly and enthusiastically served their country? For two DOJ attorneys to personally take over a case of which they had been told didn't merit attention smacked of some deep-seeded vendetta. Was it politically motivated because the present administration was of a different party affiliation than mine? Was it some action I took at some point in my career that had made an enemy that wouldn't rest until I was sanctioned in some manner?

All throughout the ongoing probe I had felt it was just the system working itself through and it would arrive at the correct and proper conclusion. That's how it's supposed to work. Facts are collected and analyzed to reveal the right answer. The difference here had become that someone at the DOJ was unsatisfied with the answer that kept coming up–that we were successfully making inroads in the drug war while acting well within the scope of the law. Unhappy with this result, they now appeared to be looking for anything with which to hang an indictment (or two).

But everything came back to why?

I-95 stops? Governor Chiles' panel had exonerated us. The NAACP had to drop their class action suit, as they couldn't find a "class" of victims to bring charges against us. Congress had listened to Selena Washington's admittedly false testimony and did not go further. Judge Anne Conway had issued a directed verdict from the bench, dismissing the civil suit against our office. The U.S. Justice Department had sent several FBI investigators who had combed our offices looking for violations, and they had come up empty.

But the DOJ had gone beyond that now. They had two of their bright young attorneys living at our office, searching for anything now to justify the time, effort and money spent.

What had my deputies or I done to generate this type of modern day witch-hunt? What we had accomplished was a tremendously successful campaign against the drug dealers exploiting this country. We had done it legally and we had done it well. For that, we were being subjected to a nightmare that didn't seem like it would ever end until our heads were on a DOJ platter.

The law is a powerful weapon. Without it, countries collapse into chaos, and unstable regimes result. In our country, the law has managed to preserve the U.S. Constitution, the sacred document that separates us from the disorder of other places. This legal charter has stood the test of time and I had been proud to be a part of this law enforcement process.

But when the force of that law is turned in full strength against any one individual, group or entity, it is overwhelming. Of all people, I knew how overmatched the average citizen is against the law. That is why we were so careful in my office not to abuse the power the people had vested in us. Now, ironically, that power had been turned on my office, and I felt as helpless as the ordinary person would be in fighting back against it.

I wondered now how many people in this country fell victim to the system. How many individuals were hounded by someone in power that had virtually every means at his or her disposal with which to turn up the heat? How many times has this happened to people who had done nothing wrong other than to belong to the wrong political party or who made an offhand comment that disturbed someone who could bring the full force of the law down around them? Did they feel the same sort of betrayal and disillusionment as I was now feeling?

There have been examples of justice gone awry in the past, where an innocent person finds himself (or herself) trapped by circumstantial evidence. There have been people jailed and even executed for crimes they did not commit.

Fortunately, this rarely happens to the average citizen, let alone an officer of the law. There is usually a "team" mentality to law enforcement that often protects it own. Clearly, with the events of the past couple of years, I was no longer considered by someone to be part of the "team."

But who? Who could have it in for my office or me so badly, they would continue to investigate us just to find anything that could result in an indictment?

Something must have happened following the completion of the Governor Chiles task force. He was no fan of mine since I was a Republican. But what had he said when he referred the case to the DOJ after his panel could find nothing conclusively wrong about the I-95 stops? Why was it elevated to this now intense level of investigation, notwithstanding facts, notwithstanding truth? Any competent attorney would have dropped the case by now.

What about Janet Reno? I barely knew of her, and only because she was from Florida and occasionally stayed with friends at New Smyrna Beach. As a state attorney for Dade County, she had a reputation for being overly tough on police officers. In a well-known case in 1986, in the midst of a war on child abusers, she went after a Miami police officer named Grant Snowden on the basis of a weak accusation of child sex abuse. His wife ran a baby sitting service and though there was no substantiation to the charge, Reno prosecuted. She paraded child witness after child witness to the stand and Snowden was acquitted, the evidence too absurd for the jury to believe.

But Janet Reno did not give up. She built another case, using most of the same child witnesses reciting the same accusations, and she was finally able to get her conviction. About to hear Judge Amy Donner's decision, police officer Grant Snowden told her, "You are about to sentence an innocent man." And so she did––to five life terms.

In 1998, the 11th Circuit Court of Appeals overturned that conviction. Twelve years of time lost, sitting in a jail cell. A career finished, a life changed forever because Reno wanted a conviction and would stop at nothing to get it. The U.S. Supreme Court refused to hear the prosecution's appeal of the overturned conviction. Former police officer Snowden was a free man at last.

Is this what I was in for? Our situation had a similar pattern. Despite the inability to build a case, the DOJ pressed on. When Reno lost the first case against Snowden, she went out and built another. Could it be she had decided she would keep the pressure turned up on me until she achieved the same result? If so, did it matter whether I was innocent or not? Did it matter whether there was any evidence or not? Was I destined for a jail cell?

It was hard to believe that the DOJ would so blatantly misuse all the power and authority they possess to come after a Sheriff's office that was successfully battling the war on drugs. But perhaps this was the motivation. To knock off the country's #1 drug interdiction program could change the face of law enforcement against this type of crime. There certainly would be some special interest groups that would be glad to see that happen. We had already heard from two of them— the ACLU and NAACP. They were traditionally Democrat-oriented, so this could be a political agenda after all. Take out our agency and those in office would receive a key political boost from two strong support coalitions.

While I had never met Janet Reno in connection with this office, she did have some past dealings with the Volusia County Sheriff's Office. Specifically, she crossed paths with my predecessor here, Ed Duff, over a murder case. She had agreed (at the urging of friends she had in Volusia County) to look into a murder case that Duff had essentially closed. She wanted it reopened. Duff wasn't about to change his mind. He was at his stubborn, country boy best when he essentially told Reno to get lost. In all likelihood, Reno formed her opinion of the Volusia County Sheriff's Office right then and there as a group of backwoods, good ol' country boy "hicks" and she appears to maintain that position today.

The *Orlando Sentinel* articles of 1992 simply re-enforced this notion, even though the people at the top had been replaced by highly educated, highly trained law enforcement officers. First impressions can be everything, however, and any reader of those *Sentinel* articles could certainly come to the conclusion that the Volusia County Sheriff's Office was run by a bunch of bigoted country bumpkins.

Across the country, our operation had been branded as one who enforces the law by abusing the rights of African-Americans and other minorities. Nothing could be further from the truth, but truth was no longer the issue. Oust us and many, if not all, of the convictions we had obtained over the last few years would likely be reversed. This would appease both the ACLU and NAACP, among others.

I shouldn't underestimate the power of drug money, either. It's a $300 billion/ year business and certainly the drug lords running the show have found ways to funnel some of that cash into important campaign contributions, well-layered and disguised for what it is. That drug dealers are influence peddlers was not particularly surprising. If they can see a way to rid themselves of an enemy, they'll do it. That the DOJ would be their unwitting ally was so ironic, you could probably hear the laughter all the way back to Colombia.

To continue their investigation despite the clean bills of health our department had received itself bordered on civil rights infringement. If our office conducted an investigation like this into any resident of our county, I think Volusia citizens would rightfully hang us from the nearest tree. Yet here was the highest law office in the land on a search and destroy mission using tactics they would never allow any other law enforcement office to ever use.

Jeannie was as devastated as I was by this targeted DOJ assault. To her, how a country that I had fought for could sustain an investigation in the face of contrary evidence uncovered from every source was unconscionable.

One other conceivable notion for the DOJ's actions was, as noted earlier, political. I am a Republican, this federal administration is not, and taking me out of office could have that type of motivation. But I am only one Sheriff in a country full of them, many of whom were also Republican. What did one Sheriff matter politically to this administration? Again, it didn't make sense. I never had any ambition to run for public office. To be Sheriff, you had to run, but I didn't look any further past the Sheriff's position. I didn't want to do anything else politically. Most politicians don't understand this. Their sole ambition is to hold a political office and many will do anything to stay there. My feeling is that we are *public* servants. That's who we worked for – the public. It wasn't meant to be a career. It is a position in which you served the citizens for a time and then someone else took over. That's the whole idea behind term limits. Perhaps someone thought I had my eyes on a bigger political prize in the future and so they were doing their best to discredit me now before I achieved a popular following due to the success of the Sheriff's Office. But it still seemed far-fetched that the DOJ would spend the money to derail a possible future political campaign I might launch. Jeannie and I simply could attribute no obvious logical motivation to the DOJ's relentless pursuit.

I have always believed that we have a great justice system in this country. There is nothing better in the world than our constitution. People from all over the globe, from all walks of life, come here looking for a better way of existence, often to get away from their own government's abuses. No one that holds a high position of authority in this country should ever be allowed to destroy or ruin lives simply because they have the power to do so. Those that run from it in other countries surely do not expect to see the same type of thing here.

I never expected it to happen to me, but I knew that I wasn't alone. There had to be other people who fell victim to this onslaught, and that thought terrified me even more. Who was out there in our country that had been run over by the runaway train of injustice that we were apparently capable of at the highest levels of government?

Up until now, our office had done a remarkable job of deflecting the criticism and continuing on with our jobs. We had compartmentalized the problem, and continued to carry on our important law enforcement tasks around the county. We had continued to make stops on I-95 in accordance with the same legal procedures we had been using and knew to be correct.

But now one couldn't help thinking about the DOJ's obsession and where it came from. It was never far from my thoughts, though outwardly I put up a good front. Fortunately, we were as busy in the office as always and this helped somewhat to take my mind off the DOJ campaign.

But the DOJ attorneys never let their investigation stray too far from our line of vision. That two DOJ attorneys would also now turn investigator when their own investigators couldn't find anything was so rare it was nearly unprecedented. That's because investigators often testify in a case and here they could be witnesses in their own prosecution of us, a conflict of interest if ever there was one.

They were interviewing all of the deputies, even former ones, and they were hearing all kinds of wild stories that some disgruntled members of the department chose to fabricate for the attorneys' benefit. Lawyers who were impartial, who could listen to a tale and separate the truth from the lie, would have dismissed the accusations being made. But the DOJ attorneys Olsen and Perez were so desperate to come up with anything, they focused on a couple of deputies that gave them what they wanted to hear.

They ignored the same testimony delivered over and over again by virtually every deputy in the department of how our interdiction efforts worked and what happened on specific stops. But the statements of our legitimately top officers carried no weight with Olsen and Perez. Instead, they listened to two dissenters with their own agenda against the department because it was, finally, what they wanted to hear. It was what they were instructed to hear from their superiors, because no DOJ attorneys take as much time and spend as much of the public's money investigating a case without the approval of someone at the top of the Department of Justice. They ignored 99 percent of the evidence and assertions from witnesses and relentlessly concentrated on the contrary opinions of two officers.

We had already seen these attorneys in action at the civil trial when they argued for a stay in the lawsuit. Wendy Olson was both arrogant and ruthless, a dangerous combination. She had been hell-bent on securing that stay, but the DOJ had compiled nothing in the way of evidence to persuade Judge Conway to hold up the civil trial. Tom Perez was less of a presence, but still an intense lawyer, ever so focused on his task – to obtain an indictment against me.

The DOJ attorneys threatened to subpoena the financial records of Jones, Anderson and I. They were convinced, especially after hearing two deputies talk, that we were siphoning off money for our own personal use. When our legal advisor Nancye Ege married Deputy Bobby Jones, they both owned houses, Nancye in Ormond Beach, Bobby in Deland. They sold them both after getting married and had a new house built for the two of them. To the investigators, this was proof that Bobby was not reporting all of the cash he seized on the interstate.

And on and on it went. Many legal experts have said that any grand jury can come up with an indictment on the weakest of evidence. Yet, weeks continued to go by and there were no formal charges brought against any of us. But they forged on, knowing that our government had an endless amount of money and resources to spend on a targeted investigation of this nature. Hard as it was to believe that there was nothing else pressing in Washington, D.C. for these two attorneys to attend to, they continued their vigilant pressure. They must have wanted me in the worst way. They didn't care how long it took, how much money was spent or whose families they wrecked along the way, they were not leaving until they had an indictment and conviction in hand. This relentlessness was frightening.

In their own minds, I was sure they believed that Sheriff Bob Vogel had directly ordered the stopping of Blacks and Hispanics on I-95. But even as a state trooper, most of the larger seizures I made were against white motorists. No matter. They were fixated on me as some type of country bumpkin, red neck Sheriff stopping people and seizing their money as the *Orlando Sentinel* had detailed, and their efforts would continue until this somehow proved true.

Janet Reno had to know what Perez and Olson were doing. No DOJ attorneys are given this much time and money to investigate without the boss knowing what's going on. This had to mean she sanctioned it, but why? A number of cases I made as a trooper were Miami cases, where she used to work as state attorney. So she would certainly know who I was. The connection had to be Governor Lawton Chiles, a good friend of Reno's. Chiles' former press secretary now worked for Reno in Washington. But that still didn't answer the question of why. What motivated Janet Reno and the Department of Justice to come after one of their own?

The individual target letters they had sent to Bobby Jones, Dale Anderson and I would have to have Reno's approval. These letters stunned attorney Jon Sale, who was assisting Nancye Jones and our office with the DOJ investigation and representing me as Sheriff in my official capacity. Jon is an extremely intelligent, highly respected attorney in the legal community and had previously worked as the first assistant U.S Attorney for the southern district of Florida. There are few people in the justice system that command the amount of admiration that Jon Sale does. He was invaluable and his knowledge of the law and especially the federal government system as it pertained to the DOJ and the Civil Rights section was crucial to us.

Jon Sale advised us that the targeted DOJ letters meant Nancye, Jon and I couldn't really talk to anyone about most department matters without there being the possibility of obstruction of justice. Just the simple matter of discussing an I-95 case with a deputy could be construed as an attempt to influence the outcome of the investigation, since we now knew that we were specifically the people the DOJ were after. Even enforcing the normal discipline process could be considered hindering the DOJ investigation as it could be interpreted as retribution against some deputies that might testify against us. Our ability to compartmentalize the DOJ was now severely compromised. The Sheriff's office could no longer conduct business as usual and this was unacceptable to me and to the attorneys assisting us.

In addition to subverting our normal everyday procedures, the DOJ investigation was costing us dearly in money and time. Deputies were constantly being disrupted during the course of their work and subpoenaed to answer questions, often covering the same ground over and over again. Every time the deputies that the DOJ had focused on (since they were telling Olson and Perez what they wanted to hear) came up with another story, a new wave of subpoenas would make the rounds. Despite their inability to corroborate their witness' stories, they pressed ahead.

I wouldn't wish these two attorneys on my worst enemy. They could listen to 40 people tell a story, 38 of which told it one way and two another, and they would focus on the two who told a different version. I could never run our office's investigations in that manner. We always took the proper objective approach as we had been trained to do. We accumulated the evidence, sifted through it, evaluated it, and let the chips fall where they may. Olson and Perez subscribed to a different theory of investigation. They knew where they wanted the chips to fall and were only interested in the evidence that could support that. This investigative method left me feeling uneasy and uncertain about the future.

Certainly anyone in a leadership position is going to make some enemies. There were deputies I had disciplined that were eager to assist the DOJ in any way they could. The majority of the deputies in the Volusia County Sheriff's Office are good, hard-working, well intentioned people. Olson and Perez chose to listen to the stories of the disgruntled few and ignore the rest. But even concentrating their investigation in that manner, the year 1995 dragged on and the grand jury still could not come up with an indictment for an I-95 stop.

Our attorneys sent Perez and Olson a letter in May of 1995 regarding the entire mess. They argued that we had amply cooperated with all of the records requests and having witnesses available to give testimony. But enough was enough. The DOJ had been at it a full year, including two complete reviews by FBI agents that gave a thumbs up to our procedures.

Our attorneys further pointed out that the witnesses the DOJ were depending on so heavily had given inconsistent testimony regarding alleged racial targeting in the civil trial already. Nothing they had said persuaded a judge to even let the case finish, let alone reach a conclusion that these accusations were correct. To rely on them as the key witnesses in any criminal case, our attorneys were warning, would be a damaging mistake.

The attorneys focused specifically on Deputy Frank Josenhanz, who was the individual alleging that there was a formal policy in our department to stop Black and Hispanic motorists. The lawyers pointed out that Josenhanz was found not credible at any time. In addition, one judge pointed out that statistical evidence did not establish racial discrimination, either when considered alone or in conjunction with other evidence.

Josenhanz had insisted that we published a procedure for the I-95 stops that included stopping minorities. He described it as a "drug courier profile" and said it detailed the characteristics of people we instructed the SET to stop. We were all mystified by this as we had never published anything and I had stopped using a profile early in my state trooper days.

We finally found what Josenhanz was talking about. He had a three-page report entitled "characteristics of a drug courier" that he had brought back from a training school held in Jacksonville. In the three pages, there was only one word that bordered on racial overtones—ethnicity. It was listed as a characteristic, but could easily have been describing Colombians or Jamaicans or others in this country that played a role in distributing drugs. It was a far stretch to saying this meant "to stop Blacks and Hispanics on Interstate 95."

Josenhanz was the only deputy with this. An attorney named Mike Alderman, who worked with the Department of Highway Safety and Motor Vehicles, published it in 1984. Although he was the original author, whoever was handing it out at the training school in Jacksonville had long ceased giving Alderman credit for the work.

So much for Josenhanz' big scoop about the Volusia County Sheriff's Office.

Also in this letter to DOJ, our attorneys noted that while the DOJ continued their dogged pursuit of an indictment for racial discrimination, other arms of the Justice Department had agreed that no such pattern of racial targeting existed. Our lawyers argued that the DOJ should speak with one voice and indeed had already spoken on this matter.

Finally, the letter demonstrated that our office was at the forefront of promoting racial diversity within our own law enforcement agency. Leonard Davis had become a recognized expert on the subject and it was he, of course, who headed up the Special Enforcement Team that made the traffic stops, as well as working to expand the ranks of the office with minority officers.

While we knew Perez and Olson never had anything of substance for the I-95 stops because there was nothing to find, there was still a concern that they might indict anyway and take their chances. They were nearing the end of the grand jury investigation and faced a tight timetable. A grand jury is convened for 18 months, after which it is disbanded if nothing is found. As the 18-month deadline approached, Perez and Olson were under the gun to come up with something. They wanted nothing better than to return an indictment for any type of racial discrimination connected to the I-95 traffic stops and in a brief moment of panic I thought they might twist one of the legitimate stops we had made to make it fit an indictment.

Clearly, they weren't about to go away empty-handed. But what would they come up with? What case (or cases) would they focus on to demonstrate that our office was violating the civil rights of minorities?

Frustrated by a lack of result on the I-95 stops, they turned their attention to a couple of other stories that they heard from those deputies who did not like the standards and discipline procedures of the Volusia County Sheriff's Office that had been implemented after I took office in January 1989. A couple of these deputies were still around because I did not have the ultimate authority to fire them myself, as has been noted earlier in this book.

These stories were about police brutality, conducted and advocated by my office. Police brutality! Those that know me understand how I feel about excessive force of any kind. It is a thin line that police officers walk, and we had disciplined and even brought about firings (agreed to by the county manager) of deputies who had stepped over that line of police brutality. I will not and have not tolerated it in our agency and the deputies clearly know my position.

That this should now be the focus of the DOJ's grand jury investigation was an even larger stretch than looking for racial profiling and targeting on our I-95 stops. But nothing the DOJ did surprised me any longer.

Typical of the cases they were now reviewing was that of Albert Hudson who, along with his wife Ruby, were stopped by the I-95 team for speeding. This was a case mentioned earlier in this book where Deputy Bobby Jones heard a "thud" when he approached the car, and as it turns out, the sound was that of a fully-loaded semi-automatic 9mm pistol with the safety off that Hudson denied was in the car. It was after that incident that Deputy Jones exercised even more caution when approaching any car he had stopped.

The Hudsons were placed in the back seat of the deputies' patrol car and Deputy Jones called for backup. Sergeant Dale Anderson, field leader of the I-95 team, and his partner Deputy J.W. Smith responded. After hearing about the gun (and four kilos of cocaine found in the trunk), Sergeant Anderson thought it best to search the suspects. They were brought out of the car and a normal search was conducted. Also on the scene were Sergeant Mark Davis with the St. John's county Sheriff's Office who was riding with the team as an observer and Deputy Frank Josenhanz who was still on the team at that time.

Josenhanz reported to our legal advisor Mel Stack that Anderson and Smith, who conducted the search, did so using excessive force. The case was investigated by Internal Affairs and there was no validation of Josenhanz' story. Josenhanz then repeated it to the DOJ attorneys. Oddly enough, Albert Hudson had died 15 months after the incident from a chronic respiratory illness. While there were no injuries or other evidence of the alleged excessive force, there was apparently some thought that the DOJ could tie the death to the I-95 stop and arrest.

Every one else present on the scene, including the third party observer from St. John's county, said it was a normal, routine, by-the-book arrest. Except Josenhanz.

Rather than listen to everyone else, attorneys Perez and Olson fervently wanted Josenhanz' story to be right. So they forged ahead to investigate other wild stories that some deputies like Josenhanz would relate to them.

Finally in May of 1995, down to the last week of this grand jury and after two years of federal investigation, the grand jury handed down two indictments. Captain Dale Anderson was indicted for two counts of use of excessive force and

Sergeant Mike Coffin was indicted on one count. Anderson was cited for the alleged beating of an individual named Ken Hill. Both Anderson and Coffin were charged with excessive force against one Doug Meagley, a man who had kidnapped his 16-month-old daughter at knifepoint in Edgewater and driven north to Flagler County and who would eventually surrender after a four-hour standoff.

Both suspects were white. But the deputies were charged under federal law Title 18, section 242. Under this statute, prosecutors will have to prove the deputies assaulted the suspects because they were foreign, or by reason of their color or race. A former civil rights prosecutor for the DOJ said the charge was odd, as both parties are white. He had only seen one case in fifteen years where this statute was used for a case where both parties were white and it never went to a jury as the charges could not be substantiated. Odd, yes, but so was everything the DOJ had done with respect to this entire investigation.

There were no indictments for anything done as part of the I-95 stops. There were no indictments returned against me. There was nothing for Bobby Jones, either. After all this time, two cases of alleged excessive force was all the "Injustice Department" could find to justify the time, effort and money spent here on behalf of "justice". While relieved that I wouldn't follow the same path as the Miami deputy Grant Snowden, I focused my concern now for Anderson and Coffin.

Under normal circumstances, I was certain that Anderson and young Mike Coffin would beat these charges. Neither individual, Hill nor Meagley had filed complaints or even accused anyone of excessive force. Meagley's case went back to 1990 and the Hill arrest was in 1993. We had no internal affairs reports to look back on, as nothing had prompted any investigation. These seemed like two fairly straightforward arrests. But, in the hands of the DOJ, who knew where this prosecution would go or what the outcome would be.

Anderson and Coffin would now have to secure legal representation and be suspended with pay until the case was finished. They would be subject to endless negative media scrutiny, their careers and reputations on the line, and for what? To get back at me? Certainly they must have thought they could somehow get to me through Dale Anderson, as he was part of the I-95 team. Yet the DOJ was playing with people's lives in their quest. The charges carried a maximum penalty of 10 years and a $250,000 fine. Dale Anderson was looking potentially at 20 years in prison. The whole mess was maddening, and totally without merit.

Dale Anderson had been a lifelong law enforcement officer. He had joined the Volusia County Sheriff's Department in 1973 and, like Leonard Davis, had seen a lot of changes over his more than twenty-year career. He had been a deputy, an investigator, had even ridden a motorcycle for a time. His selection to head up the Special Enforcement Team as the field leader for the I-95 stops, SWAT team activities and other investigations of this nature was a giant step ahead for him. He had also attended the FBI national training academy at Quantico in 1992 and had successfully graduated from that prestigious school.

Dale, his wife Debbie, and four sons took this news hard.

Dale and Debbie had known adversity in the past. Their firstborn son had died when he was 2. Their four boys now ranged from age 17 to seven months. He was a dedicated, loyal professional law enforcement officer that made the excessive force charges even more absurd. If Jeannie were ever to be kidnapped, I'd want Dale Anderson to be in charge of securing her safe return.

Mike was a five-year veteran, a young, conscientious hard-working deputy with a clean record to this point. He was career-minded, working on his college degree. This was a path I advocated having traveled it myself, studying between duty shifts. He was born and raised in Deland and would take on any task assigned him. He was never a part of the I-95 team, but handled difficult assignments professionally.

The case he was indicted for was not even mentioned in his record. He and Dale Anderson, along with the entire SWAT team, had been called to Flagler County to assist the Sheriff's Office to capture Doug Meagley. Meagley had kidnapped his 16-month old daughter in Volusia County and driven north, ending up in the smaller region of Flagler County, where he held his daughter hostage in a house. The Volusia County Sheriff's office is always willing to assist other law enforcement agencies so when Flagler called, we came.

It was a hostage case, and the SWAT team handled it appropriately, eventually getting Meagley to surrender. In keeping with procedures, Meagley was instructed to send the child out first and once she was safe to come out himself. He complied and when he finally emerged from the house, SWAT team members took him to the ground and he was handcuffed to remove any further threat. There have been cases where the kidnapper changes his mind about giving up and puts up resistance and the SWAT team actions were meant to prevent this from happening. The young girl was checked to be sure that she was OK and that was it. Meagley did not file any charges of unusual punishment or beating. But the DOJ indictment said that Anderson and Coffin did "willfully assault Doug Meagley, resulting in bodily injury."

Bodily injury? We could find nothing in our reports to substantiate that. What injury? We would have to wait for the discovery process to find out how the DOJ attorneys had drawn this conclusion.

The deputies were arraigned a week later in federal court in Orlando. They both pleaded innocent to the charges. Mike Coffin had arranged for a lawyer through the Police Benevolent Association, while Dale had hired two attorneys who had handled similar cases in the past.

The press attending the arraignment asked the deputies' attorneys about a possible plea bargain in exchange for information on the I-95 team's alleged practices as reported by the *Orlando Sentinel*. Anderson's attorney said the only plea that would be entered was the one Dale had just given—innocent. Coffin's attorney concurred and pointed out further that Mike had never been on the I-95 team so how could he help any DOJ investigation into the activities of the SET squad?

Obviously, the press was just as confused as we were. The *Sentinel* still wanted validation for their Pulitzer Prize, and could not see the connection between indictments for excessive force and the alleged racial profiling on I-95. Naturally, the *Sentinel* took time in each article to reprint their incorrect statistics about I-95, apparently subscribing to the theory that if you print anything enough times, it becomes a fact.

The indictment said that Meagley was tackled while Anderson went to rescue the child. Apparently, he broke his toe as a result. But he didn't complain of it at the time. Anderson and Coffin's attorneys would later find that Meagley had most likely broken the toe earlier during the kidnapping incident when he had kicked in the front door of the house in Edgewater the day before when he kidnapped the child.

In the other case, Ken Hill was a suspect that Dale had spotted at a nightclub. There was an outstanding arrest warrant on him and Hill noted Dale's presence at the same time Dale picked him out. Anderson chased Hill out of the bar and into the yard in back of it. Hill tripped and fell over a log and was caught and arrested. He did not complain of unusual punishment and a review of his mug shots showed nothing unusual. Anderson was accused in the indictment of an excessive beating of Hill along with dousing him with pepper spray.

As the attorneys prepared their cases, Anderson took an active role in his defense, sifting through the avalanche of paperwork. He had plenty of time on his hands during the suspension, so he thought he would put it to good use. He was having a difficult time explaining to his kids why he wasn't going to work like he always had, and where his deputy's car was located as it no longer sat outside at night. The emotional toll on the Andersons was rising. The more Dale reviewed these cases the greater his frustration with the absurdity of the charges.

Apparently, the DOJ didn't think much of the original charges either, especially since they were filed under the statute implying racism, so they filed new charges in July 1995. This time they had found what they wanted—a black suspect that was arrested by both Anderson and Coffin back in 1991. Kevin Lamar Gillislee of Deland was subdued and arrested after he fired ten shots into Volusia County Deputy Greg Piser's car. Anderson and Coffin pulled him out of a bathtub a day later, while executing an arrest warrant assigned by a judge. Gillislee kicked the gun out of Anderson's holster and Anderson hit him with his flashlight to prevent him from reaching the weapon. After all, Gillislee had already fired multiple times on a deputy. The flashlight blow worked and they were able to handcuff the suspect and arrest him.

The DOJ must have been worried they didn't have a civil rights case before they found Gillislee, since a minority was not involved in the other two situations. But Gillislee was not going to help them much. Despite the fact that Gillislee had shown no qualms about shooting at a deputy, Anderson still approached him with gun holstered to make the arrest. Gillislee was also charged with resisting arrest and the grand jury indictment against Anderson and Coffin said that they had perjured themselves during their testimony of Gillislee's arrest at his subsequent trial.

The DOJ attorneys appeared to be through. They returned to Washington, D.C. after the latest indictment, apparently giving up on finding anything else in their search for evidence against the Volusia County Sheriff's Office. What a travesty! Two years and a smear campaign later and all they have are three groundless excessive force cases. You could review every law enforcement agency in the country and come up with the same thing. The trial was still weeks away, and I knew in my heart that both Anderson and Coffin should both be acquitted. But would they be? In the meantime, they and their families would also have to endure the enormous pressure of a court appearance and ultimately the unknown of a jury trial.

It seemed to me that Olson and Perez had become nothing more than a point team for a small faction of disgruntled deputies within our office. When they spoke, the DOJ listened. When the other 95 percent of the department offered information, they were ignored. What it had created was a difficult atmosphere where a couple of rogue officers saw an opportunity to have me somehow ousted from office. With me gone, they must have believed the department would return to its old ways, leaving them plenty of room to operate in an undisciplined environment. What they didn't realize yet was the old days were long gone, replaced by an accredited, professional law enforcement agency that had to meet rigid standards to maintain the level of excellence needed to validate that endorsement. No amount of storytelling was going to restore the old order whether I was there or not.

So former SET team members like Frank Josenhanz and Lou Garcia turned against their old associates. Josenhanz' reputation as a "cowboy" was well documented and justified his removal from the SET team. What was ironic was that he was accusing his fellow team members of doing the things that got him kicked off the team.

Garcia was a different story. He had testified at one time during a trial stating that the I-95 team had no racial profile that they operated with and no edict to target Black and Hispanic motorists. A couple of years later, he apparently changed his mind and his testimony. In reviewing the differing testimonies, the State Attorney's Office asked that Garcia be investigated for possible perjury since he had told two different stories about the SET team during recorded testimony. One of the stories had to be incorrect. I'm sure there were a few hoping it would be the first story that he told that would be proved inaccurate and that he was just "covering" for his fellow officers. We knew that he told the truth then, but for some reason he elected to go the way of Frank Josenhanz with his most recent testimony.

The problem for us was how to handle this case. We could see what the State Attorney's Office saw in the differing statements, but now Garcia was a potential witness for the Department of Justice and we couldn't formally conduct the investigation requested without risking obstruction of justice charges. It was an absurd situation but that was what all of this had come down to. We would have to talk to a number of deputies to investigate Garcia's testimony discrepancies, but we had no idea who was on the DOJ's witness list for the grand jury. Speaking with any of them in connection with the Garcia matter could certainly be construed as obstruction of justice in the DOJ's eyes. The only thing we could do was to talk to the DOJ about the matter.

We advised the DOJ attorneys of the State Attorney's request and they told us to do what we had to do to normally run the department. We turned it over to our Internal Affairs Department and Garcia was suspended with pay, pending the outcome of the investigation. It didn't take them long to become convinced that Lou Garcia had perjured himself.

The next step would be to send it back to the State Attorney's Office, but they excused themselves from the case. So Governor Chiles' office had to assign someone else to look into it. Chiles picked Harry Shorenstein, a Democrat and an attorney from Jacksonville. Shorenstein spent a lengthy amount of time reviewing all of the paperwork and decided that he would not recommend prosecution of Lou for the perjury. He stated that Garcia walked "a thin blue line" and he could have been lying in his original testimony to protect his fellow officers and is now telling the truth. If he prosecuted Garcia, Shorenstein said, it could prevent other officers from coming forward and telling the truth. I had trouble following that logic as clearly Shorenstein was saying that Garcia's first statement defending the I-95 team was false. How would he know that? No other deputy (other than Josenhanz) who worked on the team substantiated anything these two guys said. But nothing made logical sense in this entire mess.

Shorenstein then began looking at I-95 cases, although he had only been charged with looking into Garcia's testimony pattern. Shorenstein was politically active with strong ties to the Governor and perhaps he had agreed to have a look at the I-95 stops in yet another last ditch effort to pull out some type of indictment from it. I reminded Shorenstein that the DOJ was already looking into the I-95 cases and he backed off.

Lou Garcia was now in a dicey position. He had reversed his previous testimony and every officer in the department knew that Lou had now lied for whatever reason. There would be a definite concern if Lou ever returned to the active ranks as to whether other officers could trust him or not. The *Sentinel* compared him to Frank Serpico, the New York City cop who testified to widespread police corruption and was the subject of a movie starring Al Pacino. Comparing Lou Garcia to Frank Serpico was as ridiculous as it sounds, but something you'd come to expect from the newspaper that falsified facts to win a Pulitzer Prize.

I had to avoid contact, as much as I could, with both Anderson and Coffin. It was routine procedure in this type of situation, but we all were astounded that it had come this far. There were even billboard signs that had been put up encouraging Anderson to "give up" Sheriff Vogel. This just strengthened Anderson's resolve and Dale received a boost in the very same month as his indictment when Florida Attorney General Bob Butterworth came to town for a memorial service for fallen officers. Butterworth gave Dale some encouraging words and I know Dale appreciated it. He and Debbie had prepared divorce papers as protection in the event that Dale was somehow convicted in this nightmarish odyssey, and he could use any amount of encouragement.

One evening Jeannie, Sheila and I went to a restaurant called Clancy's, intending to have dinner. We went there often and did so this time without thinking that it was also a favorite place of Dale Anderson's. When we saw that Dale was there, we couldn't stay, couldn't have dinner out at a place we liked because of the upcoming trial. As we left, I noticed that a van had pulled up and parked near us. When we drove away, the van followed us south on Nova Road to US 1. I made a couple of quick turns and the van stayed right with me. I made a sudden abrupt turn, heading north again on US 1 and then two other rapid turns before I had finally shaken the van. After a few minutes when all of our heart rates returned to normal, I drove back to Clancy's and there was the same van parked again. The vehicle displayed a temporary tag that wouldn't tell you who the owner was, only where the temporary tag had been issued. The van's presence back at Clancy's meant that someone had either Dale or I or both of us under some type of surveillance.

It was as if I was no longer living and working in the United States of America.

Jeannie went back into Clancy's to give Dale a heads-up that he was being watched.

While the emotional upheaval being experienced by the families of Dale Anderson and Mike Coffin was first and foremost in my mind, I knew that my own family was burdened by this seemingly endless pressure, too. Jeannie and Sheila had never complained about my work, never voiced disapproval at the long hours, at my being called out in the middle of the night, or being disrupted from a holiday meal. They were my strength, my backbone that helped keep me going. I knew of many officers whose family lives had ended in divorce, but our marriage and relationship with our daughter seemed to get stronger in the face of this ordeal.

I appreciated the emotional lift this gave me, but my family began to feel the physical toll of this nightmare by the middle of 1995. Sheila came down with mono and was sidelined for several weeks. We cared for her and worried as parents do, but it was Jeannie who spent more time with Sheila and it was Jeannie who then contracted the illness herself. We had no idea how devastating this illness was to prove for our family.

For as Sheila recovered, Jeannie did not. Her strength sapped by the mono, we figured it would only be a matter of time before she was up and around again.

But after a couple of weeks, she didn't improve. Actually, her condition worsened and I feared it was more than mono that was causing it. She remained unable to leave her bed for any length of time. Soon she had difficulty even getting up to use the bathroom. She was physically worn out, her small frame thoroughly weakened, the energy having taken leave of her body. Her eyes were rimmed with a tired blackness and she could do nothing but sleep for hours on end.

I was frantic with worry internally, but tried not to show it to Jeannie and Sheila. The staff and deputies in my office counted on my strength every day as we endured the DOJ pressure and now I had to maintain that same level of energy at home in the hopes of lifting Jeannie's spirits and power. I had never seen anyone so completely worn out that even the act of sitting up in bed was a tremendous chore.

Doctors diagnosed Jeannie with chronic fatigue syndrome and could offer little hope as to how long it would last and when she would be better. It was a relatively new disease the physicians told us, that we had to be patient and that Jeannie should keep taking the vitamins that were prescribed. We were spending $50-60 each week on vitamins, in the hopes that these pills would miraculously inject some adrenaline into Jeannie.

I wished every day that I could give Jeannie my strength. At night when I'd come home, I'd sit and just hug her, hoping that I could transfer power merely by the closeness of our bodies. I was getting up early each day, working out, trying to keep my own physical power up to a high level. There were those who would watch me every day to see if any wear and tear was starting to show, but I refused to give anyone that satisfaction. I also knew that I had truth on my side and this bolstered me more than any routine of calisthenics could ever do.

After consulting several local doctors, I finally took Jeannie to the Mayo Clinic. By this time, it had been months since Jeannie first took ill and we were all at wit's end trying to figure out how to improve her condition. Jeannie was reluctant to go, but Sheila and I insisted. They did a very thorough analysis and the first thing they told us to do was to flush the vitamins down the toilet. They were not helping Jeannie get better and she was better off not taking anything.

They prescribed a lifestyle change instead. Jeannie's schedule was as bad as mine. She was still an Elementary School Resource Teacher. This was in addition to all the public appearances to be made with me in the course of Sheriff's duties. Naturally, the lengthy DOJ embattlement and the local media pressure had also contributed to her exhaustion and Jeannie would have to find a way together to shake these things from her system.

She decided against returning to work as a School Resource Teacher. This mental decision seemed to slowly return her physical strength. It would be weeks before Jeannie was back to normal, but she had finally turned a corner.

I gave thanks for this turn of events. Jeannie meant more to me than any job and if it came down to the choice, I knew which path I'd take. For a time, I was wondering if life for us would ever be the same again. By day, I had a law enforcement agency to run despite the internal pressures everyone felt as so many were touched by the DOJ case, due to depositions and testimony. By night, I had a family wracked by illness to help. But I wasn't going to give up. All my life I've been fighting to win and my family and I were going to come out ahead no matter what. I somehow managed to get through these months and I credited much of this mental and physical strength to my training as a U.S. Marine, where when you felt like you couldn't handle any more, they gave it to you anyway. You simply found the will to complete whatever task it was. That's how each day seemed to me through 1995. Every day presented the challenge of getting through and accomplishing daily tasks as I went. It was a battle that I truly felt Jeannie, Sheila and I were destined to win and so, I hoped, by extension, would Dale Anderson and Mike Coffin.

In addition to the DOJ distractions, it was at this time that our office had to deal more repeatedly with a man named Tom Bourke. He had been a presence in our lives for a few years now, but had really turned up the heat on us during the DOJ investigation and indictments.

Tom Bourke was a letter writer. He had started out with us on a positive note, being an active supporter during my first term in office. He had lost a son to drugs and he liked the way our office was fighting this problem to hopefully avert similar tragedies from befalling others. He had even sent flowers to Nancye Jones during this early period.

He wanted to play an active role in my 1992 re-election campaign, but he presented such a slovenly appearance that he was frightening to some of our supporters. I decided against him being a part of our campaign and when informed of this, he turned on our office in a heartbeat. This was the time following the initial publication of the *Sentinel* articles and Bourke launched his own personal investigation of our office. He repeatedly sent in public records requests for our files, an action any citizen has a right to do, and kept our office busy photocopying for several weeks.

But it was his letter writing campaign that rankled most. From 1994 through 1998, Bourke sent me 87 letters. Nancye received 32, Leonard Davis 9, Dale Anderson 3, Bob Butterworth 7 and Merle Harris, editor of *Seniors Today* and a strong supporter of mine was sent 13 letters from Bourke.

Typical of a Bourke letter was one written to me in August 1994.

"Dear Sheriff Robert L. Vogel, Jr.:
You know it is a real shame that people like you are able to finagle their way into a powerful political position… There is one comforting thing to know, we have grand juries to deal with you… I wrote a 4,000 word letter about you and

your crew… It had the type of punch needed and would have the type of impact needed to politically topple you… You're a lucky man… I can't and won't send the letter out now to everyone… A certain government agency has requested of me that I not do so… I was further warned that because an atmosphere of desperation and anger exist in your office, it would be unwise for me to make such a move… I say if I see a storm coming our way from Deland that threatens the safety and peace of me or my family, I'm going to hold one person responsible… Keep your pit bulls on a leash… You're in heap big trouble and you know it… Word is no legal deals, no Butterworth bailout, no nothing… The book is getting heavy and it is going to be thrown in the next 60 days… You're a bigger fool than I thought if you underestimate the ability of the FBI…"

This was typical of the tone and content of a Tom Bourke letter. Everyone seemed to get them, every week, sometimes daily, spitting out the same venom. He wrote to Janet Reno, judges, attorneys and anyone he could think of that might exert some influence in getting me removed from office. A letter to Nancye that same month included the comments, "Tell me counselor, while attending law school at the University of South Carolina, did anyone ever instruct you in the importance of and the use of ethical restraint? Yes, I question the ethical conduct of you and the Volusia County Sheriff's Office… Oh, by the way, do you mind if I ask a quick question before I let you go? Do you know a good attorney that specializes in criminal law?"

The mail from Bourke typically came certified and was poorly written. But it was voluminous and added another layer of difficulty when trying to carry on the routine daily work of the office. In addition, he had taken aim at our friends Merle and Dilys Harris, editors of *Seniors Today*. Because of their support of me (I contribute an article each month to their publication) Bourke felt it necessary to target as many subscribers to this newspaper as he could telling them that I was "a sick man" and condemning Merle and Dilys for being supportive of my career. I apologized to the Harris's for being dragged into the sorry circle of Tom Bourke, but they assured me that nobody took this guy seriously. But Bourke pressed on, undeterred, another product of the *Sentinel*'s stories about I-95. He wanted me removed from office just as badly as Wendy Olson and Tom Perez.

Adding further to this circus atmosphere was the irony that even as the DOJ was doing its utmost to get me removed from office, that same governmental branch was bestowing awards on our agency. First it was a Public Service Award for our Weed and Seed program in Spring Hill. In this program, we concentrate on a community that has a large crime problem and use law enforcement techniques to get it back under control. It's a constant, ongoing process and we worked with the local Deland Police Department to weed out the criminal element. Prosecuting criminals under the Weed and Seed program meant taking them to court on a federal level. This meant those convicted would serve more of their sentence than if convicted in state court, and thus would serve as a deterrent for some. But our efforts were not limited to investigate and arrest. We also spent money to enhance the lighting in many parts of the community, giving drug dealers fewer dimly lit places in which to transact their illegal deals. We cleaned up vacant lots and instituted a beautification process to clean up the area. We involved the community and the crime problem receded. For this, we were recognized by the same Department of Justice that was bent on exacting some type of frontier justice on us.

The second honor was for Project Harmony, a collaborative program that involved the school system, Stetson University, the West Volusia Police Athletic League and sixth graders in Volusia County. The purpose of the program was to get young people from various ethnic backgrounds to interact with each other and develop a friendship and respect for one another. This created a more positive environment in the schools and there was less trouble as a result. We utilized the Sheriff's Youth Camp in Barberville in the western end of the county to put the children up for a week, let them get to know each other.

As a result of the program's success, President Clinton cited our organization for a Project Harmony Award. This was the first cultural diversity program to be recognized as successful by the White House. Naturally, this received no local media coverage, as it was apparently not newsworthy enough. The DOJ certainly ignored any positive happenings in our department. No matter. What was important was that we felt we were on to something with this program and if it contributed to a safer environment within the schools, we were better off as a community.

THE TRIAL

It was nearing November 1995 before the case finally appeared to be heading to the courtroom. The DOJ attorneys were compiling "like evidence" cases, collateral situations that involved a measure of excessive force so that Perez and Olson could demonstrate a pattern that would help prove that Coffin and Anderson were guilty. The cases they had to prosecute – Meagley, Hill and Gilislee – were weak and they needed to have as much as they could to expect to win this case. We maintained confidence that they could never build enough of a case, since there was nothing concrete to build on.

The DOJ was desperate now. Despite the pressure we faced in the Volusia County Sheriff's Office, it was time for Olson and Perez to deliver on the 18-month long grand jury investigation. Desperate times called for desperate measures. Wendy Olson and FBI agent Jim Price both had asked two Flagler County Sheriff's deputies to undergo hypnosis to help them remember more about the Meagley hostage case. They declined and Flagler Sheriff Bob McCarthy called the government request "bizarre." Olson then told Sheriff McCarthy that he was obstructing justice in a civil rights case. McCarthy responded by saying, "What about the rights of that little girl? Our deputies were right on the scene and know that none of the stuff the government is saying actually happened."

In addition, the DOJ had repeatedly expressed concern that I was personally intimidating several witnesses, pointing to Lou Garcia's suspension as proof. But I had suspended Garcia as he was the subject of a perjury investigation, normal procedure for any situation like that. I hated to see the DOJ pit deputy against deputy but that's exactly what had happened.

One of the collateral cases Wendy Olson and Tom Perez were hoping to use to show a pattern of excessive force was based on the testimony of Deputy Steve Rupert and involved the arrest of two brothers. Ramon and Carlos Jenkins were apprehended on drug trafficking charges in November 1988, before I had even taken office as Sheriff. Rupert said he was taking the handcuffs off of Carlos when Jenkins began fighting with Rupert. Rupert said that Anderson and Deputy Ray Almodovar came flying into the room, removed Jenkins and thoroughly beat him before Rupert could break it up. Rupert said he didn't report the attack at the time because Anderson was his superior officer and he feared retribution. Carlos was dead now and the DOJ could not find his brother Ramon to substantiate the case, so all they had was Rupert's word.

As the trial opened in November 1995, that turned out to be all Perez and Olson generally had—the word of a couple of deputies against Anderson, Coffin and a host of others willing to stand up for Dale and Mike. That these were the only cards they had to play really didn't surprise us since we knew there was nothing they could have because it simply wasn't there to find. What we didn't know is how far they could take this information in a trial and what influence it would have in a jury if they emphasized only what they wanted.

Early on, they put Deputy Erik Eagan on the stand. He was the deputy who was with Anderson when they chased down and arrested Ken Hill. Eagan admitted on the stand during the trial that he had personally punched Hill twice and then lied about it in his report to me. He then said that Anderson had kneed Hill in the back when he was lying compliantly on the ground as Eagan handcuffed him and later they knocked him over a fallen tree. But now his testimony was questionable since he already admitted he'd lied about his own actions and that he had, in fact, used what appeared to be excessive force himself. His credibility as a witness would be a preview of what was to come for Perez and Olson.

In addition to credibility concerns, Perez and Olson faced a numbers problem as well. Against the three or four witnesses that the DOJ brought up to level these accusations against Anderson and Coffin, both men paraded dozens of witnesses to the stand during the trial, stating that they had never seen either deputy use excessive force in any way.

Again, this was not surprising and the DOJ attorneys should have been prepared for this. They had listened to the small group of dissenters who told them what they wanted to hear and ignored the rest of the deputies' testimony. Naturally, Anderson and Coffin's attorney brought as many of the others to the stand to counteract the DOJ witnesses. It almost wasn't necessary since the DOJ witnesses seem to be bringing the curtain down on their case all on their own.

The crux of the trial finally came down to a case that neither Anderson nor Coffin was charged with, but illustrated how absurd all this had become. As previously noted, Deputy Steve Rupert had arrested Carlos and Ramon Jenkins for drug trafficking and later alleged that Anderson and Deputy Ray Almodovar had beaten Carlos while the arrested man was screaming and protesting. Deputy Tracy Hernlen, the former SWAT team member who had fired the fatal shot at Helen McConnell, backed up Rupert on this testimony.

Hernlen had originally told a grand jury that he had never witnessed an officer using excessive force against anyone, but recanted with his statement about the Jenkins case. Hernlen was not in on the arrest, but had supposedly come in to the examination room to assist Rupert in some way. Hernlen couldn't recall the names of the Jenkins brothers and was even incorrect about where the alleged incident took place. He said that Anderson had taken the handcuffs off the protesting Carlos Jenkins to accompany the man to the bathroom and then, in the hallway, beat and kicked him. Hernlen said he heard a thump and then rushed out of the room and saw Anderson beating Jenkins and yelling, "He's resisting! He's resisting!" Hernlen went to break it up and said Anderson kicked him, too.

Hernlen's trial testimony was a mess. He contradicted himself endlessly, said he couldn't recall anything he had previously told the grand jury, and told a different story at the trial. He claimed to have kept a separate diary of events and said that he had written about this incident some months after the event. He had never reported it to Sheriff Duff at the time it happened in November 1988 and then said he had shredded the diary with the appropriate pages in it. Robert Leventhal, one of Anderson's lawyers expertly pointed out the credibility problems with Hernlen's testimony mostly by letting Hernlen sink himself on the stand.

But the biggest blow in this case came from Ramon Jenkins, the other brother who was arrested that day. Carlos had since died and for some inexplicable reason, the DOJ attorneys never bothered to find Ramon, who was also present that day and could either substantiate or contradict the Rupert and Hernlen testimony. But nothing these DOJ lawyers did made any common sense.

Anderson and Coffin's attorneys left nothing to chance. They found Ramon in Texas and brought him in to testify. Put on the stand, Ramon told an entirely different version of the events as had already been described by Rupert and Hernlen. He said that no deputy touched Carlos. Ramon was shown pictures of Anderson, Hernlen and Rupert and said that he didn't know who Anderson was and that he had never seen him. He did identify Rupert and Hernlen.

Ramon Jenkins took the story further. He testified that while Carlos was not beaten by anyone, he was—but by Rupert. He said that Hernlen released his handcuffs and then started shouting, "He's resisting! He's resisting!" — words Hernlen had attributed to Anderson — and then Rupert took over. He punched Ramon repeatedly as the suspect tried to cover up and absorb the hits as best he could.

The courtroom was shocked by this turn of events. Wendy Olson sat transfixed, listening to Ramon Jenkins' statement, as if she could see her case disappearing among the stream of words that was Ramon's testimony. Later, Jim Price, the FBI agent who had suggested hypnosis to Flagler County officers to help them remember the Meagley incident better, followed Ramon out into the hall to ask him when Anderson's lawyers had found him.

It was Rupert and Hernlen's word against Jenkins, but Ramon had nothing to gain from lying about the incident. The deputies had plenty to conceal apparently and had laid off this use of excessive force on Anderson. Hernlen had made no secret of the fact that he blamed Anderson for a lot of the problems he had, both from a career (demotions and reassignments) and personal (divorce, bankruptcy) standpoint and perhaps he saw this as an opportunity for some type of revenge.

That was the end of the case. The testimony was all in. Flagler County officers did not substantiate the excessive force claim against Coffin and Anderson in the case of Doug Meagley. Deputy Eagan admitted to beating Ken Hill himself, impugning his credibility. And, in their collateral case evidence, Ramon Jenkins had descended on the court like a ghostly apparition out of Rupert and Hernlen's past to dispute their evidence. It seemed to us that Dale and Mike stood a better than even chance of beating this misguided rap. But it was still in the hands of a jury, no certain thing.

On November 22, 1995 the verdicts came in. Standing within a few feet of each other were the DOJ attorneys and Anderson and Coffin, flanked by their attorneys.

Anderson's charges were read first and an anxious Dale awaited the jury result. After each charge came the words, "Not Guilty." Dale Anderson was a free man.

It was now Mike Coffin's turn. The first charge was in the Meagley case. Jurors ruled that Mike never assaulted Meagley in any way. His other charges met with the same "Not Guilty" tag line. Mike Coffin had also been acquitted on all counts against him. His ordeal was over.

This trial never should have happened. What a waste of time and taxpayer money! Even Bob Leventhal, Anderson's attorney and a former federal prosecutor said that it was the weakest case he had ever seen federal prosecutors bring against anyone. I would bet that the careers of Wendy Olson and Tom Perez were not going to be long ones with the U.S. Justice Department. Perhaps the DOJ should have been indicted for defrauding the taxpayers of this country.

Probably the saddest part of the whole trial was to see a couple of our deputies take the stand and perjure themselves. What their motivation was can only be guessed at, but I'll stand behind my belief that these were officers not pleased with the way I ran the department, instituting disciplinary measures all professional law enforcement agencies need to have. I would have to re-examine some of the cases in light of what was said in court as deputies Rupert, Hernlen and Eagan appeared to have been involved in excessive force cases personally that had never been brought to the light of day until now.

Wendy Olson left the courtroom in a hurry and would not comment on the affairs. Of those that stayed behind, they pointed out that the investigation into my department was still going on and was not yet closed. Even after all of the evidence had been sifted through and evaluated from many different ways, with the same negative results, the DOJ was still singing the same refrain—the Volusia County Sheriff's Office is still officially under investigation.

Our Confiscated Funds account would be tapped to pay for the bulk of Anderson's defense. I'm sure drug dealers would have enjoyed the irony of that. These funds had been heretofore used to upgrade the department's technology and equipment to make us more effective fighting crime. Now, we would have to use it to defend two capable officers against groundless charges brought by our own U.S. Justice Department. If this story were a novel, readers would likely dismiss it as being too far-fetched.

We had to now put this behind us and continue on with the process of law enforcement. Dale and Mike were anxious to get back to work. That would be the easy part. What would be difficult is trying to patch up a department that has a few deputies whose truth telling had now been brought into question. There would be no retribution against these men, and normal procedures would be utilized to evaluate what to do about some of the statements made that incriminated them.

Due to Rupert's apparent involvement in an excessive force situation with Ramon Jenkins, I removed him from the SWAT team pending an Internal Affairs investigation. But he resigned shortly thereafter to return to the Midwest where he grew up. I also had no choice but to suspend Hernlen with pay until an Internal Affairs investigation could examine the Jenkins case. Oddly enough, rumors had long persisted that Hernlen and Rupert, close friends, had both got a SWAT team tattoo. That concerned me then as being a little too intense for this type of work and apparently my worries were justified.

Eagan was already on administrative leave and I formally suspended him with pay due to the statements he made about personally using excessive force. This was not any type of personal backlash from me, but normal procedure as dictated by our accreditation standards we uphold as a professional law enforcement agency. I knew the newspapers would never understand this (or print it), but I was bound to follow proper procedure.

Congressional representative John Mica was disturbed by what our office had been subjected to by the Department of Justice in their years-long probe. Calling the process a "witch hunt" he formally asked the chairman of the House committee that oversees the DOJ for an accounting of its actions in this case. I appreciated this gesture on behalf of the Volusia County Sheriff's Office.

As it turns out, we needed Congressman Mica's help a short time later. President Clinton had authorized additional funding for law enforcement agencies to put more officers on the street. But our share of that funding was being held up as we were under investigation by the DOJ. I called John Mica to ask why as the indictments had now been settled. He was upset and made some calls and obtained the money for the Volusia County Sheriff's Office.

Lou Garcia had filed a federal "whistle-blower" lawsuit after he was suspended due to the state attorney's office investigation into perjury charges against him. He claimed that he was suspended due to the fact that he was going to testify against our department. Of course, that wasn't true. He had told two entirely different stories under oath and perjured himself, leading to his suspension in accordance with department rules. Any deputy would have had the same consequence. He was suspended with pay, pending the outcome, and the county was trying to find him another job after the state eventually decided not to file formal charges against him.

Garcia finally gave up the whistle-blower suit idea in early 1996. He also resigned from the Sheriff's Office after the now 20-month suspension. Hernlen's suspension was lifted in late January and he was reassigned to the judicial services division.

Dale Anderson's first day back on the job had brought a smile to his face even before he left his house. After putting on his deputy's uniform for the first time in more than six months, his youngest son exclaimed, "Daddy, you're a policeman!" He had been too young earlier in the year to realize that his dad wore a uniform and Dale hadn't been able to wear it since his suspension pending the outcome of the trial. His son was delighted with his father's occupation, and so was Dale.

Incredibly, it would be another year and a half before the Department of Justice would officially end their probe of our office. There were no charges filed, other than the flimsy indictments of Anderson and Coffin, and no evidence ever uncovered that our office had handled matters in any way other than professionally and legally. By then it had been four years that they had examined our procedures from every conceivable angle.

And they finally just walked away.

They left with a few parting shots, of course. You couldn't put four years of federal time into an investigation and merely give it up quietly at the end, apologize and say you made a mistake. That isn't how DOJ operates as I had come to find out.

They indicated that it was recommended that I be charged back in March 1995 with civil rights violations to **make an example** of me. But they never filed charges, were never confident enough of building a case on the word of a few disgruntled deputies. They took this failure out on Dale Anderson and Mike Coffin and made a shambles out of their lives for a few months to justify their obsession with the Volusia County Sheriff's Office.

To make an example of me? You don't charge people with crimes in this country to make an example out of them! That's scary stuff, almost Big Brother-ish in concept. This is the type of behavior that fires up the militia groups across the country, directing their rage at a branch of federal government run amok.

I doubt we'll ever know why. What was disturbing to me was that if I was doing things wrong, then I would have accepted that and altered our procedures accordingly and taken whatever punishment it deserved. But to go by the book, to follow legal procedure as carefully as we did, and then have a newspaper print a series of falsehoods as distorted as the *Orlando Sentinel* articles were in June 1992, was beyond comprehension. Then, to see the fallout from these articles and the injustice it spawned was to endure a living nightmare.

Worse, there was no way to successfully combat that tactic. No matter what you did, people who read those stories formed an opinion of me from their reading, and it wasn't a positive one. It's hard to see people look at you, wondering if you're some kind of abusive racist running the Sheriff's department, when the truth was as far from that as it could be.

What could you do? All there was for me was to simply operate as I always have and trust that most of the people in the county would be swayed by the full investigation into the department without any negative result. We had been cleared beyond any shadow of any doubt, and it was my hope that when the election of 1996 came around, people would remember that the agency was vindicated every long, torturous step of the way. I knew there would be some votes lost along the way, but still put great faith in the people to discern the difference between truth and falsehoods.

What I felt when it was over was a kind of humility. I know that as a public servant, I'm going to be subject to a certain amount of criticism. Even the letter writing of Tom Bourke unfortunately comes with the territory. And while what I (and other deputies in the department) had been subjected to was completely unfair, it was a not-so-gentle reminder that there are always better ways to do things, better ways to serve the public.

Bitterness about this is not a useful emotion. There are always things to learn, new ways of operating that make us more efficient and effective. The criticism of our department helped us to focus on how to perform our jobs and turn those negative statements into positive ones.

I think we were doing that quite well. My first term in office had been primarily spent professionalizing the department. This term in office had been a nightmare of accusations and ultimate absolution.

I was hopeful that if I could win a third term in office, I could focus more on further improving how the Volusia County Sheriff's Office served and protected the citizens of Volusia County.

ELECTION NIGHT, 1996

Jeannie and I held hands in the back room of the Riverside Pavilion. All of the precincts had now reported in and I was still behind. All that remained were the absentee ballots.

The mood in this part of the Pavilion was down beat. Dale Anderson sat with his arms crossed, lucky cigar still out of sight. He had been twirling it the first part of the evening, but his hands merely clasped his arms now. Terry Sanders was totally pale and I was concerned that he might pass out. Connie Locke had her hands folded in front of her most of the night, but now they gripped the back of a chair, knuckles whitening in tension. Bob Rickmyre sat stooped over, almost in a stance of prayer – hands folded, head down, eyes closed, probably seeking support from a higher power. Leonard Davis was standing like a statue, seemingly unable to move. Jody Palermo held his head in his hands, perhaps trying to summon some more inner strength.

Jeannie and I looked at each other. We didn't need words. We were searching each other for answers, but there were no more for now. We were in mutual disbelief. We didn't expect to lose this race. With all that happened, we believed it would be close, but not that we'd be on the losing end.

Our eyes told us that we weren't concerned for each other if these results stood. We knew we could get through whatever lay ahead. But it would be difficult to face all those wonderful people who had sacrificed to support and campaign for us. That would be the most difficult test of all.

Sheila was outside, talking to her friends in the parking lot. Upset, she made her way back into the main room and found Carol and Mike Kilman, who owned a local jewelry store where she worked part time. They had planned to come for about an hour or so, but with the results so close, they stayed in support as many others had.

Sheila suggested that maybe if they went outside and prayed, her dad's luck would change. Carol and Mike agreed, but they weren't the only ones who'd heard Sheila's suggestion. As they moved to the front entrance, a groundswell of people began to move with them, to take their prayers outside as one last resort. Someone nominated Cecil Hunter to lead the group prayer. Cecil had been our designated prayer guide and always led our campaign meetings with a prayer.

Suddenly, there were more people outside than there were in the main room. From the celebration and the cheerleading inside to the determined people of all denominations now gathered in a giant circle outside, the mood of the night abruptly changed. John Smart, a retired Methodist minister and former mayor of Lake Helen, another small town in Volusia County, encouraged everyone to hold hands while he recited a prayer.

While Jeannie and I looked into each other's soul for answers to our future, Protestants, Catholics, Jews and other religious orders stood in unison, holding hands, straining to hear John Smart's words of prayer. Everyone wanted to get in the circle and be part of what was going on. John asked God to help the Sheriff come through this night.

People were driving into the parking lot, hopping out of their cars and coming into the circle to be involved in this extraordinary prayer. When he finished, everyone hugged, tears coming down the faces of many. It was a magical, mystical feeling for those that were there.

The excitement outside of the Riverside Pavilion must have traveled inside where Jeannie and I stood holding hands, feeling some of that uplifting spirituality. The reverie was broken by the noise of the phone, ringing one last time that evening. It was Gary Davidson. The precincts had all reported in and the absentee ballots had been counted. I had been re-elected!

Shouts of joy broke from the members of that back room, pent-up pressure discharged all at once. Everyone was hugging and laughing, the tension released, relief taken over. As we celebrated, I heard Gary say over the phone that we had won by more than one percent, which meant there would not be an automatic recount.

Ron Johnston had grabbed me in a bear hug and lifted me off the ground. I thought he was going to break a couple of my bones in his excitement. The atmosphere was suddenly jubilant, when only moments ago you could hear every creak in the room it was so quiet.

I caught Dale Anderson's eye and he just gave me a wide-eyed grin, took an exaggerated deep breath and pulled the cigar out, drawing it across his nose. It was lucky, after all. Connie was embracing Leonard, then Jody; Bob Rickmyer hugged Jeannie.

Suddenly, we heard the shouts of joy from outside. We went into the main room and were surprised to see people coming into a half-filled room. Where had everyone gone? Out to pray we found out moments later from Dilys Harris.

"Where's Sheila?" I asked someone, and then I saw her, trying to get to the main room stage, boxed in by well wishers. I turned to look for Jeannie and she was right next to me, holding my arm and we embraced for joy. We could hear a reporter from Channel 9 say to Nancye Jones, "Who's the Sheriff hugging?" Jeannie couldn't resist, and yelled out, "His girlfriend!" We were all in a "let it loose" mood.

The sight of the many people who had now crowded into the Pavilion stunned me. They were crying; they were laughing; they were holding hands; they were still cheering. Dilys Harris led a cheer called, "People like us don't want Gus!" a direct retort to Gus Beckstrom's campaign slogan, "People like us want a Sheriff like Gus." Others were singing, "Get on the bus, Gus!" a takeoff from an old Paul Simon song. It was bedlam.

Sheila was trying desperately to get to the stage, tears streaming down her cheeks. The poor kid, I thought, what a night she'd had! I felt a tremendous sense of relief and knew Jeannie did, too. We struggled to get to the microphone so we could thank all of these great folks for coming out and showing their support in a real time of need. I have no doubt that the energy of this gathering pushed me over the top to win.

Jeannie had found Buddy Ridgell, our office manager for all three campaigns, a senior citizen who worked actively each campaign to help us out. She steered her towards the stage. It seemed to take forever, there were so many hands to grasp on the way. I saw Brent and Becky Millikan. Brent had been our campaign treasurer for the first two elections and had been an advisor this campaign. He shouted that he and Becky had seen the news on television, that we were losing, and they couldn't stay away. I thanked them both and moved on.

Finally, we reached the stage. I hugged Sheila as tight as I could and realized she was still trembling. Jeannie hugged her, too, and they were both saying "Dad won! Dad won!" That brought more tears of joy to Sheila's face. We were running on pure euphoria now.

I took the microphone and thanked everyone who had come out, and all those who had worked hard and those that had voted for me. I said that we would work even harder to earn back the votes we didn't get. My staff and I were dedicated to making Volusia County the greatest and safest place to live.

Sheila didn't even make it through the brief speech. She needed air and went outside, wanting a glass of water, only to start hyperventilating. Jody Palermo's wife, Tracy, was a nurse and rushed over to see what was wrong. As soon as Jeannie knew, she was by her side immediately. Jeannie took Sheila's hand and said, "Let's pretend we're doing yoga" and they went through their breathing routine. "Dad's got a job," Jeannie assured Sheila, "you can go to Stetson! Your vote really counted today, honey!" Jeannie's cheerleading seemed to have a calming effect.

Ironically, Signe Earhart, the nurse who eighteen years ago had been present at Sheila's birth, was here at the Pavilion. She came to Sheila's side as well, saying, "I brought you into this world, you're not going anywhere yet!" Sheila's friend Michelle's father was a Sergeant in our office, Dave Hinshaw, and he called an ambulance. By the time they arrived, Sheila was better. The paramedic wanted to know why Sheila couldn't breathe and she looked up at him and said, "Why don't you think I can't breathe?" as if the man should have known exactly what had transpired here tonight.

Before the winning announcement, the news media had been circling like buzzards, sensing the expiration of their target. But after I had been declared the winner, they collectively seemed to soften. Nigel Cook of the News Journal was on bended knee, trying to take our picture and he looked friendly, a sight we had not often seen from the local journalists this campaign.

In the early hours of Wednesday morning, the Riverside Pavilion finally began to clear out. Sheila was feeling normal again and Jeannie was feeding the members of the media who were still there - and famished. Gus Beckstrom came on the television and said he wouldn't challenge the vote (it was not an automatic recount) and would go with the will of the people.

A TV reporter asked me for an interview and I agreed. The video media had always been fair with me, so I answered some questions. At one point during the questioning, as tiredness began to overcome me, I did let loose at the print media. I called their stories of the past few months slanted and untruthful and hoped that no one would ever be subject to that kind of reporting ever again. During this interview, someone had said that John Holland of the News Journal was on his way out to the Pavilion.

He never showed.

As we left the Riverside Pavilion that night, hand in hand, Jeannie, Sheila and I had felt as if we'd won a great battle. What we didn't know was that the war was not over.

CHAPTER SIX:
GUARDING THE BALLOTS

THE WILL OF THE PEOPLE

Gus Beckstrom's acceptance of the will of the people lasted about 24 hours.

From a nearly 4,000 vote deficit after all the precincts had reported in, I held a 14,962 to 10,086 absentee ballot advantage to win the election. Almost 25,000 absentee ballots was an amazing number in itself. But many that vote absentee are seniors, and this age group was a firm base of support for me. A large number of my campaign workers voted absentee as well so that they could campaign uninterrupted on Election Day. That considered, the margin of absentee ballot victory was not surprising to me.

The true wonderment was that these votes would turn out to be so crucial.

Deanie Lowe, Supervisor of Elections for Volusia County, typically counts these votes in advance of the election. So, after all of the precincts report in, this number total can be added quickly for final results.

The carefully crafted media campaign to blitz me out of office was nearly successful. The accusations about our I-95 stops, the Sentinel reports, the Governor's Panel, the NAACP suit, the civil trial and the long, drawn-out U.S. Justice Department investigation had finally taken its toll on the average Volusia voter. Add in a final two-week print media assault by the Daytona Beach News Journal and I was indeed fortunate to survive all of that.

Lost in the shuffle of all these negative, inaccurate and misleading stories was that crime in Volusia County continued to spiral downward even as its population grew significantly. This was the true accomplishment of a dedicated professional law enforcement agency.

It's just not news that Volusia citizens get to read.

Instead, we were in for one more battle, this time over the election results. Beckstrom did not ask for a recount. Instead, a day after saying he was returning quietly to his lieutenant's post in the Winter Park Police Department, he formally asked for a review of the absentee ballots to check for improprieties.

A total of 27,310 absentee ballots had been returned, some of which did not contain a vote for the Sheriff's position while others came in too late to be counted. The total sent in was more than 80 percent of the ballots requested, a record according to Deanie Lowe.

I had no idea where this re-examination of the ballots would lead and I wasn't concerned. I had been returned to the Sheriff's office by a very slim margin and all I could do about that was to continue doing my job as Sheriff and try to win some of those votes back. The ballot challenge would be a distraction, just as the DOJ and Sentinel stories diverted our concentration. But we had overcome those difficulties, had time after time been found to be properly doing our jobs, and we would continue on that same course. I was contemplating some internal changes to improve the efficiency of the department, but we would keep doing the things that helped bring the crime numbers down in our county.

Beckstrom's challenge to Deanie Lowe was met with her publicly stating that she understood Beckstrom's frustration at losing by just 798 votes, but insisted the election had been conducted fairly and this review would show that. Beckstrom wanted to personally compare lists of absentee voters to those who voted at the polling booths to ensure there was no duplication. Lowe denied that request, saying Beckstrom was no longer a candidate and by law cannot examine the lists.

I can't imagine people voting twice. If they did, they'd be found out soon enough. The Elections office routinely compares the lists anyway each time out to be sure that didn't happen. Beckstrom didn't have to issue a challenge for that to occur; this was normal procedure.

At this same time, the Daytona Beach News Journal wrote a story about the deputies that had guarded the absentee ballots, noting that they were all strong Vogel supporters. They said the deputies had physically handled the ballots and even helped count them. The inference was obvious – that these deputies had somehow altered the absentee ballot actual results.

I shouldn't have been surprised. The print media hasn't played fair in more than four years, why should they change now? The angle of the story, slanted so desperately at me, was typical of the lack of balance in the way the News Journal and the Sentinel had constructed their stories.

What they didn't say was as important, if not more, than what they did. Deputies always handle the safety and security of the absentee ballots. They did this in 1996 and every election before that for as long as anyone who has been involved in this political process can remember. All of the ballot handling was done under supervision of the Elections Office, as is always the case, and nothing different happened on the days leading up to the election and Election Day itself than on any other previous year. Finally, I never know who will be actually assigned to this task. The request came from the Elections Office and was forwarded to the civilian clerk who routinely handled these assignments. The deputies were requested by name because they had previously worked in the Elections Office before. This request was made without my knowledge or approval, which is customary with this kind of request.

Knowing these facts might change your perspective on the story the News Journal published, which is exactly why they left it out. All we've ever asked of the media is to be fair, report the entire story for the public and let them decide how they feel about it. Apparently, the News Journal and others didn't believe the average American reader was

smart enough, that they needed a little help in deciding how they should feel about an issue or a story.

That Christmas, 1996, Jeannie and I gave ourselves one of the more memorable presents in our lives. We canceled delivery of the News Journal. There was no further reason to keep reading this newspaper. There were much better ways to start the day than

having to refute the misleading remarks made in a newspaper that clearly wanted me out of office as much as the Sentinel did. Some one else could read the stories and comment on them. I had work to do.

Having accepted the will of the people, Beckstrom was now challenging their integrity. He hired Jacksonville attorney Don Weidner to help with the ballot review challenge. Weidner immediately filed a petition asking to see the absentee ballots. I'd long thought that Beckstrom had some financial support that lurked in the background, possibly some people who disliked me and whom helped back Beckstrom in his run for office. Why else would a lieutenant from Winter Park (in Orange County) want to run for Sheriff in Volusia County? He barely qualified as a legal resident having a second home in our county that he rarely spent time in. Who was going to pay for Don Weidner's services, I wondered? Did Beckstrom have that kind of money?

Interesting questions, but it was a challenge the newspapers were not going to take on.

This was Beckstrom's first run for office of any kind. He had been associated with the Winter Park Police Department since 1967 and held a Bachelor's and Masters degree from Rollins College. He was a large, rude, overweight, grammatically challenged man and definitely fit the look of the stereotypical Southern Sheriff label that many had tried to affix to me. His campaign volunteers worked hard during his campaign but essentially relied heavily on the negative press furnished by the local print media. Beckstrom's core of supporters were more anti-Vogel than pro-Beckstrom. They were driven not by their belief in Beckstrom as much as their hatred of me. That helped his cause, no doubt. He also earned the endorsement of the News Journal and Sentinel, no major surprise.

Beckstrom had said during his campaign that he was going to cease all I-95 stops. He stated he would get rid of our helicopter that was partially funded by Halifax Medical

Center as an air evacuation vehicle. He was also going to end the Marine patrol and sell the boats. Interestingly, these were all methods by which we had successfully fought the drug war over the last few years.

He had accused our department of being top-heavy with too many Majors (we had five) and said he would have no Majors and use that money to hire more deputies. We had nearly 400 deputies now and I had established an important chain of command to ensure that proper supervision would take place. It had, for the most part, and the results were a more disciplined group. As previously noted, not all of the deputies I inherited liked the supervision and the disciplinary measures that were put in place to encourage good results. These individuals would move over quickly to Beckstrom's camp in the hopes that I would not be re-elected and the office could return to its old ways.

During the campaign, Beckstrom supporters accused ours of running a campaign of intimidation, a charge that made a good sound bite but lacked substance. It's not my style to intimidate people and do not tolerate that from the deputies and employees who work with me, nor would I allow a campaign worker to do anything that remotely approached this tactic. But his supporters repeated the charge throughout the campaign, and received much support from the print media who essentially made the same accusation.

Now Beckstrom was accusing my deputies of wrongdoing in their Elections Office duties and he promised repercussions. Weidner followed up the petition request with a motion that a judge rule on the validity of the ballots. He claimed that dead people received ballots, that ballots were opened improperly and without Election Office supervision, and that absentee ballots were missing. A Circuit Judge agreed to hear Beckstrom and Weidner's arguments on the Wednesday following Deanie Lowe's report. The election results were headed to court.

In the days leading up to the appearance in Judge John Doyle's courtroom, Deanie Lowe revealed some of the routine practices involved in the absentee ballot counting process. They are counted in mass about four days before the election. The ballots that are rejected by the machine are reviewed and touched up for electronic counting because there wasn't enough lead to record a result. Some ballots (about 200) that were completed but mailed with unsigned envelopes were counted. One of the Volusia County deputies guarding the ballots, Sergeant Robert Menrisky was left alone with the ballots at one point.

None of these actions was unusual, according to Lowe, and happened regularly each Election Day. The larger issue for Judge Doyle was whether these actions violated any state election statute. When he heard all sides on Wednesday, he decided to pursue it further. He ordered Lowe to turn over the ballots to the court where they would be reviewed for validation. He told the courtroom that the public needs to have confidence in its electoral process and that the accusations made by Beckstrom of gross negligence needed to be investigated. He scheduled a public inspection of the ballots beginning, Thursday, November 15 and lasting for two weeks.

I had won the absentee ballot count by a 60-40 margin, the substantial majority of which were marked and sent in before the News Journal's final print assault during the days leading up to the election. I think some poll voters were clearly influenced by this attack and, combined with all of the other news of the past four years of Governor's Panels, civil suits and the DOJ investigation, helped to make up many minds.

Lowe had been a public servant for nearly 20 years and was an honest, competent person. She had served on the Volusia County Council for several years and was even chairperson at one point. Her father had been and her two sons still were in law enforcement (one working for us) and she had always been supportive of law enforcement, an attitude I had always appreciated.

But now she was caught up in a maelstrom of events beyond her control. Procedures she and her predecessor Kathryn Odom had followed for several years were now being questioned, newspapers were vilifying her, and county citizens publicly questioning her motives. She was not alone. The News Journal also publicly questioned the actions of Sergeant Menrisky, who was taking some heat for being left alone with the ballots. News Journal reporters dug up some background on the 15-year veteran deputy that showed he had previously worked years earlier as a locksmith in New York.

The inferences the newspaper wanted people to draw were obvious the way the stories were written. Deanie Lowe is a supporter of mine and thus could influence the election and Sergeant Menrisky could easily pick a lock and alter ballots in my favor. Of course, they would have to know well in advance of Election Day that I was going to have trouble winning the election, something that no pre-election poll had predicted. Then they would have to risk their careers to alter the election results. The whole thing was ludicrous. That my loyal deputies would even think of breaking a law to mark ballots

was absurd. Making it even more so was that this story followed the News Journal pre-election assertion that no one in the Sheriff's office was loyal to me and openly advocated my being ousted from the position.

Worse, to infer that a deputy was dishonest in this manner was a new low even for these local "journalists." These deputies were all proud of their integrity and in a short period of time, they had been painted with the brush of illegality. Let's face it, this isn't a "get rich quick" employment opportunity. The main thing a law enforcement officer has is his credibility. You take that away and you might as well put a .45 in their hands and let them shoot themselves. Without their integrity, their whole career is jeopardized. Having to testify in court about this matter adds an unwelcome and unnecessary sentence to their resume. This cut deeply for these deputies and I felt sorry for them, especially since I, not them, was the intended target. They would never touch a ballot. They know that this is the people's election. What the people say, goes. End of story. The ability to freely elect officials is what makes this country great. Calling these deputies (and Deanie Lowe's) credibility into question was desperate at best.

Clearly, this was destined to become another battleground.

≈ ≈

TAINTED BALLOTS

When is a ballot a questionable one?

This became the all-important query as the assessment of the election results continued through November and into December. It was certainly true that ballots had been touched up, due to the voting machine's inability to read the markings. This could mean that there wasn't enough ink used or the wrong kind of marker filled in the spaces on the ballot. This is what Judge Doyle had to determine.

Initially,there was a hand recount of the absentee ballots. After that was done, the results gave me an even wider margin of victory.

So, they counted them again.

I won again, and picked up a few more votes. Beckstrom was right, the vote count was initially wrong. I should have won by more votes than I had been credited. Maybe I was the candidate that should have insisted on a review of the election process.

That different tabulations could result each time the votes were counted does speak volumes about outdated voting procedures in Volusia County. Deanie Lowe had already said that she intended to request additional updated equipment, expressly for the purpose of being able to read any kind of type and avoid the necessity to help fill in the intended circles on the absentee voter's behalf.

Naturally, only my side was pleased with the vote recount. Beckstrom followed up with a lawsuit against Volusia County and the Canvassing Board (that oversaw the election and that included Deanie Lowe) and then he sued me personally. By doing so, he was not suing me as Sheriff, just as an individual. This meant I had to now arrange for personal legal representation. I picked a Deland attorney whose office was close to the courthouse to handle this responsibility. I also knew Jeannie would be at every hearing. Personally, I was going to stay as far away from it all as possible and concentrate on my law enforcement duties. There was much to be done, including my contemplated reorganization and I didn't want to lose time away from the job.

Again, I wondered where the money was coming from to fund this legal activity. Was Don Weidner's practice so quiet, he could devote himself full-time for this case? Was he doing it pro bono? Not likely, and Beckstrom had held a fundraiser to help finance it, except few people came and not much money was raised; certainly not enough to pay attorney fees. Believe me, I know how much attorneys cost. It remained a significant question for me, but no obvious answers were forthcoming.

In reviewing and recounting the ballots, about 5,000 of them were considered "tainted." What this meant had varied meanings, depending on whom you asked, but ballots that found their way into this initial 5,000 count displayed one or more of the following characteristics:

a pen was used, instead of the required specified pencil
if a circle was completely and precisely filled in
marking outside the circle in attempting to fill it in
only voting in the Sheriff's race
if an answer looked like it had been erased

After looking at these criteria, it was a wonder there weren't more "tainted" ballots than 5,000. After all, you either filled in the circle or you didn't, yet according to two of the descriptions that cast doubts on a ballot, either circumstance would be warrant consideration of tampering.

Many of the absentee voters were seniors. Both sides acknowledged this. Many simply wished to avoid the crowds at the polling sites. Many have difficulty writing, or have poor eyesight. Some can't hold a pencil well. Some have trouble reading directions. In all of these circumstances, there was a good chance of having sent in a "tainted" ballot. But the longer you looked at a ballot, the more it was obvious that the ballots that needed filling in were marked in the same spot as they had been originally. The county attorney had even suggested a forensics expert be brought in to validate where the original voter markings had been. I was all for that.

The "experts" scrutinized all of these ballots several times. It was a public process and Jeannie attended every session. She had also been present at the recounts and had challenged several ballots being counted that were placed in Beckstrom's pile when they should have been put with mine. By order of Judge Doyle, the Clerk of Court became responsible for the recount.

Beckstrom's lawsuit sought to overturn the election because absentee ballots had finally decided my victory. They wanted to disqualify all of the absentee ballots. That meant disenfranchising some 27,000 people of their vote. Failing that, he was hoping to at least have the ballots that were identified as "tainted" thrown out. All of this because, his lawsuit stated, there was altering of ballots, that Sheriff Vogel's deputies guarded these ballots, and that many votes had not been tabulated, allegations spurred by the News Journal.

If the latter statement were true, the recount would have showed that discrepancy. Instead, the recount gave me more votes that I was not credited with on Election Day. But, we still had to defend ourselves against the lawsuit.

It was now late December and there would be no courtroom appearances until after the first of the year. Judge Doyle didn't even want to hold a hearing until there was a statistical review of the ballots to see if the ratio between good and "tainted" ballots was high enough to potentially constitute fraud. Deanie Lowe intended to examine the ballots that were being questioned to see what exactly she and her staff were being accused of in the lawsuit.

The average Volusia County citizen, especially veterans and seniors, were outraged over this process. They wanted their vote to count and couldn't believe that Beckstrom wanted to toss them out. Jeannie and I were both stopped on numerous occasions that holiday season with people expressing exactly these feelings. We truly appreciated the support.

In the meantime, I was busy being Sheriff. I elevated Leonard Davis to the position of Chief Deputy, a spot that put him second-in-command of the Volusia County Sheriff's Office. I had a lot of confidence in Leonard and knew that he would run the daily operations quite well. I intended to spend more time in contact with Volusia citizens and the employees of the agency to ascertain their needs and see that they were being met in a reasonable manner.

Staff Support and Administrative Services were combined into one division called Support Services, to be headed by Major Bob Rickmyre, current head of the Administrative Services Division. Major Jim Lockwood, who had headed up Staff Support, was moved into Leonard's now vacated position of commander of Law Enforcement Services division. Additional staff changes were all designed to streamline, flatten and strengthen the organization.

On New Year's Eve, Judge Doyle set a trial date of January 27 to hear the suit. That was two days before my birthday and a week before our 24th wedding anniversary, two occasions that would apparently be marked in court. Beckstrom was extremely unhappy about this trial date and publicly said he would try to have my swearing-in blocked.

There was a problem with Beckstrom's logic. There was no formal swearing in necessary for an incumbent Sheriff. I was already in office and was simply staying in the same position. There could have been a ceremonial event, but it wasn't needed. But we were now faced with the threat of Weidner filing an injunction to prevent me from taking office until this matter was resolved. This threat hung heavy with us throughout the month of January.

The real challenge was in the ultimate result of all this fuss. If Judge Doyle did end up throwing out enough ballots to reverse the election result, then it would be chaos at the Sheriff's office. Technically, all of the arrests made from the point where Beckstrom would have taken office until the time he was installed by the Judge could be called into question. Defense attorneys probably would have had challenged the legal authority of the deputies.

Beckstrom had once said he'd accept the will of the people – and didn't. Now he'd said he would accept the will of a judge, but was starting to backpedal on that pledge, too. Politicians!

To overturn the election, Judge Doyle would have to find real evidence of fraud. There was no such thing as limited fraud. Once proved, it would invalidate the election result. Because of that, the Judge wanted to take time and examine every ballot called into question by Beckstrom and Weidner.

Weidner finally decided against filing an injunction against my taking office, relieving one worry from our minds. It would have, he said, unnecessarily complicated the upcoming January 27 trial. This injunction would require an immediate hearing, all evidence assessed and the Governor's Office involved. It would also delay the January 27 trial further and neither Weidner nor Beckstrom wanted that.

The vote analysis continued throughout January. There was an assessment of the overall vote, which at the fourth recount stood as an 819 vote margin victory for me. There were now 8,994 disputed ballots. I was voted on 62.6 percent of these and Beckstrom on 37.4 percent. If they were really tainted by me, why would Beckstrom win any of these votes? He wasn't being accused of tainting ballots, yet he had been the recipient of a vote on a number of these ballots. The experts said there was a significant deviation in the tainted ballots from the total absentee ballots where I had won 59.9 percent of those. It would be up to the Judge to ultimately decide, and then he would have to rule that fraud was evident.

The trial didn't start January 27. Oddly enough, it was Weidner who asked for a continuance to February 3, the day of our 24th wedding anniversary, to complete his study of the ballots, something he had been doing since early November. The court-ordered vote recount now had me winning by a total of 1,111 votes, up from the previous 819. The longer this went on, the more votes I continued to have put in my corner.

But it was to be a Judge that decided the final outcome.

～ ～

THE WILL OF THE JUDGE

On the morning the trial began, Jeannie, Sheila and I all felt "here we go again." It seemed like our lives had been one long trial since 1992 and we wondered if it would ever end. That being said, we knew we were survivors. We were fighters and we were winners. We could have packed it in a long time ago. Stronger people would have been crushed under the onslaught we had faced. But we don't give up that easily. Not when we know that we have right on our side.

The trial lasted eight days. Beckstrom and Weidner started off with their statistical experts, who essentially testified that the difference in the election was the result of the tabulation of "tainted" ballots. They brought in a political consultant and a Jacksonville University math professor. The political consultant, Witt Ayres, had no real statistical background and Volusia County attorney Dan Eckert made a motion to have his comments stricken from the record. Judge Doyle postponed his ruling on their motion, which could mean he was having second thoughts about the man's qualifications as an expert. In fact, the Judge himself pressed Ayres about the chances that the higher number of ballots that had to be marked over could be because a large number of seniors voted in this manner. Wouldn't they be more likely to not have pressed down hard enough for the computer to tabulate the vote? Ayres reluctantly agreed there could be other reasons for the large number of marked over ballots other than voter fraud.

Weidner managed to find two Volusia County voters to put on the stand. One said that she had requested an absentee ballot but never received it and when she went to vote, was turned away because she had been marked as having been sent an absentee ballot. She tried to clear it up with the Elections Office to no avail. According to her, she didn't get to vote that day.

Others stated they received unsolicited absentee ballots in the mail, but didn't complete them. Instead, they went to the polls and had no problem voting.

At the end of the first day Weidner teased reporters with news about a possible last minute witness who had earthshaking comments to make. If brought to the stand, this person could change the whole perspective of this trial. Naturally, Weidner didn't name the individual, he only said he was still interviewing the person and evaluating the testimony. Translation: the first day hadn't gone exceptionally well for him and he needed to drop a few hints of big things to come to sustain his stalled momentum.

The second day of the trial belonged to Assistant Elections Department Director Lana Hires. The majority of the time was spent scrutinizing procedures with Weidner trying to prove every action was a cut corner, a break in security rules and thus election fraud, the reason to overturn the election. Weidner received concurrence from Hires that about 170 envelopes containing absentee ballots did not have the proper information on the outside of the envelope, but were counted anyway. He also pointed out several cases where the voter's signature on the ballot didn't match the signature in their voting record. Hires said that was true in some of the cases, but allowances were made for elderly voters whose signatures change with age and frailty compared to how they signed years earlier. That was not a reason, Hires said, to deny these people a right to vote.

When questioned about the deputies that helped with the ballots when they were simply supposed to be guarding them, Hires said it was her idea, not theirs. We had so much to do, she said, since there was a record number of absentee ballots coming in. They were paying the deputies $25/hour, so why not put them to work? They helped, but they were not allowed to mark ballots, she testified.

Weidner brought the deputies to the stand on the third day of the trial. Each of them testified that they didn't mark any ballots. They essentially watched TV, read, and checked on the four outside doors. They guarded the ballots. But Weidner went after them with both barrels blazing. All Weidner could do was attack their credibility and hope that the Judge came to the conclusion that this meant they had deliberately perpetrated voter fraud.

Then Weidner brought up one of the Sheriff's Office employees, Sandy Campbell, a victim's advocate coordinator. Her testimony was surprising. She said that she had overheard Deputy Bob Grim say that Vogel was ahead the day before the election and that he had actually demonstrated how they helped to mark ballots. Weidner also brought up a Crossing Guard Supervisor, Janice O'Neal, who said she heard rumors prior to the election that deputies had marked the ballots. Both Campbell and O'Neal said they were afraid to testify because of possible repercussions.

There was already testimony from everyone in the Elections Office and the deputies that they hadn't participated in the marking of the ballots. They were likely present when Elections officials marked them and they may have helped put them through the vote machine again, but this doesn't constitute fraud.

I was concerned about what the women had said about job repercussions. Their immediate boss was Major Connie Locke, who oversaw the Community Services Division. Connie wouldn't take any actions, but to be on the safe side, we gave her administrative leave, so that Campbell and O'Neal would feel free to testify and that nothing was going to happen as a result. I only wanted them to tell the truth.

Weidner introduced a piece of paper that he insisted indicated evidence of intimidation by Sheriff's Office employees. It was an unsigned note to Campbell that was allegedly left on her car windshield, saying, "Lying under oath is a dangerous thing to do. Why did you do it?" Campbell received a round of applause from Beckstrom supporters when she stepped down from the stand and left the courtroom.

Deanie Lowe took the stand next. Weidner called into question her entire absentee ballot process which she fought hard to defend every step of the way. Weidner told her the Elections manual did not allow absentee ballots to be re-marked. Lowe agreed, but pointed out that ballots that are not properly marked at the polling places are allowed to be touched up to record the vote and she simply transferred this practice to the recording of absentee ballot results.

Finally, Weidner brought up Beckstrom's campaign manager, Walter Mentzer, a former poll clerk. Weidner showed him ballot after ballot where the markings were made with two different types of ink or lead. Mentzer said they were improper and shouldn't have been counted, indicating they were tampered. Under cross-examination, my attorney asked how did Mentzer know who had touched up the ballot? Mentzer just looked at him and asked what he meant. He reiterated that wasn't it possible the two types of ink could have been made by the voter? What if they realized they had made a mistake with the type of writing instrument they used, and went over it with the proper marker to be sure their vote was counted? Wouldn't that explain the ballot markings as well? Mentzer said that was just speculation and County Attorney Dan Eckert remarked, "Isn't your entire testimony speculative?"

Eckert then showed Mentzer that he had made a mistake on two out of 40 ballots he had just reviewed. These ballots that he claimed had double markings did not. Mentzer re-examined them and was forced to agree he had made an error. Eckert pointed out that this meant Mentzer, a former poll clerk was wrong about 5 percent of the time. Wasn't it possible that voters made mistakes at least as often and re-marked their ballots? Human error alone could account for a significant number of the "tainted" ballots.

Weidner had finished his case. He had no more to present. He was hoping that he had thrown enough circumstantial shading on the situation to convince Judge Doyle to toss the absentee ballots and give Beckstrom the victory.

It was now Dan Eckert's turn. He brought Debra and Jay Musser to the stand. They were employees with Global Elections Systems who provides Volusia County with the voting equipment. They were among the people in the elections Office re-marking ballots to be sure they were properly read. They described how an oval circle had to be filled in on the ballot in order for the machine to register it and said that it was not uncommon to have to retouch up some of the ballots. But they insisted they simply completed the circle that had been started by the voter. They also testified that they saw no deputies marking ballots.

He also brought Sandra Campbell back to the witness stand. Eckert was concerned about her earlier testimony not being correct. During this questioning, Campbell finally admitted that her testimony during this trial was inconsistent with the deposition she had taken in preparation for court.

And the beat went on. This was the longest election of my life. We had been fortunate to win on Election night, 1996 but those results usually stand. The election is over and you get on with it, one way or the other. Not liking the results, Beckstrom was determined to get into the Sheriff's Office another way – through the court system. While I had done well in court in the past, you never really know what a judge or jury will be thinking about when they ultimately make their decision. To me, Weidner and Beckstrom had done nothing to prove that fraud had occurred.

The local print media was having a field day with all of this. They were now reversing field from their pre-election reporting. They had painted a picture before the votes were tabulated of a Sheriff's Office deeply divided, where most deputies were not in my camp and hoping for a change. Now, they were working on the opposite track; that my office was filled with loyal deputies who were trying to intimidate people into voting for me, to put Vogel signs up in their yard, to contribute to the campaign. Whatever suited their mission at the moment was what they printed.

And their mission, which they had definitely decided to accept, was to change this Sheriff's Office from an elective to an appointed position. Nothing would satisfy them beyond that. They needed either a badly incompetent or a crooked Sheriff to take the next step to accomplishing this objective. They had failed on the "badly incompetent" and now went for the "crooked" allegations. A Sheriff that changed the outcome of an election by fraud would be a strong case to use to make this an appointed office.

I had thought there was likely no precedent for this type of case in Volusia County. But there had been a previous instance of voter fraud here. In 1936, a Judge's election ended with an opponent named Tappy defeating the incumbent, one John Peacock, by 300 votes. Peacock charged fraud in the vote counting process and demanded a recount. Tappy charged that Peacock had joined in a conspiracy with the Sheriff and the Supervisor of elections to make sure Peacock won. If that was the case, they had obviously done a lousy job of it.

Two Florida Supreme Court justices actually came to Volusia County to supervise the recount. When the votes were tallied again, Peacock won. There were allegations that someone had stolen ballots from New Smyrna Beach and that many of these were in favor of Peacock. Judge Peacock had a reputation as an honest man, and was a fighter of political corruption. And, when it was all over, he had held onto his Judge's seat.

I liked it when the good guys won.

Eckert brought in his own statistician to refute claims from Weidner's witnesses. James McClave of Gainesville testified that there certainly didn't seem to be evidence of fraud that he could see. He looked to demographics as a more likely explanation. His contention was that men, people over 70 and Republicans are more likely to vote for Vogel and vote absentee and that would favor me in any counting of absentee ballots. He said that without even looking at the absentee results; that should give me 59 percent of the absentee vote based strictly on demographics. (I had 59.9.)

He also made an interesting point that spoke volumes about what had happened in this election. He illustrated by graph the results of the absentee ballot count day by day. He noted that the early ballots were heavily in my favor, but as the election neared, the later ballots that came in showed a continued drop in the support level for me concurrent with the bad publicity I had been receiving in the News Journal. If there were fraud going on with the absentee ballots, there would have been a spike in the ballot count in my favor, not the progressive downward trend that had been recorded. Instead, the absentee ballots reflected what was going on in voters' minds in general.

What was going on was a concentrated last-ditch News Journal effort to oust me from office. About ten days before the election, they began a series of articles that hammered me, the Sheriff's Office and brought back all the history that had gone before – I-95, the DOJ, the NAACP and a sprinkling of new stories to illustrate that I was a power-hungry Sheriff gone mad. In as much as it was during a time frame when the average voter reads the paper to get a handle on candidates and the issues to determine how they are going to vote, it was timed for release to maximum effect.

The News Journal pre-emptive strike was distressing. A News Journal reporter's hostility had started, I believe, back in 1991 with the Helen McConnell shooting. As previously noted earlier in this book, a young News Journal reporter named John Holland had called me repeatedly about the follow-up to that tragic incident resulting in me finally hanging up on him when he called during Thanksgiving dinner after telling him I had nothing more to add. Apparently for Holland, this was unforgivable.

Holland had reportedly made comments to a veteran journalist at the News Journal about "getting" the Sheriff. The other reporter was shocked at this attitude and told Holland that you don't just go out and "get" someone in print. There has to be an underlying reason to start some type of investigative reporting effort on somebody. Holland, an investigative reporter himself, must have had that reason in his own mind because he asked to be assigned to the Sheriff's race. Given his journalistic preferences, this was an unusual request but one that the News Journal apparently accepted at face value and he landed the assignment. Holland might have known the police beat in some way since his father was a law enforcement officer in Massachusetts.

He began attending all of our events. He came to every function we attended from candidate forums to luncheon speaking engagements. His presence was felt everywhere. If he weren't a reporter, you'd have good cause to think he was a stalker. He first started in on us in a meaningful way in his reporting on my handling of a couple of promotion requests within the department. These promotions involved deputies who were also veterans. I picked others over these individuals based strictly on staff recommendations and who warranted the promotion. In my mind, these individuals did not.

Deputies that want a promotion and don't get it are, as you can imagine, disappointed in the result. Most of them go back to doing their jobs a little harder, trying to make every effort to earn the promotion the next time around. Others take a different track. In this case, Deputies Hank Beck, James Zierman and Chuck Keller all felt they had been discriminated against and began pursuit of this with the Department of Labor.

There is a federal mandate that veterans be given preference in promotions, all things being equal. But here all things weren't equal and there were clear reasons these individuals were not as outstanding as others who were more qualified for promotion. Zierman, for example, had been the subject of several citizen complaints and an Internal Affairs investigation. I have to take all facts into consideration, not just their veteran status. I'm a veteran myself and 41 percent of the Sergeants in the Sheriff's Office are veterans, hardly evidence of veteran discrimination.

But the Department of Labor disagreed. Their investigation was poorly run and didn't review all of the factors involved in the decision-making process. It was as if the "veteran" status was the sole characteristic to be examined. That is not my reading of the federal statute nor was it the reading of the Volusia County Personnel Director.

But reporter, John Holland had a field day with it. In August 1996, as the election campaign began to heat up, the headline in the News Journal ran "Vogel faulted over veterans." There were follow-up articles that re-hashed it during the weeks leading up to the vote.

Taken alone, this issue was reportable and not likely to dent my base of elector support. I try to be as fair as possible in all personnel decisions that I am able to make in the Sheriff's Office. But to Holland, this was only the first shot in the war to come, laying the groundwork for his attacks.

Holland approached me early in the campaign to ask if I had anything on my opponent Gus Beckstrom. I told him I did not run that kind of campaign and would not release any kind of negative information if I had it. This is my third election run and we've tried our utmost to keep the first two on a positive plane, focused on the issues the voters want to hear about. This campaign would be run no differently. This did give me an indication of the sort of person Holland had the potential to be, and I'm sure he asked Beckstrom the same thing. How Beckstrom reacted, I couldn't say.

Incumbents have a definite advantage in running for office. They have name recognition, a base of support, and know how to run an election campaign. But they are not invincible. What could seriously hurt is a scandal or a torrent of bad publicity in the last couple of weeks during the election. The timing is crucial. Negative candidate publicity has proven effective in the past when delivered too late in the campaign for the individual to rebut the information. Some candidates purposely hold "bombshells" if they have them until the last few days to time them just right. We've never done that and refuse to run our campaign that way. To date, our supporters ignored the negative stories and voted for me based on our record. I expected some erosion of support. You couldn't go through four years as we had and expect that everyone would ignore the negative articles speaking out against the Sheriff's Office, and me personally. But I still thought that we had a good chance to win by a safe margin.

Those feelings were borne out during a campaign appearance at the Volusia County Home Show at the Ocean Center. We had some bumper stickers that were printed incorrectly. They did contain a Sheriff's star, so we thought that rather than waste them, we could hand out the stars at this gathering and ask people to wear the stick-on stars as a show of support if they so chose. There was a tremendous amount of enthusiasm for it and, as the day wore on, the great majority of people (probably 70 percent) were sporting Sheriff's stars in support.

John Holland had attended this event and spent his time in Gus Beckstrom's booth as my opponent had also marked this show as a good opportunity to campaign. With the visual support of the star and the verbal approval we were getting from the attendees, he must have wondered what Beckstrom's chances really were, without some key assistance. We felt that this was a good gauge of where we were with only a few weeks to go before voters went to the polls.

But even we couldn't have anticipated the type of reporting that followed. Holland first focused on Jeannie, of all people, in the first of several articles implying that we run a campaign of intimidation and misused the Sheriff's Office for election purposes.

Dale Anderson, who was always active in our campaign, had been working on a case with a FDLE analyst named Jeannie Pounds and they had numerous telephone conversations and follow-up regarding it. My Jeannie had called Barbara, one of the staff at the Sheriff's office, to thank her for a birthday card she had sent to her. After a few minutes conversation catching up on family and friends, Jeannie innocently asked Barbara to remind Dale that there was a campaign meeting that evening. Barbara wrote that up on a message pad and left it for Dale. It was apparently picked up by someone along with several "Jeannie called" messages that were from FDLE investigator Pounds.

Holland's conclusion was that Jeannie was misusing the Sheriff's Office by constantly calling with campaign news and information. Nothing could be further from the truth. We asked John Holland to check the return phone number on those "Jeannie called" messages to verify who Jeannie really was. There was no follow up like that from him. Once the story attacking Jeannie and our campaign had been printed, the damage was done and there was no interest in checking it further for accuracy.

I was upset that they had singled Jeannie out. You can take any shots you want at me, but not my family. This was an incredible low in journalistic ethics.

But there was more. We had permission from an owner of numerous gasoline service stations, to put up a "Vote Vogel" sign on his properties. The campaign office sent Angelo, one of our workers to do that. He put up the sign as directed, as long as the manager of the station did not object. At one of the stations, Angelo got into a debatable conversation with a Beckstrom supporter about the qualifications of the two candidates. In an article written by John Holland, published and entitled, "Vogel runs campaign of intimidation", this was construed as Vogel campaign supporters threaten local service stations to display our campaign signs. The article also contained the allegation about Jeannie improperly using the Sheriff's Office for the campaign.

It was difficult to fight back against this type of reporting. It's one thing to shade things in a particular manner. It's another to print misleading information.

If anyone ran a campaign of intimidation, it was Beckstrom's camp. We had numerous reports of Beckstrom supporters ripping down "Vote Vogel" signs, shades of the Ralph Henshaw campaign four years earlier. They would put Beckstrom signs up in front of Vogel signs. One supporter told us that she was cleaning out her garage and a Beckstrom supporter going house to house came up to her and told her not to vote for Vogel, that he had houses in the Bahamas and was rich with drug money. Even at the aforementioned Home Show, Dilys Harris was working at the Vogel booth while Jeannie, Sheila and I were circulating and an ex-deputy now working on behalf of Beckstrom approached Dilys and told her that she wouldn't be getting any promotions next year. The woman obviously didn't know Dilys was not employed at the Sheriff's Office, and she delivered his message loud and clear. Yet these were similar to the things we were being wrongly accused of in conducting our campaign.

Fortunately, there was other media in the area. Marc Bernier, the host of his own talk radio show on WNDB-AM from 3-6 PM every day, had me on numerous times during this siege to air my side of the story. The tone, nature and inaccuracy of the articles stunned him. He asked me the questions that Holland wouldn't and we were able to get the other side of our story out to listeners who may have by now been leaning towards voting Beckstrom.

So, too did Dilys and Merle Harris come to our rescue. Their newspaper, Seniors Today, reached a lot of our constituents and I was concerned about how they were taking this negative News Journal onslaught. Merle and Dilys also ran our side of these stories in an effort to get the truth out.

Both Marc and the Harris's risked a lot by letting us use their media outlets as a bully pulpit to get our word out. Marc is a well-respected local talk show host who had exposed Ralph Henshaw as a weak candidate four years earlier and had also let us put the truth out about the Sentinel stories. He went to bat for us again here and I remain deeply indebted to him for giving us his show to air the truth. Merle and Dilys risked losing circulation and advertising in their newspaper, but they never even considered the ramifications. They just wanted to get the other side of the story out and let the chips fall where they may.

So, as James McGlave pointed out on the stand, there was plenty of reason to see a decline in the Sheriff's popularity as the election drew close. That absentee ballots paralleled this decline was sufficient for him to argue against any kind of voter fraud.

It was powerful testimony.

Eckert also called to the stand Elections Supervisors from two other counties who said that their procedures were similar to Volusia County's practices with regards to absentee ballots. They also re-marked ballots, much of it done by the canvassing board in their respective counties. One of the men, Ion Sancho, Elections Supervisor of Leon County (the home of Florida's capitol city of Tallahassee), said that the election laws were the most poorly written of any of Florida's statutes. He testified that his office weighs the rights and will of the voter higher than strict adherence to election policy. This echoed Deanie Lowe's comments. Sancho also said older men are the most likely to improperly mark their ballots.

After hearing much of this, it occurred to me that this kind of improper ballot marking which forced "remarking" commonly occurred in every election. The difference here was that these votes meant so much more for a change.

Dan Eckert recalled Deanie Lowe again to take her through a step-by-step rebuttal of all the charges Beckstrom and Weidner had leveled against her and her employees. She explained some of the testimony from the women who said they received unsolicited absentee ballots as likely confusing the actual ballot with the request form for a ballot. Many candidates sent out request forms and her office was deluged with calls asking why they received absentee ballots when it was only a request for one.

Concerning the allegation that deputies guarding the ballots overnight could alter them, she dismissed it quickly. She said it was an incredible stretch to believe that a deputy could find the keys to the vault, the absentee ballot room and the tabulating room and then make changes to the ballots. She said the machines were checked each night and again in the morning to be sure no additional ballots had been fed through. Strict records were kept and there was no way a deputy could have altered or destroyed ballots without it being discovered almost immediately.

Lowe concluded by saying, and looking directly at Beckstrom that "my staff and I put our hearts and souls into this election and that nothing was done illegally or to harm any candidate. It was a fair election," she concluded.

That was it for the trial. Weidner brought in a few more rebuttal witnesses, but it was finally turned over to Judge Doyle for his long-awaited decision. Essentially, he would decide whether voter fraud was present or not. If so, he had a 1975 Florida State Supreme Court ruling in a Hillsborough County (Tampa) case to fall back on, which stated that ballots could be overturned only if there is fraud, intentional wrongdoing or gross negligence that disturbed the "sanctity of the ballot."

There was eager anticipation in the air the day of Judge Doyle's ruling. Beckstrom supporters were confident that Weidner had done his job of proving the case of fraud. I went to work as I had done each day of the trial, knowing that I would hear from Jeannie as soon as the verdict was announced. We had all been here before and felt that we had proven just the opposite, that no fraud had occurred and that I had won the vote fair and square, by an increasing number each time they recounted the ballots.

Doyle ruled quickly on Wednesday, February 12. He did find that the Elections Office was guilty of negligence as far as the election went, but could detect no evidence of voter fraud and said the ballots would stand as is. He emphasized that Sheriff Vogel was properly re-elected to a third term. He said that he dismissed Beckstrom's most significant charges, namely that ballots were fraudulently cast for Vogel, that unauthorized workers helped process ballots and that faulty tabulation procedures destroyed the sanctity of the absentee ballots. As far as he could see, none of those things transpired.

We had won!

Beckstrom's immediate response was to say that there were a lot of problems in this county and that someone other than him also needs to bring them to the attention of the public.

Jeannie, Sheila and Dilys Harris needed an escort to get out of the courtroom and Dale Anderson provided a shield as they followed deputies out a side door and away from angry Beckstrom supporters who fully expected to be calling him Sheriff Gus today. Their "escorts" rode to the Sheriff's Office and found that Beckstrom supporters were demonstrating there as well, but Dale once more provided cover for the ladies as they made their way up to my office. After that harrowing trip, they discovered I wasn't there. Instead, I was hearing details from my attorney over at his office.

Judge Doyle had exonerated me, but was clearly unhappy with Elections Office procedures and Deanie Lowe would have to alter the process for the next election. Lowe personally was glad to see the election results upheld and vowed to address all of Judge Doyle's concerns. As far as Sheriff's Office employee Sandra Campbell's testimony was concerned, he termed it as conflicting and gave it no credence. In the final analysis, he found the election to be a "full and fair expression of the will of the people. Vogel won."

What the Judge found most disturbing was over 1,000 ballots weren't counted at all by the Elections Office until the court-ordered and supervised manual recount. Those ballots alone, when counted, were in my favor by more than 200 votes. To Doyle, "if banks counted money the way the Supervisor of Elections counted votes, our financial system would collapse."

Those were tough words, but Deanie Lowe has worked long and hard for the county and would do everything she could to improve the situation for the future. I know she felt bad about my election being called to question because of the Elections Office problems, but I knew her difficulties was not the sole reason people were challenging my victory. There was such a hunger to get me out of office and this was yet another setback to those that wanted to make this happen. Well, I was still here and planned only to continue working harder.

⇒ ⇐

THE WILL OF THE FLORIDA SUPREME COURT

The will of the judge did not turn out to be enough for Gus Beckstrom, either. He decided to appeal the decision of Judge Doyle. My attorney was surprised insofar as Judge Doyle had given such a detailed ruling and is well versed in the law. He didn't see anything in the decision that could be overturned.

But that wouldn't stop Beckstrom or the publicity. The distractions would continue. His attorney, Don Weidner, said he would appeal the decision to the 5th District Court of Appeals in Daytona Beach as soon as possible.

One change I planned to make immediately was to remove the job of guarding the ballots from the Volusia County Sheriff's Office. The Elections Office would be better served to have a private security firm handle it. I certainly didn't want any other deputies subject to the same scrutiny as those who took the 1996 detail endured. Deanie Lowe understood immediately. She was even considering eliminating the human element all together and putting in an alarm system or using a guard dog or both.

Bizarre elements continued to dog this never-ending case. Sandra Campbell, who had testified at the trial, had a car incident on the last day of the trial. Her right front wheel apparently came loose while she traveled down US Highway 92. Stranger still, the tire was missing three of its five lug nuts and the other two were lose. I turned the investigation over to FDLE. I wanted us out of anything involving this election, and since she'd testified, I thought we'd be better served having an outside agency look into it.

Beckstrom's formal appeal was made on March 12, 1997. It was done on the basis of one of Judge Doyle's statements that the integrity of the election was irreparably harmed. If so, Beckstrom argued, he should have overturned the race. The appeal dragged on for a time, as Beckstrom needed the transcription of the original trial to cite his points for appeal and delayed paying the $7,500 transcript fee. He had until May 21 to get his full appeal done and he filed a 21-day extension, meaning it was now due June 11.

In the meantime, Deanie Lowe was not thrown out of office. Governor Chiles' staff reviewed the trial transcript and decided there was nothing that warranted her removal from her post. Deanie was at work upgrading the vote tabulation machines and getting a new computer chip that more easily read the voter's markings, whether in pen or pencil, and thus prevent the re-marking process that had been so controversial during the trial.

Beckstrom finally finished his appeal by the June 11 deadline. He was not saying, however, that he would accept the will of the Appeals Court. His attorney, Don Weidner, already was making statements to the press that this was strong enough to bring to the Florida Supreme Court, if necessary. This was going to drag on much farther than anyone thought. The November 1996 election that I had now won a couple of times, was still up for grabs to Beckstrom's way of thinking.

In June, Sandra Campbell reported a fire in her garage. Apparently, a towel covering car stereo equipment in a cardboard box was smoldering. She happened to awake at 3:00 AM and discovered the problem. She awakened her husband, who then disposed of the stereo components from the box. This was added to the FDLE investigation, as they were still trying to wrap up the car incident. Laboratory analysis did not find any combustible material on the towel itself.

During this time period, Chief Deputy Davis recommended the victim's advocate program that she worked in be transferred to the State Attorney's office, due to cost savings and duplication of effort. State Attorney for Volusia County John Tanner ultimately decided to take in the volunteers who worked in this program, but not the paid employees. We then had to find places for these individuals, including Campbell, who had refused beforehand to go to the State Attorney's Office. We assigned Campbell to work in the Central Records at the Sheriff's Office.

Four days later, Sandra Campbell reported another incident. She claimed someone had thrown an object at her car, while she was driving on Interstate 95. There was a four-inch diameter crack in her windshield as a result of this vandalism. She could not give any information about the individual who threw the object, except to say the person was riding in a sport utility vehicle. She then pulled into the Port Orange rest stop off I-95 to call in a report on the incident. She was unable to provide any other details and the object that was thrown was not recovered.

There was ample opportunity for the news media to note that a person who testified against the Sheriff was having all of this trouble. The Sentinel ran with the story, but I had heard nothing from John Holland lately.

The FDLE couldn't solve the Campbell mishaps. They felt her car, a Lincoln Town Car with 138,000 miles on it, could have lost the wheel due to excessive wear on the tire. There was no evidence of human involvement in the loosening of the lug nuts, and there was nothing further for them to investigate. The FDLE investigator later told me and testified in a deposition that he felt she was responsible herself for all her mishaps.

By November, Beckstrom had an answer from the 5th District Court of Appeals. They declined to hear his case and instead referred it to the Florida Supreme Court. This was the DCA's way of fast-tracking the case to the Florida Supreme Court, since they would ultimately be hearing the case anyway. The Supreme Court would not get to the case for a while and I feared this thing could continue to drag on and on. But the Court agreed to consider it quickly and said they would hear oral arguments in December 1997. They wouldn't rule for several months, but the oral arguments of the merits of each case would be handled in rapid fashion. It was Beckstrom's last shot. He could go no further with this case than the Florida Supreme Court.

Beckstrom claimed that a ruling against him by the Supreme Court would send a message to other counties that it was OK to violate election laws when processing absentee ballots in the state of Florida. If that was Beckstrom's argument, I sensed he would be in trouble. Judge Doyle had called for changes in the processing of these ballots in the future. He wasn't saying they couldn't have been handled better. The Judge said there was no intentional fraud in the handling of the ballots and that's what Beckstrom needed to prove to get a reversal. But you never know what can happen in a courtroom so this election was still some time off before being finally decided.

Some of Beckstrom's supporters chartered a bus and drove to Tallahassee to cheer on his oral arguments even though no decision would be issued. Only our attorneys went. My supporters and I stayed home.

The seven judges were well prepared. They had thoroughly read up on this case and began firing pointed questions at Weidner and Dan Eckert. One of the most interesting questions asked was that if they threw out only those re-marked ballots where it was impossible to tell where the original markings had been, would it change the election result? Since this numbered only 200, and I had won by over 1,100 votes, the answer was no.

The court finally decided on March 20, 1998, nearly a year and a half after the election had been held. In its unanimous decision, the seven-justice Florida Supreme Court ruled, rejecting Beckstrom's appeal and upheld Judge Doyle's ruling. No one expected it to be a 7-0 vote, but it was. Unquestionably, the Supreme Court found that fraud had not taken place and left the right to vote with the people of Volusia County instead of a courtroom.

We had won again! Beckstrom was out of options. The election that wouldn't end was finally over.

≈ ≈

WHISTLEBLOWER

No matter how you try to operate the office in a normal manner, the distractions presented by the ballot controversy made it supremely difficult to do so. I had wanted everyone to focus on the job at hand and these fine folks had done their best. But, at last, after nearly six years of extracurricular activity that couldn't help but divert some attention away from the usual daily tasks, routines had returned to the Volusia County Sheriff" Office. There was no trial to prepare for, no investigator's questions to answer, no news stories to comment on. It seemed like a time warp back to 1989. While there certainly was an emotional toll, this lack of complication would make the job a lot easier for everyone.

This didn't mean all the problems had disappeared overnight. Reminders of the past six years still held positions within the Volusia County Sheriff's Office. Frank Josenhanz, the DOJ's best friend whose lack of credibility had helped destroy the house of cards they had built their case upon, was still around - and unhappy.

He filed a whistleblower lawsuit in 1998 against the Sheriff's Office, saying that he had been unfairly treated because he had testified against several deputies and myself during both the civil trial and the Anderson-Coffin excessive force cases.

This book has already mentioned Josenhanz' "cowboy" approach to law enforcement. It was Josenhanz whose behavior as a member of the I-95 team had forced us to remove and reassign him.

Nancye Jones remembered Josenhanz when they were both at the Daytona Beach Police Department, she as the agency's legal advisor and he as a police officer. Josenhanz was involved in a situation where his partner had ended up being killed. They had worked an off-duty shift and headed to a nearby bar for a couple of drinks. Three "yahoos", who had come in to the bar and began causing trouble, interrupted their libations. The bar's bouncers asked Josenhanz and his partner Sorensen to help, knowing they were police officers.

The officers managed to get the three men out into the parking lot, but Josenhanz' cowboy attitude got the best of the situation and rather than leave it at getting the men out of the bar, a confrontation resulted. The three men were in a Pontiac TransAm, and Josenhanz was hanging on to one side of the car and Sorensen the other when it appeared one of the men was reaching under the seat for something. The car suddenly took off, and Josenhanz jumped while Sorensen hung on. He couldn't hold for long and when he fell, he cracked his skull. Sorensen never recovered. He was in a coma for months before finally passing away.

The entire matter could have been handled differently. Josenhanz doesn't belong in law enforcement. It involves self-control and a calm demeanor in many cases.

He left the Daytona Police Department a short time later and went to work for Sheriff Ed Duff in the Volusia County Sheriff's Office, which is how I inherited him. Josenhanz wanted to be the next "Trooper Vogel" on the highway, arresting drug dealers.

I believe his resentment or jealousy of me motivated him to mislead the Department of Justice and the lawyers in the Selena Washington case. He repeated false statements to others that at one time I had consulted with him about running for the Sheriff's Office prior to my 1989 campaign. This conversation never took place, but in his delusional world he may believe it did.

The belief that I prevented him from becoming a top law enforcement officer due to his testimony was part of his whistleblower lawsuit. He claimed that I had shuffled him around the department to force him to quit.

After a year of sporadic negotiation back and forth, the attorneys settled the lawsuit in exchange for his resignation and a dropping of the suit. He was then no longer affiliated with the Volusia County Sheriff's Office.

This didn't mean we saw the end of Josenhanz. As election 2000 neared, Gus Beckstrom is challenging for the Sheriff's Office one more time. Assuming that I'm going to run, Josenhanz thought he'd assist Beckstrom if he could. Only, as is typical with Josenhanz, it's the kind of help that's not worth it in the long run.

Beckstrom had set up a web site, one of the new mediums in campaigning as we enter the 21st Century. Josenhanz posted a couple of negative articles about me on Beckstrom's web site. The articles were very negative. Following a newspaper account of this action, Beckstrom had the articles removed from his web site.

This is a problem with the Internet. It's not regulated for accuracy or truthfulness. Anyone can print anything they want.

Sandra Campbell wasn't finished, either. After the Victim's Advocate program was transferred to the State Attorney's Office and she was reassigned, she had another incident. She claimed a battery charge against one of her supervisors, an accusation that could not be substantiated by an internal investigation comprised of independent witness interviews. Her battery claim was that a supervisor grabbed a pencil from her hand and left a mark. There was some degree of concern for her mental health following that circumstance in addition to the other incidents that had dogged her following the election trial.

Nobody could prove anything one way or the other. The culmination of much of this information plus reports from her supervisors convinced Chief Deputy Leonard Davis to place her on medical leave in July 1998.

She filed her own lawsuit in September of that same year, claiming that because of her testimony, members of the Sheriff's Office had harassed her. The lawsuit was filed against Volusia County and Sheriff Vogel. It all seemed so familiar. I did not operate that way, nor did the employees and deputies of the Sheriff's Office. I didn't pretend to understand her motivation in testifying, the Judge himself had questioned her conflicting testimony, but retaliation is not what I'm about. We've always had a major advantage in any of these situations – the truth. Nothing else really matters other than that. It's so easy to file a lawsuit today if things don't go your way.

No one will ever likely understand all the motivations of these individuals. It may not be explainable. It was just part of the job you had to deal with every so often. I'm willing to bet most large companies of 800 or more employees end up involved in the same types if things. Perhaps it's human nature. With that many people working in one place, there are bound to be some conflicts.

⌐⌐

TRUTH, JUSTICE AND THE AMERICAN WAY

In 1996 and again in 1999, the Volusia County Sheriff's Office was renewed as a nationally accredited law enforcement agency. I was proud that we'd been able to maintain that status especially in light of all the diversions since our previous accreditation in 1991. But this showed we had maintained our standards of excellence and we would continue to do so for as long as I remained Sheriff.

It was this professionalism that threw the DOJ attorneys when they came to Volusia County. They expected to see some rag-tag, hillbilly hole-in-the-wall office. Instead, they found a progressive, highly trained group that is a standout in the state and one of the few accredited agencies around the country. The team that renewed the accreditation specifically cited the court security system, traffic unit, evidence facility and Project Harmony in its summary.

During the evaluation, they encourage comments from local citizens on their opinion of the Sheriff's Office. These remarks were all positive in nature and helped us obtain this important distinction of merit.

Since the Florida Supreme Court ruling on the absentee ballot controversy, morale has returned to its first-term high. After over 20 years of representing the Sergeants and deputies, the Police Benevolent Association has been ousted as a representation party for the deputies. The members instead voted in the Fraternal Order of Police, a less confrontational group and more willing to work cooperatively. Before being ousted, the PBA finally completed its 1998 contract and deputies received retroactive raises due to the length of negotiations.

I'm not sure the union has any value to the officers. In a state where you have a "right to work" law and no binding arbitration, the effectiveness of the unions is questionable. Members may be better off representing themselves. The County Council likes the deputies, but do not look favorably at the union. Unions endorse candidates and create bad feelings that accomplish little.

I absorb a lot of blame for the lack of pay raises, but I have nothing to do with it under the Volusia County charter arrangement. I have no ability to negotiate. I'm invited to attend the sessions, but that's about it. We give our opinion in support of the deputies, but the County Manager and the Council have the final say. What finally worked this year is comparing Volusia County deputy pay rates to other Florida counties our size. Our deputies were definitely underpaid. That's been somewhat rectified, but the deputies didn't need the union to make that successful argument.

Leonard Davis' appointment as chief deputy has helped me immensely. He's well liked and well respected and runs the day-to-day operations smoothly. He gives me time to devote to other key issues. In addition, he now handles the media chores. I evaluate our programs on an ongoing basis to see which are working and those that are not. I network with other agencies in the state to see what's effective for them or to stay tuned to news and crime patterns that could affect our county.

We established a Sergeant's Advisory Panel within the department to give the leadership feedback on operations. Sergeants from all the various units and divisions participate and have the opportunity to air their comments. It's helping us to keep a pulse on things and be sure all facets of the Sheriff's Office are functioning properly. We're still working on automating more of the operations. We're installing Mobile Data Computer Terminals in patrol cars, paid for with $800,000 of confiscated drug dealers' funds. We are working well with all of the local law enforcement agencies to coordinate training and task force operations.

There's now a countywide homicide investigation team that works with all of the law enforcement agencies. They will not only solve current crimes, but will look into older, unsolved cases, too. I'm excited about the potential of this unit. Having all of the agencies working together like this can save taxes, improve efficiency, and avoid unnecessary duplication. It's a great time for Volusia County law enforcement.

Youth programs are critical to any community's well being. Steve Deluca, owner of an oil company and a group of citizens established a Youth Foundation to raise money to develop a better connection and working relationship between the police and our children about the problems associated with criminal behavior, drugs and substance abuse. We have many school partnership programs in addition to the successful School Resource Officer program, the Sheriff's Youth Camp, and 100 Deputies/100 Kids. It's the preventive end of law enforcement.

We still battle the war on drugs. In December 1997, a seven-county Central Florida area that included Volusia County, was designated by Congress as a "High Intensity Drug Trafficking Area" (HIDA). With the designation, part of a bill sponsored by Bob Graham in the Senate and John Mica in the House of Representatives, $1 million dollars was awarded as seed money to address the problems associated with being a HIDA. Sheriff Don Eslinger of Seminole County was named chairman, assistant U.S. Attorney Rick Jancha vice chairman and I am on the committee representing Volusia County. There are 22 HIDAs across the country, including South Florida. It certainly bore out our belief that our area is certainly used to distribute drugs. The fight goes on.

There are reminders of the past from time to time. In April 1999, Esquire magazine ran an article called DWB (Driving While Black) that re-emphasized that minorities, especially blacks, are singled out by law enforcement in highway stops. In this piece, I am called a pioneer of highway drug interdiction techniques and there is a menacing photo of me sitting in a patrol car. Well, perhaps it will keep drug traffickers out of Volusia County.

I was not the object of the article for a change. The writer, Gary Webb, was attacking the practices of some other law enforcement agencies and their alleged singling out of blacks in these highway stops. Highway drug interdiction remains in the forefront of law enforcement today.

It has been a long hard fight. All my life I've waged a battle against various circumstances from the woods in Pennsylvania to the jungles of Vietnam to the urban crime of Florida. I've always felt that I was put on earth for this reason, to help corral the chaos of crime. Despite the setbacks and the distractions, the Volusia County Sheriff's Office is at the top of its game and doing more than ever to make this county safe for everyone.

The question now became: do I want to run again in the year 2000 for Sheriff? I had been wearing a uniform – with the Marine Corps, the Florida Highway Patrol and the Volusia County Sheriff's Office – for 31 years.

We'd come a long way since 1989. The journey was not always easy or smooth, but the County is in excellent shape for law enforcement. Y2K was behind us. But the 2000 campaign looms large.

I had several opponents already. In addition to Beckstrom taking another shot, a former Volusia County Sheriff's deputy named Ben Johnson had thrown his hat in the ring. During the latter part of Johnson's career personal problems spilled over to his work product, which caused his departure from the Sheriff's office.

In January 2000, Johnson received an interesting boost that the newspapers loved. My father, a resident of Volusia County, donated $25 to his political campaign.

The newspapers loved it. "Vogel Family Feud" was the headline run in the Orlando Sentinel. It would normally be a big story – except for the fact that I've never been close with my parents. As I've already pointed out, they have never really been parents to me. It might as well be a complete stranger's donation to Ben Johnson.

Johnson had befriended my parents when he was District 4 Commander in Deltona back in the mid-90s. He would frequently ask them about me personally and about my childhood. This was not my style of campaigning.

The year 2000 had barely begun and the gloves were already off. Let them have at it! Jeannie, Sheila and I had survived much worse the last several years. The Volusia County Sheriff's Office had strengthened considerably, as proven by our successful re-accreditations in 1996 and 1999. I was proud of all these accomplishments and felt that I could easily stand on my record.

The problem was I hadn't decided yet whether I would run for a fourth term. Twelve years is a long time in a high profile public life and while I was pleased with how far the Sheriff's Office had come, the possibility that I could leave it at this high level would be a good way to go out. Whatever I decided, I knew this was not a decision I would make alone. Jeannie and Sheila would certainly have their input.

Other candidates were waging their campaigns. I wasn't all that concerned about catching up. There were plenty of loyal supporters who were more than willing to back another run and I truly valued their support and friendship.

I had spent considerable time thinking about the campaign and the next four years. My family and I were praying about the choice I would soon have to make. I was concerned about the inevitable toll a campaign would take on all of us. The question still lingered as to whether it was finally time to pursue ventures in private life.

In June, Jeannie and I attended the annual National Sheriffs Conference, held in Kansas City. We had time to think and discuss our future.

A few days later I had made my decision. The Sheriff's Office was in great shape. Volusia County's crime rate had dropped steadily in my years in office.

And, while I am still relatively young, the excitement about opening my own business is a strong attraction.

All of these factors collectively helped me decide not to seek a fourth term. I announced a press conference for Friday, June 23 on the courthouse steps where I was first sworn in January 1989. Jeannie and Sheila would be there with me as they had been a dozen years ago.

I contacted Merle and Dilys Harris of the publication Seniors Today and advised them of my decision. I wrote a letter to them that they would publish in the release of their every other week issue that was to be distributed that day. This would give them a first scoop over the other media who couldn't run a printed version of the story until Saturday.

The letter read:

> "My family and I would like to personally thank Seniors Today and especially Merle and Dilys Harris for their loyal support and friendship since I have been Sheriff. The Sheriff's Office has never been in better shape and employee morale is at an all-time high. We have accomplished much for the citizens of Volusia County, including a lower crime rate, a thrice nationally accredited agency, and implementation of state-of-the-art crime-fighting equipment. Our many innovative programs to reduce violence, school intervention, and volunteerism have been recognized throughout the state and nationally with many awards. The Sheriff's Office is at the top and the agency is in great shape. My current term ends December 31, 2000 and I will not be seeking a fourth term as your Sheriff. It is time for my family and I to go forward with our personal lives. We deeply appreciate our steadfast supporters who have encouraged us along the way. Thank you for allowing me to serve you – the citizens of Volusia County. It has been a great honor and privilege."
>
> —Bob Vogel

State Attorney John Tanner, Assistant U.S. Attorney Rick Jancha, Daytona Beach Police Chief Ken Small, and my Chief Deputy Leonard Davis, among others, all tried to talk me out of this decision. But my mind was made up. I had received several calls from local police chiefs and admittedly it was hard to walk away from all we had accomplished together as a team. Communication between various law enforcement agencies in Volusia County was excellent. But this was a family decision. While it was a difficult choice to make, now that it had been done, I was very much at ease with it.

Once he realized I was not running again, Leonard Davis made his own decision to try for the top job. I was encouraging; Leonard had the experience and the credentials and he was familiar with all the inner workings of the agency and had established rapport with other agencies. He was the logical choice from my perspective.

Within ten days, Leonard announced his decision to run for Sheriff.

The days went on and as the September primary election loomed closer, Leonard found himself trailing both Beckstrom and Johnson by significant margins.

The primary whittled the candidates down to just two for the November election. Gus Beckstrom was the top vote getter, probably due more to name recognition on the part of voters than to increasing support. Ben Johnson ran second and Leonard Davis, Paul Crow and Wendell Bradford were officially out of the race. Leonard ran third. Johnson ran ahead in only one area – Northwest Volusia County.

Beckstrom constantly criticized the agency as part of his campaigning, and this bothered a large number of the rank and file. As a result deputies then gravitated towards Johnson's campaign.

This was underscored by an unusual endorsement for Johnson on the same courthouse steps in September. All three of the defeated Primary Sheriff's candidates – Davis, Crow and Bradford – appeared with Johnson to uniformly pledge their support for him. This was a boost of publicity Johnson needed. Beckstrom's name recognition would not be as much of a factor in November.

Besides, Beckstrom was not a consensus builder. The deputies knew it would not be easy to work for him. It was his way or no way.

Johnson, for his part, simply kept his head down in the weeks leading up to the general election. He said what people wanted to hear and quietly courted support from behind the scenes. This, along with Beckstrom's style, helped Johnson get elected on November 7. The race was over relatively early and projections gave it to Johnson by mid-evening. However, this did not mean it was a dull night at the Election Office.

I was in bed asleep when I received a phone call from that office saying that someone had driven away from the Election office and had ballots in the car. By the time I arrived there, it had progressed farther than that. A judge had ordered the Elections Office sealed off entirely and the dumpster out back, too. Deputies were required to guard the office around the clock. The Bush-Gore recount controversy was just beginning.

I couldn't help but shake my head over the whole thing. Four years ago, Sheriff's deputies were being accused of doctoring ballots for me. Now, they were required to stand guard over them once again, something I didn't believe we'd ever have to do.

We quickly located the car that had left the Elections Office. It was just a worker going home in an empty car. No ballots had left the building.

Secretary of State Katherine Harris had ordered a recount and at first there was only a concern about hand-counting a precinct in DeBary that had a glitch with its machines. Everywhere else in the county a machine recount was done. But the decision finally was made to recount every precinct by hand. It would take some time and a lot of overtime for county workers, but Volusia County moved ahead with it.

Media was everywhere you turned. Satellite dishes, trucks and other media paraphernalia decorated the county offices in Deland for several days. Everyone was looking for a story edge and one day after the election, an older man turned up in a car and went into the Elections Office with a sack of ballots over his shoulder. The media went crazy, but it turned out he was a poll worker just delivering a last bag of ballots that had been previously overlooked in his car. It looked bad, and it was certainly careless, and not done with any specific malicious intent, but the media had a field day with this incident.

At least Volusia County had a recent experience with recounts. When they recounted the Sheriff's race in 1996, I ended up with several hundred more votes than those that had been registered by the machines. So it was no surprise that the count changed slightly after the hand recount, giving Vice President Gore a few more votes.

Gore had carried the county handily, and now had a few more for his total. This vote count went in for Katherine Harris' final certification as ordered by the Florida Supreme Court.

As the Presidential election was being contested in the courts, I was busy preparing for the transition to Ben Johnson. It would be a far cry from the transition I had (or didn't have), when outgoing Sheriff Ed Duff refused to let me in the building until after I had been sworn in, and even then he just left the keys on the office floor. Johnson would have our full cooperation and I envied the situation he was walking into as opposed to what I found waiting for me in 1989.

Johnson had said during the campaign that he would wait until he was in office to make any personnel changes, but he announced his appointment of Bill Lee to Chief Deputy shortly after the election. A new era had begun.

In late December, I received a great surprise with a retirement party held in my honor at the Ocean Center in Daytona Beach. I was humbled by the presence of nearly 700 well-wishers and a variety of speakers for a prepared program. I couldn't believe the size of the crowd. How could so many people show up for me? I wanted to personally thank each person for attending. I couldn't pass up the opportunity to announce my future including this book and my new business – Vogel Security – doing full service installation of security equipment, monitoring services, security guards, investigations and background checks and the like. It was exciting to hear myself talking about the new venture and I looked forward to actively pursuing the idea of running my own business.

There were many great moments that evening that I'll treasure forever. Jeannie had arranged for my old Vietnam buddy, Harold "Ace" Hendricks, to be a special guest of honor. It was great to catch up with him and we promised to visit after the holidays. It was a "This is Your Life" celebration and I was grateful that so many people were here to experience it with me.

Putting the final touches on the evening for me was a speech delivered by my daughter Sheila. She had endured so much during the last 12 years and had literally grown up in a public spotlight that was not very friendly. Her words that night meant so much …

"One of my very first memories of my dad being a Florida Highway Patrol Trooper was when I was three years old. I would take his large brown and tan shirt from his uniform and put it on my small frame. It would fit me as a dress with its tails dragging on the floor. As if that wasn't enough, I would put on his shiny black size 9 1/2 shoes on my little feet and try to walk on them. They would flop all over, but I didn't care because now I was dressed just like my dad – the one person I looked up to most.

" As I got a little older, around four or five, I quickly learned about my dad's radio in his patrol car. I wanted to talk on it and wait and listen for the people on the other end to speak a few letters and numbers back. Of course, dad said I wasn't allowed to do that. So, he and a fellow State Trooper, George Wilkinson, each got a CB radio. I thought that was the greatest thing in the world. Dad would let me sit on his lap and pretend I was driving his patrol car while I, Honey Bee, spoke to George, Smokey the Bear, through the CB. Every time I got in dad's patrol car, I would pick up that CB to see if Smokey the Bear was listening.

" As time went on, my dad continued to be a Trooper, but things got a little more serious. My dad started making a lot of drug stops on I-95. He always worked the night shifts and was continuously by himself out on the road. I can remember him putting on his bulletproof vest before he left for work and me asking him questions as to what it was. He also had to remove his wedding ring from his finger and my mom's picture and his credit cards from his wallet. He also removed his driver's license as it had our home address on it. In addition to the bulletproof vest, he was now carrying an extra gun strapped around his ankle. All this was so new. It was his way of protecting us just in case a drug bust went the wrong way.

"Unbeknownst to me, there were a lot of death threats against my parents and I from various drug dealers. I did know that I wasn't allowed to get the mail out of the mailbox in case of mail bombs, not to open any packages left by the front door, and not to play outside unless mom was there to watch me. We had one rule in our house at this time. Mom would say, 'make sure you tell daddy you love him and say good bye to him before he goes to work tonight, just in case he doesn't come back to us tomorrow.' I followed this rule every night.

I would reach my little arms up around his neck and hug him tight as he lifted me in the air. Then I would stand by the door as he drove away.

"My dad had decided to announce that he would be running for Sheriff at the northbound rest area near Port Orange. This was the place where he made most of his drug busts. It was a beautiful sunny day. My mom's parents – my grandparents – were there and granddaddy videotaped the whole thing. I stood right next to my dad as he made his speech. I watched my dad, not as my dad, but as this man who had changed from a young State Trooper to a respected gentleman. I didn't know it then, but this was the first day of my new life.

"My dad successfully won Sheriff of Volusia County in 1988. I learned so much about campaigning and I learned much about life in general by watching my dad. At this young age of 11, my dad taught me things most kids my age didn't know. I knew about campaigns and election law, drug laws, and about how to analyze people. But most of all I learned what type of person it takes to give so much of themselves to help a community of people and expect nothing in return. I learned that this is a person who will continue to fight for what he believes is right no matter how many times he gets knocked down. This person is my dad.

"On a cool breezy day in late 1988 my dad was inaugurated as Sheriff. The night before I had stayed up and eaten all my Christmas chocolates and was covered in hives by the time I woke up in the morning. I remember wanting to put Calamine lotion and telling my mom that it would match my pink dress. In front of the Volusia County Courthouse, I held the bible as my dad was sworn in as Sheriff of Volusia County by Attorney General Bob Butterworth. This was a day I'll never forget. The birds flew in the shape of a V over the courthouse.

"Life changed so much after this day. My dad became an extremely busy man and a devoted Sheriff. No other daughter in this world could love her dad as much as I love mine. I love him not just because he's my dad, but also because he gives so much of himself to others. I've seen in his eyes that he truly cares about each and every person here. He's taught me to stand up for what I believe in, to never give up, to always strive to be the best I can be, and most of all always stop and show the people around you that you love them.

"So, at this time, the time of my dad's retirement, I'm happy that he's retiring, not sad. His life is taking on a new chapter and I can assure you, this is not the last you are going to see of him. He's going to continue to fight for what he believes in. But he will also take time to relax and this is the part that I like the most. Because this is the part that gives me my dad back.."

—Sheila Vogel, December 4, 2000

The other comments that evening that have stayed with me were the words of U.S. Attorney Rick Jancha. He said that I was blessed with a clarity of purpose and that through good times and bad, I never lost sight of the purpose for which I was elected.

Another comment came from Merle Harris when he said that instead of taking polls, Bob Vogel took an oath, to perform the duties incumbent upon him and he did this with honesty, integrity, wisdom and character, and with an absolute disregard for personal consequences.

What a great way to be remembered! I've always believed in doing the right thing, not just the popular thing. You must have clarity of purpose to do that and I thank God for whatever gifts I possess. If this is to be the legacy I have left law enforcement, I couldn't be happier or prouder to have served the public in this way. I will still be protecting people with Vogel Security. I know Jeannie and Sheila feel the same.

Semper Fidelis!

LUKE 10:19

Printed in the USA
CPSIA information can be obtained
at www.ICGtesting.com
JSHW022320140824
68134JS00019B/1210